Daoist Dietetics

Food for Immortality

D1738810

by

Livia Kohn

Three Pines Press
P. O. Box 609
Dunedin, FL 34697
www.threepinespress.com

9   8 7 6 5 4 3 2 1

First Three Pines Edition, 2010
Printed in the United States of America
⊗ This edition is printed on acid-free paper that meets
the American National Standard Institute Z39.48 Standard.
Distributed in the United States by Three Pines Press.

Cover art: Private photo of Daoist porridge.

_____

Library of Congress Cataloging-in-Publication Data

Kohn, Livia, 1956-
Daoist dietetics : food for immortality / by Livia Kohn.
— 1st Three Pines ed.
   p. cm.
Includes bibliographical references and index.
ISBN 978-1-931483-14-8 (alk. paper)
1. Cookery, Chinese. 2. Dietetics--China. 3. Taoism. I. Title.
TX724.5.C5.K64 2010
613.20951?dc22
            2010000017

Contents

Acknowledgments

This book grew over several years in an ongoing dialogue with my friend and colleague Ute Engelhardt. As sinology students at the University of Munich in the 1970s, we both focused on the work of Sima Chengzhen, then moved on in different directions. As I continued to explore the various modes of self-cultivation in the Daoist tradition, Ute became a specialist in Chinese dietetics, examining and presenting—usually in cooperation with practitioners of Chinese medicine—the characteristics, workings, and therapeutic application of all different kinds of food.

We had variously talked about putting together a book that would bring our expertise together and when, early in 2009, her new book on Chinese dietetic recipes appeared and I visited her in Munich, we decided to move ahead on the project. Then and there, we created a preliminary book outline and began the writing process. In the event, since I had more time and could dedicate myself fully to the work, I ended up writing it myself. But her published work on dietary therapy, her continued encouragement, her sharing of references and research materials, and her corrective readings have been essential in creating *Daoist Dietetics*. Modesty prevented her from accepting the position of cooperator, but her presence is felt throughout the work.

I would also like to thank Andreas Noll for encouraging the project and suggesting that I teach dietary methods at the TCM Congress in Rothenburg, Germany. Last, but certainly not least, Stephen Eskildsen and Vivienne Lo have been very supportive and made numerous suggestions for correction and improvement.

Introduction

The body always move; your food always reduce.
Moving, never reach extremes; reducing, never get to naught.
Eliminate fat and heavy things; control all salt and sour tastes.
Diminish thoughts and worries; lessen joy and anger.
Get out of hectic rushing; watch out for sexual exhaustion.
Do this always—and you'll see results!
—Master Blue Ox (*Yangxing yanming lu* 1.10b)

Daoism is special among the world's religions in that it places particular emphasis on body cultivation for spiritual attainment. This peculiarity is due to the traditional Chinese conception of the body as joined with the greater universe through the medium of a vital energy known as *qi* 氣.

Qi is the concrete aspect of Dao, the material root power of the universe, the basic stuff of nature. In ancient sources it is associated with mist, fog, and moving clouds. The character for *qi* as it appears in the oracle bones of the Shang dynasty (1766-1122 B.C.E.) consists of two parts: an image of someone eating and grain in a pot. Combined, these parts signal *qi* as the quality which nourishes, warms, transforms, and rises. *Qi* is, therefore, the life force in the human body and the basis of all physical vitality, found foremost in the air we breathe and in the foods we eat. This means that dietary practices are at the very core of the Daoist undertaking. They form an essential way toward being healthy in the world, living for an extended period, and transcending to the ultimate state of immortality.

Healing, Longevity, and Immortality

Daoists and medical writers in Chinese history have formulated the cosmology of the body in many different terms and established numerous theories of how exactly the various parts and aspects function and work together. While it will be the exciting task of future research to explore their work and understand their circumstances and different histories, it is possible to summarize the fundamental tenets of the Chinese vision to present a general framework of Daoist cultivation practice, understanding fully well that this is an approximation and does not claim to show it as an immutable system of either theory or practice.

Thus, generally traditional Daoist and medical thinkers agree that there is only one *qi*, just as there is only one Dao. Many understand it to come in two forms: a basic primordial or prenatal *qi* that is inborn and connects us to the cosmos and the Dao; and a secondary, earthly or postnatal *qi* that is replenished by breathing, food, as well as social and sexual contact and helps the body survive in everyday life. Both forms of *qi* are necessary and interact constantly with each other, so that primordial *qi* is lost as and when earthly *qi* is insufficient, and enhancing earthly *qi* is no longer necessary when primordial *qi* is complete (as in the case of the embryo in the womb). Once people are born, they start this interchange of the two dimensions of *qi* and soon start losing their primordial *qi*, especially through interaction with the world on the basis of passions and desires, sensory exchanges, and intellectual distinction.

As people lose their primordial *qi*, they begin to decline and eventually die. Should they lose it at a rather rapid or unbalanced rate, they experience a weakening of their defenses which grows into minor symptoms that may lead to acute or chronic conditions. Just as sickness is therefore a form of *qi*-loss, so healing is the replenishing of *qi* with medical means such as dietary therapy or food cures as well as drugs, herbs, acupuncture, massages, and various other means at the physician's disposal.

Longevity, next, comes in as and when people have become aware of their contribution to internal imbalances and take their healing into their own hands. Being initially helped by medical means, then developing a life-style more congruent with their energetic needs, they attain a state of good health. However, they do not stop there but proceed to increase their primordial *qi* to and even above the level they had at birth. To do so, they follow specific dietary principles as well as work with breathing, healing exercises (*daoyin* 導引), self-massages, sexual control, and meditations—practiced to a large extent today under the name of qigong 氣功 (see Kohn 1989; 2006; 2008a; Cohen 1997). Applied regularly and systematically, these methods ensure not only an extension of natural life expectancy but often lead to increased vigor and youthfulness.

Immortality, third, raises the practices to a yet higher level. To attain it, people have to transform all their *qi* into primordial *qi* and proceed to increasingly refine it to even subtler levels. This finer *qi* will eventually turn into pure spirit (*shen* 神), with which practitioners increasingly identify to become spirit-people and immortals. The practice that leads there involves intensive meditation and trance training as well as more radical forms of diet and other longevity practices. Immortality implies the overcoming of the natural tendencies of the body and its transformation into a different kind of energetic constellation. The result is a bypassing of death so that the end of the body has no impact on the continuation of the spirit-person. It also leads to the attainment of magical powers and eventually to residence in the heavens and paradises of the immortals.

Chinese longevity and dietary practices, as first described in manuscripts of the second century B.C.E. (see Harper 1998; Lo 2010), occupy a middle ground in this system. They stand between healing and immortality and are usefully applied on either level. Although essential as medical techniques and in health improvement, they also play an important role in Daoism, but with some modifications. For example, diets on the medical and health levels involve moderation in food intake as well as overall life-style as well as the conscious use of inherent food qualities such as warming, cooling, sinking, or rising to balance seasonal climates, geographical variations, and personal tendencies—either working in harmony with them or using food to counteract their tendencies and alleviate their impact. Practitioners are encouraged to avoid excess eating and heavy foods, to eat properly cooked meals in small portions, and to be mentally calm and consciously aware as they eat. As they are conscientious in their practice, their *qi* continues to become stronger and they need ever less food, until—in immortality practice—they can cut out all main staples and replace food first by herbal and mineral concoctions, then by the conscious intake of *qi* through breath. This technique is called "avoiding grain" (*bigu* 辟穀) and is still undertaken today.

Similarly, healing exercises, self-massages, and breathing techniques serve to stretch and loosen muscles, stimulate the circulation, and aid the smooth flow of *qi* in the body. They are never strenuous, but change in nature as people proceed from healing to longevity and immortality levels, becoming more cosmic in pattern and more counter-intuitive. Breathing for health and long life thus involves inhaling all the way to the diaphragm, which expands as one inhales. Breathing for immortality, on the other hand, may lead to something called "reversed breathing," which uses the diaphragm the opposite way, contracting it on inhalation. The practice leads eventually to a method called "embryo respiration" (*taixi*

胎息), in which no obvious breath enters or leaves the nostrils. Instead, practitioners absorb *qi* through their entire body and circulate it within.

Sexual techniques, too, are used on all levels, first with a partner, later internally in celibate solo practice. In all cases, adepts experience sexual stimulation but then, instead losing it through orgasm, revert the rising *qi* of arousal, commonly called essence (*jing* 精), and move it up along the spine with the help of meditation and massages. This is called "reverting the semen to nourish the brain" and is supposed to have strong life-extending effects. In more technical Daoist practice of later centuries, it might even lead to the gestation of an immortal embryo (see Wile 1992; Kohn and Wang 2009).

Balancing Qi

Before one attains any of these higher stages, though, one has to lay the groundwork. It consists largely of balancing *qi*. Chinese medical textbook may discuss *qi* in terms of quantity, since having more indicates a stronger metabolic function. This, however, does not mean that health or longevity are a byproduct of storing large quantities of *qi*. More commonly they note that there is a normal or healthy amount of *qi* in every person, and health manifests in its balance and harmony, its moderation and smoothness of flow. The texts envision this flow as a complex system of waterways with the "Ocean of *Qi*" (Qihai 氣海) in the abdomen; rivers of *qi* flowing through the upper torso, arms, and legs; springs of *qi* reaching to the wrists and ankles; and wells of *qi* in the fingers and toes. Even a small spot in this complex system can influence the whole, so that overall balance and smoothness are the general goal.

Human life is the accumulation of *qi*; death is its dispersal. After receiving a core potential of primordial *qi* at birth, people throughout life need to sustain it. They do so by drawing postnatal *qi* into the body from air and food, as well as from other people through sexual, emotional, and social interaction. But they also lose *qi* through breathing bad air, overburdening their bodies with food and drink, and getting involved in negative emotions and excessive sexual or social interactions.

 To balance *qi*, it is thus best to breathe deeply and eat moderately in accordance with the seasons, to move smoothly, exercise without exertion, and match activities to the body's needs. This is how one keeps harmony, maintains health, and achieves long life. Health in the vision of Chinese medicine and Daoism is thus more than the absence of symptoms: it is the presence of strong vitality and of a smooth, harmonious, and active flow of *qi*, a state known as "proper *qi*" (*zhengqi* 正氣).

Its opposite is "wayward *qi*" (*xieqi* 邪氣), *qi* that has lost the harmonious pattern of flow and no longer supports the dynamic forces of change. Whereas proper *qi* moves in a steady, harmonious rhythm and effects daily renewal, helping health and long life, wayward *qi* is disorderly and dysfunctional, creating change that violates the normal order. When it becomes dominant, the *qi*-flow can turn upon itself and deplete the body's resources. Then the person no longer operates as part of a universal system and is not in tune with the basic life force. Waywardness typically appears when *qi* begins to move either too fast or too slow, is excessive or depleted, or creates rushes or obstructions. It disturbs the regular flow and causes ailments.

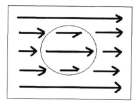 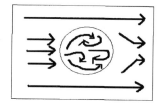

More specifically, *qi* can become excessive through outside influences such as too much heat or cold or through inside patterns such as too much emotion or stimulation. Excessive *qi* can be moving too fast or be very sluggish, as in the case of excessive dampness. Whatever the case, from a universal perspective there is no additional or new *qi* created, but localized disharmonies have arisen because the *qi*-flow has become excessive and thus harmful. Still, even describing it in this way we are thinking in terms of *qi* as an energetic substance, which it really is not. A better way of expression would be to say that the process itself of turning hot or angry is *qi*, that the way things move and change is what constitutes our being *qi*.

Similarly, *qi* can be in depletion. This may mean that there is a tense flow of *qi* due to nervousness or anxiety, or that the volume and density of *qi* have decreased, which is the case in serious prolonged illness. However, more commonly it means that the *qi* activity level is lower, that its flow is not quite up to standard, that there is less than normal concentration of *qi* in one or the other body part. In the same vein, perfection of *qi* means the optimal functioning of *qi* in the body, while control of *qi* means the power to consciously guide the energetic process.

That is to say, healing is the correction of *qi*-flow from a deviant or wayward pattern back to a harmonious or correct flow, matching the rhythm of Dao, creating well-being in the person, and aiding social interactions. Longevity is the enhancement and strengthening of the proper flow of *qi*, allowing people to fully go along with all the movements of Dao in order to enjoy health, retain vigor, and live long and successful lives. Immortality, finally, is the move toward Dao as the creative power at the center of the universe, the transformation of proper, healthy, and harmonious *qi* into the subtler levels of cosmic power, into a mysterious and ineffable state of being that goes far beyond the natural world. Eating and drinking are at the very center of this *qi*-work, an essential way of relating to nature and society, a key method of helping or hurting the body's internal systems and thus either enhancing or diminishing health, long life, and immortality.

Moderation

The foundation of balancing *qi* and eating to one's best advantage is a peaceful and harmonious life (Huang 2007, 40). From early on, and well into today (e.g., Liu 1990), books on longevity, of both aristocratic and Daoist origin, specify how to go about it. They tend to begin with mental attitudes.

Thus, for example, Sun Simiao 孫思邈 (581-682), the famous physician, Daoist, and alchemist of the early Tang dynasty, in his *Zhenzhong ji* 枕中記 (Pillowbook Record, DZ 837)[1] specifies that one should maintain a serene state of mind by cultivating an attitude of awe and care. He refers to the fourth-century *Shenxian shiqi jin'gui miaolu* 神仙食氣金櫃妙錄 (Wondrous Record of the Golden Casket on the Spirit Immortals' Practice of Eating *Qi*, DZ 836) to define this as "the gateway of life and death, the key to rites and good teaching, the cause of existing and perishing, the root of good and bad fortune, as well as the prime source of all auspicious and inauspicious conditions" (14b).

If awe and care are lost, "the mind will be confused and not cultivated, the body will be hectic and not at peace, the spirit will be scattered, the *qi*

---

[1] Texts in the Daoist canon, abbreviated DZ, are cited according to Komjathy 2002; Schipper and Verellen 2004.

will go beyond all bounds, and will and intention will be deluded" (14b). This condition, which we now call "stress," is the ultimate antithesis to health and long life. Awe and care combat it effectively since they are the basis of moral action and virtuous thoughts. They provide great benefit. As Sun says:

> One who is able to realize awe and care is safe from harm by dragons when traveling on water and cannot be hurt by tigers or rhinoceroses when traveling on land. Weapons cannot wound him nor can contagious diseases infect him. Slander cannot destroy his good name nor the poisonous stings of insects do him harm. (Sivin 1968, 118; Engelhardt 1989, 281)

To live in this mental serenity of awe and care, moreover, one should practice moderation in all aspects of life and avoid overindulgence in food and drink as well as in other sensual and sexual pleasures.

Many longevity texts in the middle ages place a great emphasis on moderation.[2] They frequently express it is in the format of twelve things to do only a "little" bit at a time. They are:

> Think little, reflect little, laugh little, speak little, enjoy little, anger little, delight little, mourn little, like little, dislike little, engage little, deal little.
> If you think much, the spirit will disperse.
> If you reflect much, the heart will be labored.
> If you laugh much, the organs and viscera will soar up.
> If you speak much, the Ocean of Qi will be empty and vacant.
> If you enjoy much, gall and bladder will take in outside wind.
> If you get angry much, the fascia will push the blood around.
> If you delight much, the spirit and heart will be deviant and unsettled.
> If you mourn much, the hair and whiskers will dry and wither.
> If you like much, the will and qi will be overloaded.
> If you dislike much, essence and power race off and soar away.
> If you engage yourself much, the muscles and qi-channels will be tense and nervous.
> If you deal much, wisdom and worry will all be confused.
> All these attack people's lives worse than axes and spears; they diminish people's destiny worse that wolves and wolverines. [3]

---

[2] It plays also a key role in Xi Kang's 嵇康 *Yangsheng lun* 養生論 (On Nourishing Life). See Henricks 1983.

In other words, harmony with Dao manifests itself in mental stability and physical wellness, and any form of agitation or sickness indicates a decline in one's alignment with the forces of nature. Various mental activities and strong emotions harm key psychological forces and thus bring about a diminishing of *qi*, which takes one further away from the Dao and reduces life. As the fourth-century *Yangsheng yaoji* 養生要集 (Long Life Compendium) by the aristocrat and official Zhang Zhan 張湛, best known as commentator to the Daoist philosophical text *Liezi* 列子 (Book of Master Lie; trl. Graham 1960), says: "Dao is *qi*. By preserving *qi* you can attain Dao, and through attaining Dao you can live long. Spirit is essence. By preserving essence you can reach spirit brightness, and once you have spirit brightness, you can live long" (*Ishinpō* 23.17ab; Stein 1999, 172). [4]

Along the same lines, the *Baopuzi yangsheng lun* 抱朴子養生論 (Nourishing Life According to the Master Who Embraces Simplicity, DZ 842) has a set of six exhortations to release mental strain and sensory involvement. It says:

      1. Let go of fame and profit.
      2. Limit sights and sounds.
      3. Moderate wealth and possessions.
      4. Lessen smells and tastes.
      5. Eliminate lies and falsehood.
      6. Avoid jealousy and envy. (1b)

While all these ensure mental stability and calm in social interaction and the professional life, the texts also recommend concrete measures of

---

[3] The version translated here appears in the fourth-century *Yangsheng yaoji* (which survives in fragments and citations), as cited in chapter 29 of the *Ishinpō* 醫心方 (Essential Medical Methods), a key Japanese collection of longevity sources, dated to 984 (Stein 1999, 170-71). It is also found in the Daoist sources *Baopuzi yangsheng lun* (DZ 842), 1b-2a and the *Shenxian shiqi jin'gui lu* 16a. In the environment of Sun Simiao, it is cited as from the *Xiaoyou jing* 小有經 (Scripture of Lesser Existence) in *Yangxing yanming lu* 養性延命錄 (On Nourishing Inner Nature and Extending Life, DZ 838), 1.5b.

[4] The *Yangxing yanming lu* similarly notes: "Life is the foundation of spirit; the body is its tool. If you use spirit a lot, it will be exhausted; if you exert the body a lot, it will perish" (pref.1a). For more on the *Yangsheng yaoji*, see Sakade 1986b, 10; Kohn 2008, 64-65.

physical moderation. Thus, citing the ancient immortal Pengzu 彭祖, the *Yangsheng yaoji* points out that heavy clothing and thick comforters, spicy foods and heavy meats, sexual attraction and alluring women, melodious voices and enticing sounds, wild hunting and exciting outings, as well as all strife for success and ambition will inevitably lead to a weakening of the body and thus cause a reduction in life expectancy (Stein 1999, 178; also in *Yangxing yanming lu* 1.10b-11a). It says:

> The method of nourishing long life consists mainly in not doing harm to oneself. Keep warm in winter and cool in summer, and never lose your harmony with the four seasons—that is how you can align yourself with the body. Do not allow sensuous beauty, provocative postures, easy leisure, and enticing entertainments to incite yearnings and desires—that is how you come to connect to spirit. (*Ishinpō* 23.3a; Stein 1999, 169)

In terms of diet, it recommends that practitioners avoid specific combinations of food, such as anything hot and cold, sweet and raw, or more specifically wheat and oats, onions and honey, celery and pig's liver, dried ginger and rabbit (Stein 1999, 200-04). They should use alcohol sparingly, boil water before drinking, and take care not to gulp down cold drinks when hot. The text also has specific recipes for beneficial food combinations, descriptions of the qualities and healing properties of herbs and food stuffs, as well as a series of instructions for pregnancy (1999, 208-10). In many cases, it provides remedies for certain conditions, notably stomach and digestive problems, including cramps, flatulence, constipation, and diarrhea (1999, 226-28).

Even in the middle ages, therefore, working with *qi* was seen very much in terms of food regulation. Medicinal diets served as the foundation of healthy living, extended life expectancy, and the attainment of immortality. Daoist dietetics, deeply embedded in Chinese culture and the medical tradition, thus always begin with food cures and the harmonization of eating. Only after the body has achieved balance and harmony can the transformation to higher levels begin.

Kinds of Food

Certain foods are more conducive to these higher levels than others, as various kinds of nutrition will enhance different characteristics and thus be favored by different species in nature. This notion is part of the general Chinese tradition, and already the *Kongzi jiayu* 孔子家語 (Kong Family Annals) of the first century C.E. says:

> Those who feed on water swim well and withstand cold.
> Those who feed on wood are strong but undisciplined.
> Those who feed on plants are good at walking but foolish.
> Those who feed on the mulberry are graceful and enterprising.
> Those who feed on meat are brave.
> Those who feed on *qi* are pure and long-lived.
> Those who feed on grains attain superior intelligence.
> Those who do not feed become divine and immortal.
> (Despeux 2007, 28)[5]

Chinese medicine picks up the same idea and classifies food into four categories that serve different aspects of individual health. As the *Huangdi neijing suwen* 黃帝內經素問 (The Yellow Emperor's Inner Classic: Simple Issues) says:

> Poisonous drugs are good for attacking wayward *qi* while the five grains will nurture [proper *qi*]. The five kinds of fruit support it, the five kinds of meat increase it, and the five kinds of vegetables complete it. As you combine these food groups with proper regard for their specific nature and their unique tastes and ingest them regularly, you supplement essence and enhance *qi*. (22.4)

In addition to drugs, this divides food stuffs into the four groups of grain, fruit, meat, and vegetables, which each have a unique impact on the per-

---

[5] The same notion also appears in the *Huainanzi* 淮南子 (Book of the Prince of Huainan, DZ 1184; 7.8b). See Major 1993, 172; Campany 2005, 108. Later the idea is picked up in Ge Hong's 葛洪 *Baopuzi* 抱朴子 (Book of the Master Who Embraces Simplicity, DZ 1185; dat. ca. 320): "Those eating greens are good at walking but foolish; those eating meat are strong and brave; those eating grains are wise but don't live long; and those eating *qi* have spirits within who never die" (ch. 15; Ware 1966, 243-44; see also Mollier 2000, 76-77). He continues by saying that none of these food methods ever guarantees true transcendence but that the concoction of an alchemical elixir is essential.

son's *qi*-flow and overall health. Each kind of food in this system is thus from the very beginning medically potent and seen in therapeutic terms, serving different aspects of the person and also different people within society.[6]

Daoists also classify foods, focusing even more consciously on their potency for health and immortality. Although one will encounter drinking Daoists today, many historical sources are adamantly against the consumption of meat and wine. The *Huangsu sishisi fangjing* 黄素四十四方經 (Scripture of Forty-Four Methods of Yellow Simplicity), cited in the seventh-century encyclopedia *Sandong zhunang* 三洞朱囊 (Pearly Bag of the Three Caverns, DZ 1139), is one of the most radical:

> The five kinds of meat are axes and hatchets that murder the organs. Wine and sex are inner and outer coffins that bury the body. Only if you eliminate the harm done by the axes, block the death represented by the coffins, and find inner restfulness can you walk on the path to long life and gradually follow the road to immortality. (4.5a)

Just as wine and meat are not conducive to advanced states, so different foodstuffs have varying effects and are consumed by different kinds of practitioners. As the ancient *Taiping jing* 太平經 (Scripture of Great Peace; see Hendrischke 2006), notes in its classification of immortals according to the foods they eat:

> Question: The upper, middle, and lower [immortals] who attain the Dao and go beyond the world—what do they eat?
> Answer: Those of the first level absorb wind and *qi*; those of the second level ingest medicinal flavors; those of the third level eat little, reducing what passes through their stomach and intestines. (Wang 1960, 716; Campany 2005, 109)

This sets up the basic distinction of Daoist practitioners: those in the beginning stages eat vegetables and simple grains that are digested the normal way but support the balance of *qi*. More advanced folk practice a diet that involves the supplementation and increasing replacement of vegetables through concoctions or "herbal formulas" (*yao* 藥). Those who

---

[6] This is also obvious in the Han manuscript *Wushier bingfang* 五十二病方 (52 Recipes for Diseases) which contains numerous concoctions that can just as easily be read as soup recipes (see Harper 1998; Engelhardt and Nögel 2009, 6).

work to achieve oneness with Dao and move closer to immortality, finally, eliminate all food and material intake and just live by absorbing *qi*, a method that reorganizes the internal system of the body and bypasses normal digestive processes (see Jackowicz 2006).

The same system is also, in some more detail, presented in the *Laozi shuo Fashi jinjie jing* 老子說法食禁戒經 (Prohibitions and Precepts on Ceremonial Food as Revealed by Laozi), a Tang-dynasty manual of Daoist food rules found among Dunhuang manuscripts (P. 2447). It notes that "in high antiquity, people ate only primordial *qi* and managed to live for millions of years," and states categorically that the highest form of eating—after not eating at all—is living on *qi*.

Beyond that, however, the text ranks different kinds of food, adding the omnivore or "see food" diet at the bottom, adding grains and mushrooms above the vegetable category, and redefining "herbal formulas" in terms of minerals:

> Eating everything is not as good as eating vegetables. Eating vegetables is not as good as eating grains. Eating grains is not as good as eating mushrooms and excrescences.[7] Eating mushrooms and excrescences is not as good as eating gold and jade.[8] Eating gold and jade is not as good as eating primordial *qi*. Eating primordial *qi* is not as good as not eating at all. By not eating at all, even though Heaven and Earth may collapse, one will survive forever. (Kohn 2004b, 124-25)

Following this, the text specifies five basic kinds of food in more detail: *qi*, herbal formulas, grain, fruits, and vegetables. *Qi* as a form of nourishment, it states, consists of practicing "healing exercises and embryo respiration, expelling the old and taking in the new, and generally harmonizing the body with the help of the six breaths," forms of exhalation that match individual organs and are today known as the Six Healing Sounds (see Despeux 2006; Chia and Chia 1993). Herbal formulas, second, include both minerals and plant products. They replace ordinary nourishment and serve to "harmonize blood and body fluids, preserve and

---

[7] The term *zhi* 芝 refers to mushrooms in general as well as to the fungus growing on the sides of trees (Stuart 1976, 271). *Ying* 營 means "splendor" and can also refer to "excrescences," another non-cultivated natural product.

[8] Gold and jade, or metals and minerals, are at the base of the immortal elixir as described in the *Baopuzi* (Ware 1966; Huang 2008a).

nourish body and spirit, calm the spirit soul and settle the will, and in general expel all wind and dampness, thus greatly enhancing life and extending old age" (Kohn 2004b, 125).

Next, the text defines grains as including "corn, millet, hemp, wheat, wild and cultivated rice, as well as various kinds of beans." It acknowledges that they can be useful for strengthening the inner organs, enhancing qi, and in general helping to harmonize the body. The last two food groups are fruits and vegetables, which should all be eaten in appropriate portions and well prepared. All these kinds of food make up what the text calls "ceremonial food" (zhaishi 齋食) i.e., food eaten in Daoist institutions at the main meal of the day, usually held shortly before noon as part of a major ceremony that also includes scripture readings and the formal sharing of merits with the donors, the gods, and all beings.

Eating in the Daoist environment thus involves all kinds of foods used in Chinese dietetics, joining it in its exclusion of dairy products and cold foods, such as ice cream or sodas popular in the West. It follows the same principles as Chinese dietary therapy, selecting food combinations and cooking methods to balance the individual's qi both in terms of personal tendencies and geographical or seasonal variants. Also like Chinese dietetics, Daoist cooking uses herbs and spices, selected for their qualities as much as for their taste, and emphasizes life-style basics, such as serenity of mind and moderation in sensory and culinary experiences.

While building on a solid base of traditional Chinese dietetics and medicinal foods, Daoist eating also has its own peculiarities. For one, it favors the use of more subtle herbs and avoids highly heat-producing agents, such as garlic and onions. For another, it sees its goal as reaching beyond health and long life to a state of energetic and meditative transformation described as immortality. To this end, it encourages practitioners to reduce and eventually eliminate the ingestion of grains, replacing them increasingly with medicinal concoctions and breathing techniques. Ultimately Daoist eating becomes non-eating, the pure absorption of qi in accordance with the greater universe, the attainment of oneness with Dao and a subtler, more spiritual form of self-identity.

Part One

Medicinal Diets

Chapter One

Principles of Chinese Diet

> The root cause of the hundred diseases and untimely death in many cases lies with food and drink. The afflictions people suffer due to their indulgence in food and drink are worse than those caused by sights and sounds. Sights and sounds people can give up for years together, but food and drink they cannot do without for even a single day. (*Yangsheng yaoji* 6)

Unlike Western nutritionists who see food in scientific terms as quantitative and measurable entities and classify it according to calories, carbohydrates, and proteins, Chinese medical writers use traditional parameters and focus on its qualitative characteristics. Their main concerns are whether certain foodstuffs will have a warming or cooling, rising or sinking, expanding or contracting, calming or stimulating effect on the *qi*-flow in the body and whether this is conducive or detrimental to the overall health of the person. Food in China is thus from the very outset a means of therapy rather than just a nutritional substance that has more or less favorable ingredients (see Kleinman 1980).

The understanding of diet in China works according to certain key principles. Most fundamental are the cosmological concepts of yin and yang, terms that describe the alternating tendencies of *qi*-flow and allow a classification of foods into three main categories (yin, yang, and neutral), each applied under several key characteristics, such as temperature and movement. A second major principle is that of the five phases, a systematization of the movement of yin and yang, symbolized by five material entities not unlike the elements of ancient Greece and India. A core notion of Chinese cosmology, the five phases allow a classification of food according to taste and an association with relevant body organs, senses, and other physical aspects, which in turn connect to the *qi*-channesl of Chinese medicine and link dietetics to acupuncture and herbal treatments.

Beyond the main cosmological systems, food in China is also classified according to main food groups outlined earlier, each further defined in terms of therapeutic effect. A final principle is the way of preparation, which comes in five major forms (cooked cereals, stews, stir-fries, soups, and decoctions) and modifies the energetic impact.

Yin and Yang

Yin and yang are at the root of traditional Chinese cosmology. "One yin, one yang, that is the Dao," says the *Yijing* 易經 (Book of Changes), the ancient divination manual of the Zhou dynasty (1122-221 B.C.E.) that still serves to tell fortunes today. Yin and yang are commonly presented in the well-known circle with two black and white curved halves, plus a white dot in the black section and a black dot in the white section. The image shows the balance and yet interlocking nature of yin and yang, the fluidity of their interchange.

The amount of white or black on each side of the diagram starts narrow and becomes wider, then ends in a narrow line. Where the white part is largest, the black begins to emerge. This shows how the two change into each other, how yang emerges at the highest point of yin, and vice versa. The symbol emphasizes the need for being inclusive and whole, to strive for balance yet be ready to change. Yin and yang form the bipolar base of a complex system of correspondences, a numerical way to explain the world. They provide the organizing concepts for all ancient proto-sciences, such as astronomy, music, divination, medicine, and dietetics.

Yang and yin originated from geographical observation, indicating the sunny and shady sides of a hill. From there they acquired a series of associations: bright and dark, light and heavy, strong and weak, above and below, heaven and earth, ruler and minister, male and female, and so on. In concrete application, moreover, they indicate different kinds of action:

yang	active	birth	impulse	move	change	expansion
yin	structive	completion	response	rest	nurture	contraction

These characteristics were in turn associated with items in daily life:

yang	heaven	spring	summer	day	big states	ruler	man
yin	earth	fall	winter	night	small states	minister	woman

father	life	unfolding	noble	marriage	soldiers	speech	give
mother	death	stagnation	common	funeral	laborers	silence	receive

It may at first glance seem that yang is "better" than yin. In the Chinese view, however, neither is better, stronger, brighter, or more preferable, and the two forces do not represent good and evil. On the contrary, the yin aspect of things is just as important as the yang, because one cannot exist without the other. They are not opposites but complementary phases of *qi*-flow, one bringing forth the other in close mutual interdependence

In terms of food, this means that one should partake of both yin and yang substances. Yin foods tend to grow in the earth and in dark, shady locations; they are sweet in flavor, fatty in consistence, and rich in potassium. Yang foods grow in air and sunshine; they are salty in flavor, lean in consistence, and rich in sodium. Yin foods include raw food, leafy vegetables, fish, and mellow tasting substances; with their cooling, moisturizing, and decongesting effect, they promote fluid production while mitigating heat accumulation. Yang foods include anything fried, boiled, fatty, or spicy, as well as meats; they are warming, drying, and stimulating in nature. Absorbing the cooking fire, they generate heat in the body and stimulate circulation (see Anderson 1988, 188-89; Farquhar 2002, 65).

Within this general system, food has three major properties:

1. stimulating (yang/heating/*qi*-enhancing)—e.g., apricots, barley, cherries, pineapple, plums, celery, coconut;

2. calming (yin/cooling/*qi*-calming)—e.g., bananas, tofu, cucumbers, eggplant, lettuce, mushrooms, pumpkins, tomatoes, watermelon;

3. neutral (neither yin nor yang/*qi*-maintaining)—e.g., apples, cabbage, carrots, papaya, grain, beans, eggs (Lu 1996; 2000).

These properties are associated with the four seasons, with people's ages, and with particular mental states. Thus, foods eaten in spring should be stimulating and neutral; in summer, they should have a calming and cooling effect; in the fall, they should serve to retain fluid (more meats); and in winter they should stimulate and warm the body. In other words, food is used to balance the pattern of the seasons, and people should favor yin foods in yang times and yang foods in yin times.[1] However, at all times one should avoid raw and cold substances, since their extreme yin properties deplete the system, weaken the spleen, and harm the small intestine.[2]

Another modification of the food intake is according to age. Young people tend to be warmer, more energetic, and more yang in quality, while older folks have increased yin. Small children, being the most yang, often crave sweets to mellow their yang-*qi*. Older people, on the contrary, tend to like meats, stews, and warming foods to counteract their yin-nature. Beyond this, food also has an effect on the mental attitude. If we lack in confidence and depend much on others, more yang food may be indicated; if we tend to be aggressive, assertive, and stubborn, a mellowing yin-rich diet would be beneficial. Overall, yang foods increase valor and strength, while yin foods will have a calming and slowing effect (Craze and Jay 2001, 19, 23).

---

[1] By the same token, foods also balance the geographic situation of a person, so that people in hotter climates should take more yin foods, while people living in colder, more northern, places should eat more yang.

[2] This is already emphasized in the fourth-century *Yangsheng yaoji*. See Stein 1999, 188-93.

The Five Phases

The yin-yang system becomes more complex and sophisticated through its subdivision into five phases: minor yang—major yang—yin-yang—minor yin—major yin. In other words, the rhythmic pattern of rise and decline in the structure of exchange is finely tuned.

The changing pattern of heat and cold in the course of a day makes a good metaphor. As morning rises, the sun begins to warm the earth and yang is in its minor phase. As the sun comes closer to its zenith, it gets brighter and the temperature increases: the major phase of yang. After reaching the zenith, just as the sun begins its descent, there is a balance between yin and yang, neither quite one nor yet the other. In the course of the afternoon, as the sun begins to sink, light gets less and the temperature cools: the phase of minor yin. When night falls, finally, the sun is not visible anymore, darkness and coolness pervade, indicating the state of major yin. From here, the next sunrise comes and the cycle repeats. As much as day and night, yin and yang are in constant motion, one part necessarily following from the other without pause—a pattern that also applies to the rhythm of daily life in the individual and society, the cycle of the seasons throughout the year, and the overall patterns of growth and decay in nature and the human life cycle.

This system of five minor and major stages of yin and yang is then linked with five organic substances that symbolize stages in the process:

minor yang	major yang	yin-yang	minor yin	major yin
wood	fire	earth	metal	water

These are known as the "five phases" (wuxing 五行). They are often also referred to as the "five elements," because they have a superficial similarity with the Greek or Indian elements—water, fire, earth, and air. However, properly speaking the appellation "element" is incorrect, since unlike in India and Greece where they refer to solid substances and firm, unchanging building blocks of the world, in China they indicate phase energetics and dynamic processes in a constant state of transformation.

In the early Han dynasty, around 200 B.C.E., the five phases were associated with a variety of other characteristics and physical entities, including directions, colors, and seasons, as well as various functions in the human body, such as yin (storing) organs, yang (processing) organs, senses, emotions, and flavorsThe basic chart, which has been at the root of Chinese cosmology ever since and also forms the foundation of Chinese medicine and dietetics is as follows:

phase	direct.	season	color	organ1	organ2	sense	flavor
wood	east	spring	green	liver	gall	vision	sour
fire	south	summer	red	heart	sm. int.	touch	bitter
earth	center	late sum.	yellow	spleen	stomach	taste	sweet
metal	west	fall	white	lungs	lg. int.	smell	spicy
water	north	winter	black	kidney	bladder	hearing	salty

Just as the sun rises and sets in a certain order, so do the five phases move in certain cycles. Chinese cosmology distinguishes two main cycles, a productive and a controlling one—also known as the generative, creative cycle (*sheng* 生) and the conquest, control cycle (*ke* 克). The cycles are as follows:

Productive: wood —fire —earth —metal —water (1 2 3 4 5)

Controlling: wood —earth —water —fire —metal (1 3 5 2 4)

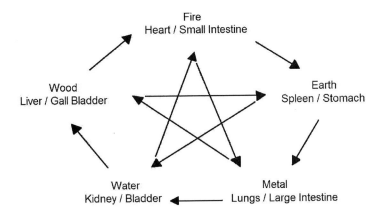

In other words, any imbalance anywhere in the body's system has an effect on the whole, bringing either excess or depletion to the various organs—and thus the senses, fluids, tissues, etc.—around it (see Huang 2008b, 101).

Within this context of the five phases the most important food classification is according to the five flavors which describe the inherent natrual tendency of the food which may or may not be the taste as noted on the tongue.[3] As already outlined in the *Huangdi neijing suwen* (7.23), they are:

1. Spicy (metal)—linked with lungs and large intestine as well as with sorghum and dog—tends to disperse *qi*; it induces perspiration and promotes *qi* and blood circulation. For example: scallions, chives, cloves, parsley, peppermint, cinnamon, chili, curry.

2. Sweet (earth)—associated with spleen and stomach as well as with panicled millet and beef—tends to relax *qi*; it slows down acute symptoms and neutralizes toxicity. For example: string beans, cherries, chestnuts, bananas, honey, melon.

3. Sour (wood)—linked with liver and gall bladder as well as with millet and mutton—tends to pull *qi* together; it slows movement and helps to control diarrhea and excessive fluids, such as perspiration. For example: apples, grapefruit, lemons, pears, plums, mangoes, vinegar.

4. Bitter (fire,)—related to the heart and small intestine as well as with beans and fowl—tends to harden *qi*; it reduces body heat, dries body fluids, and expels excess liquids, may induce diarrhea. For example: hops, lettuce, radish leaves.

5. Salty (water)—associated with kidneys and bladder as well as with millet and pork—tends to soften *qi*; it warms the body, softens hardness, and treats lymph problems and other symptoms involving hardening of muscles or glands. For example: seaweed, pickled vegetables. (7.23; Huang H. 2000, 14-16; Huang Y. 2007, 35; 2008b, 99-100; Lo 2005, 164, 167)

The five flavors should be balanced in every meal to match the individual's condition, stimulate the organs, and eliminate wayward *qi*. Dietitians use food to regulate the *qi*-flow in the channels, much like acupuncturists stimulate certain points, after providing a diagnosis in terms of *qi* excess and depletion and analyzing the condition in relation to the major organ systems involved.

---

[3] For example, lettuce is "bitter" in inherent flavor but may taste neutral or even sweet to different individuals. By the same token, grains are generally classified as "sweet," but may taste bitter or salty.

Energetic Properties

In addition to the combination of yin-yang and the correspondences of the five phases, there are two further main principles of food: temperature and movement.

First, all foods have a specific effect described in terms of temperature:

cold/cool	neutral	warm/hot
stomach yin	center	spleen yang
lung yin	triple heater	kidney yang
liver yin		heart yang
kidney yin		liver yang

(Engelhardt and Hempen 1997, 409)

While most foods naturally have a temperature quality, some also change depending on their state. Thus, for example, raw wheat has a tendency to be cool and neutral, supporting the center of the body. When sprouted, it becomes cold and acquires a slightly pungent flavor, serving to alleviate heat conditions. As cooked porridge, wheat is neutral and sweet, enhancing *qi*. When baked as wheat flour, finally, it obtains a warm temperature and aids in treating cool or cold body conditions (Engelhardt and Hempen 1997, 411).

The different temperature qualities of food are intrinsically related to the five phases and their corresponding organs. For instance, a liver weakened by too much yin food can develop an imbalance with the spleen and may cause it to overwork. This in turn may lead to an overflow of acidic secretions in the stomach, felt as heartburn and acid reflux. On the other hand, the warming and cooling qualities of food can be used to modify already existing imbalances, increasing the *qi* through warm or hot food in a weakened *qi*-channel or depleting it through cool or cold things in one that shows signs of excess or inflammation.

Second, again using the basic yin-yang matrix, the quality of food is evaluated according to its dominant movement:

1. outwards: induces perspiration and reduces fever; use in summer; spicy or sweet (pepper, ginger);

2. inwards: eases bowel movements and abdominal swelling; use in winter; bitter or salty (lettuce, clams, crabs, seaweed);

3. upwards: relieves diarrhea, prolapsed anus or uterus, falling stomach; use in spring; spicy, sweet, or bitter (apricots, celery, cherries, grapes, olives, potatoes, peanuts);

4. downwards: relieves vomiting, hiccupping, and asthma; use in fall; sweet or sour (apples, bananas, cucumbers, grapefruit, lettuce, peaches, strawberries).

All these serve to remedy certain conditions. For example: to disperse cold, use ginger or wine; to improve the appetite, eat green/red pepper or ham; to induce a bowel movement, take castor beans or sesame oil; to reduce fever, eat star fruit or water chestnuts; to relieve pain, take honey or squash.

Also, for a headache due to increased heat, use cooling and downward moving foods, such as wheat, beans, bamboo sprouts, radish, spinach, and tomatoes. To help in cases of blood- and *qi*-stagnation (e.g., angina pectoris), use foods that stimulate and move blood and *qi*, including leeks, onions, vinegar, crabs, and small quantities of wine. For erectile dysfunction, often caused by a depletion of kidney-*qi*, take walnuts, cinnamon, anchovies, mussels, mutton, and game (Engelhardt and Hempen 1997, 576-85). In all cases, the ideal is to create a diet that balances the body's symptoms through the movement as well as flavors and energetic tendencies of food.

Because of its strong emphasis on balance which includes also the need for hot, energy-giving yang foods, Chinese physicians—unlike monastic Daoists—do not support a vegetarian diet. Vegetarians eat too many cooling, yin foods, thus depleting their *qi* to levels suitable only for recluses who are not physically active. By the same token, the addition of fish to a vegetarian diet, although it provides protein according to the Western system, will not increase yang, since fish is a cool food that relates to water and therefore yin. On the other hand, a diet overly heavy in proteins and meat is not beneficial either, since highly caloric, strong yang foods may deplete the body's *qi* by causing certain organs to overwork and creating depletions in others. It is best, therefore, to eat some meat, but not too much and if possible organic, healthy specimens free of hormones and stimulants.

Food Groups

The most fundamental division of Chinese cuisine is into the categories of *fan* 飯 and *cai* 菜, literally "rice" and "vegetables" or, more broadly, the grain base of nutrition and various supplementary dishes that are mostly vegetable-based but also include, besides mushrooms and seaweed, meat, poultry, fish, fruit, and so on. Grains tend to come in whole or milled form; appear as staples, buns, cakes, or noodles; and are typically boiled, steamed, or baked. Supplementary dishes involve varying degrees of water and oil for either steaming, boiling, or frying (Chang 1977a, 7-8; Huang 2000, 17-28, 70-74; Lo 2005, 175).

While grains are the main staple of the diet, vegetables enhance and complete nourishment, allowing the *qi* won from food, literally "grain *qi*" (*guqi* 穀氣), to work properly. Beyond that, fruit supports the body's system, ensuring that fluids are plentiful and flowing smoothly, while meat strengthens and invigorates the *qi*, especially indicated in cases of weakness (Engelhardt and Nögel 2009, 20).

Although the terms "grains," "vegetables," and so on are familiar, the definition of what belongs into each category is not quite the same. For example, grain in China not only includes the standard grains, such as rice, wheat/barley (*mai* 麥), oats, millet, corn, and buckwheat, but also all beans, legumes, nuts, and seeds. For the most part, they have a neutral tendency in terms of temperature, i.e., they can be used to cool or warm depending on their mode of preparation and on accompanying ingredients. Their taste tends to be on the sweet side, which means that they strengthen and support the spleen and stomach systems in the center of the body—allowing spleen-yang to rise and excess dampness to drain—while also enhancing body fluids, such as sweat, saliva, tears, and lymph.

More specifically, round-grain rice is the most neutral and balancing among the various kinds of rice; wheat tends to help cool overheated channels, usually associated with the heart; millet warms and helps balance the large intestine and supports the *qi*. In terms of preparation, grains are usually cooked; however, patients with any kind of weakness should take them softly in gruels rather than *al dente*. Also, any grain processed into flour generally has a warming and drying effect, making it suitable at times of diarrhea or dampness and not a favorite for continuous consumption.

Beans and legumes, most importantly soybeans and peanuts, are neutral or cooling in terms of temperature and tend have a sweet flavor. Like grains, they support the spleen and stomach in the center; even more than grains, they help drain dampness. Their more processed forms such as soymilk and tofu have a slightly more cooling potency. Nuts and seeds, such as almonds, pine nuts, and sesame, are usually sweet and neutral but tend to moisturize rather than dry. Once roasted (and, more so, salted), their temperature changes to being warm or even heating, rendering them unsuitable for any kind of heat condition. On the other hand, they can be useful in dispelling "wind," a fast-moving condition, physically linked with cool, windy conditions and emotionally associated with fear and anxiety, that attacks especially the kidneys. Helping greatly with stabilizing the body, nuts and seeds are much beloved by longevity seekers and Daoists alike.

Vegetables here also include key spices and divide into six categories (see Huang 2000, 95). First are pungent vegetables that are spicy in flavor and heating and yang-inducing in quality, e.g., onions, scallions, leeks, peppers, fagara, ginger, and garlic. Loved by ordinary people and very helpful in cases of cold and weakness, they can lead to depletion when overused and are for the most part shunned by religious practitioners, whether of the Daoist or Buddhist persuasion, due to their powerful impact on the body's system.

Second are root vegetables, typically warming and sweet, with a balancing effect on the body's center as well a supporting quality for liver and kidneys. Here we have things like carrots, potatoes, cabbage, beets, fennel, rutabaga, and turnips—the kinds of things Americans associate with Thanksgiving dinner and fall coolness. Also in this group belong celery, cooling but enhancing liver-yang, and radish (*daikon*), the yin counterpart to ginger which is cooling, sweet, and pungent, strengthens spleen and stomach, enhances digestion, and aids the lungs by lowering *qi*, decreasing phlegm, and detoxifying the body (see Fang 2000).

The third class are soft and slippery vegetables, including leafy plants like spinach, kale, Swiss chard, dandelion, and lettuce. Usually bitter and sweet as well as cooling, they alleviate heat conditions and enhance the digestion. Fourth are nightshades, such as tomatoes, eggplant, pumpkins zucchini, cucumbers, and squash: neutral and sweet, they relieve swellings and moisturize the tissues. They are followed by mushrooms—widespread and of innumerable variety in China—which, with their sweet and cooling qualities as well as numerous nutrients, are very good for long life and frequently used in Daoist cooking. Last, but not least, are the various kinds of seaweed, widely used in Korea and Japan; in China they are believed to have deep effects on the body's system, notably the liver and kidneys, and which even in the West are known to have antioxidant and cancer-preventing properties (Engelhardt and Nögel 2009, 23-25; see also Huang 2000, 32-43).

None of these vegetables is usually eaten raw in China. The most common way of preparation is steaming, closely followed by boiling in soups and pan-frying in stir-fries. This has to do historically with the avoidance of bacteria and infections, but is due just as much energetically to the effort of making them easier to digest and helping the body to maintain a proper balance.

Fruit is the third major food group. For the most part sweet or sour in flavor, they can be used flexibly in terms of temperature: cooling when eaten fresh or warming when steamed. Rich in liquids, they support the body's fluids but can also, when taken too frequently, result in increased dampness. Especially pears are much favored, especially also among Daoists who like them best steamed with various nuts, berries, and herbs, since they strengthen the stomach and lungs and eliminate dampness and phlegm (Huang 2000, 43-54; Peng 20006b, 14-15, 19, 31).

Fourth and finally there are meat, poultry, and eggs, as well as fish, shellfish, and other seafood. While seafood is more yin and helps eliminate dampness, meat and poultry are yang in nature, enhance *qi*, and may increase dampness. In all cases, fat parts should be avoided, blood should be drained before cooking, and they should be fried only very briefly then steamed for best consumption—not barbequed, grilled, or deep-fat fried. Also, serving meat or fish in small pieces makes it easier to eat and digest.

More specifically, chicken and eggs—as much in China as in the West—are the strength-givers *par excellence*, gently warming and supporting the central spleen and stomach systems and usually recommended for convalescence after illness. Mutton and goat meat helps the kidneys and thus sexual dysfunction and muscle problems. Pork tends to moisturize yin, aiding lung conditions such as a dry cough. Seafood, in contrast, contains a salty flavor which aids the kidneys and a cooling effect that helps loosen dampness and heat and thus serves best in cases of night sweat, vertigo, and diabetes. It is also noticeable that most seafood when smoked, dried, or pickled, does not lose its fundamental characteristics and can thus be used in many different forms.

In addition, Westerners also tend to use a great deal of dairy, which is all but unknown in traditional China, with the exception of the Mongolian yogurt-drink called *kefir*. To examine them briefly in terms of Chinese dietetics, dairy products are classified as having a sweet flavor and neutral temperature. They increase dampness, lower *qi*, detoxify, and cool heat syndromes. Any condition involving downward movements (diarrhea) and phlegm (colds) will be made worse when taking dairy. Also, usually goat and sheep's milk are easier to digest than cow's; so are fermented products, such as curds and yogurt. A regular, moderate consumption of milk products may have a strengthening and invigorating effect on the person; any overuse or the ingestion of highly processed varieties, on the other hand, leads to abdominal tension, enhanced dampness, and weakness.

Overall, the recommendation is for a well-cooked and well-mixed diet consisting of all different food groups, as much as possible "clear" and "pure," i.e., organic and locally grown. Their diet is strongly based on grains and vegetables, with fruits, meat, seafood, and dairy added regularly but in limited quantities. Many ailments, both today and in history, go back to the tendency of overeating and indulging in processed, cooling, and yin-based foods (Huang 2007, 48, 85). As already Sun Simiao says: "Many diseases in the body can be traced back to an excessive consumption of cold food in spring and summer. Also, many dishes containing raw meat and cold foods do harm to people in a variety of ways. Thus one should avoid them" (Engelhardt and Nögel 2009, 30).

Forms of Preparation

Food preparation in China involves boiling in covered pots—made from earthenware in antiquity—steaming in bamboo trays or steamers, baking in ovens or roasting over open fires, and frying in large pans often known as woks (Andersen 1988, 152). The stove is considered not only the center of the family's activities but also a sacred place that connects humanity with the powers of Heaven, and the stove god is traditionally believed to ascend to heaven on the last day of the year to report the family's behavior to the celestial authorities (see Chard 1995). Within this framework, the Chinese create five major kinds of dishes: cooked cereals, stews and noodle-soups, stir-fries, soups, and decoctions. They are each, moreover, best suited for certain times of the day (see Engelhardt and Nögel 2009, 31-33).

Cooked cereals (porridge, gruel, or congee; *zhou* 粥) involve grains used either whole, in flakes, or ground. They are boiled until they reach a half liquid consistency. Herbs, fruits, vegetables, and meats or seafood may be added to increase taste and dietetic efficacy. Rather than being boiled with the grain, however, these should be steamed, fried, or otherwise prepared separately and added in the end. To top the dish off, one may add various spices for flavor, thus allowing the possibility of creating a large variety of meals. Therapeutically, cooked cereals tend to be warming and support the center. They set a steady, positive tone for the day and are especially recommended at breakfast. Another common application is during convalescence and after childbirth.

Stir-fries and other main dishes (*caiyao* 菜餚) use a great variety of foods, including all the different groups but strongly based on vegetables. Mostly applying a combination of different foods, they include simple and complex stir-fries as well as roasted meals and briefly seared ingredients that are then combined in salad-like dishes. Depending on the desired effect, various spices are added to the meal, including ginger, onions, garlic, as well as wine, vinegar, salt, and sugar. Also depending on the ingredients and the intensity of cooking and spicing, the therapeutic effect may vary from strongly heating through mildly warming to neutrally supportive. They are best taken in the middle of the day, when the body needs most vibrant energy.

Stews (*mian* 麵; *geng* 羹) consist of rice or noodles which are steamed or boiled and served with some liquid and a selection of vegetables and meats, either cooked immediately with the grain or prepared separately by steaming or frying and added later. They, too, tend to be warming and supportive of the body's center, creating a strengthening environment and enriching the blood. They can include various kinds of seafood, such as shrimps, and are often made with mushrooms. Calming and easy to digest, stews are ideally suited for consumption at night, several hours before bedtime, to ready the body for a good night's sleep.

Soups (*tanggeng* 湯羹) are based on meat, seafood, and vegetables, all boiled together in water for an extended period of time and seasoned with a variety of spices and herbs. Consumed either separately or in combination with other dishes, they add a warming and intensifying quality to any meal. They also serve as a major source of moisture and are well known for their strengthening effect. Soups can be eaten at all times, supplementing other dishes, and are often part of the main meal of the day.

Decoctions or herbal drinks (*tangji* 湯劑), finally, are the main way of administering traditional Chinese herbs. Various plant, mineral, and even animal substances are boiled together over a period of time—from ten minutes to an hour—often creating some rather intense odors around the house. Used therapeutically, decoctions are commonly but not necessarily applied under medical supervision and directed to alleviate and cure certain conditions. Some common decoctions include the mix of ginger, scallions, and brown sugar efficacious in cases of the common cold, as well as the joint boiling of fresh ginger and dried orange peel to calm the stomach and alleviate nausea. A variant form of decoction is syrup (*gao* 膏), made by cooking yin-moisturizing foods such as fruit, then taking the resulting juice and boiling it down to a dense consistency. Adding honey or sugar, one lets the juice simmer further until it reaches a gel-like stage. Any syrup of this sort, taken as medicine by the table spoon, will enhance moisture and support the strengthening effect of other foods. An example is apple syrup for stomach and lungs.

In terms of their daily application, the Chinese recommend various forms kinds of prepared food. In the morning, for example, when yang is low and yin is dense after a night's sleep, one may feel tired, bloated, or distended, and have an increased coating on the tongue. One eats to get the yang-*qi* moving, which is best achieved by taking warm, dynamic foods that do not burden the central organs of spleen and stomach. The ideal form of preparation is accordingly a cooked cereal, closely followed by whole-grain bread, while anything cold (juices, cereals) or heavy (bacon and eggs) tends to be counterproductive.

At noon, the body needs to replenish its *qi* and continue to be warmed and energized. Lunch should, therefore, be warm and plentiful, consisting of steamed food and stir-fries, with soups as a supplement. Dishes should be mainly made from vegetables with minor amounts of lean meat, seafood, or eggs. Cold food (salads, yogurt) or heavy dishes (fatty meats, cakes), increase dampness and phlegm and will create tiredness rather than aid the positive flow of *qi*.

In the evening, yang should begin to calm down and yin be allowed to rise. To this end, the best food is gentle and quieting, and one should avoid all kinds of intense yang as found in hot spices and fatty, heavy dishes. Stews are ideal, but easy stir-fries and soups may also serve. It is important not too eat too late to allow the body time for digestion before going to sleep. Also, many medical and Daoist texts recommend taking a short walk after the evening meal to stabilize the energetic pathways (see Engelhardt and Hempen 1997, 613-17).

Beyond cooking and eating consciously, dietary manuals also recommend the frequent consumption of tea, especially green tea. Mentioned already in the *Shijing* 詩經 (Book of Odes; c. 800 B.C.E.), tea has always been a mainstay of Chinese culture. Botanically a member of the Camellia family, tea grows as various shrubs that can reach fifty feet in height and commonly bear shiny leaves whose ends form pointed, spear-like tips. Picked and dried or roasted, and occasionally mixed with blossoms or flowers, the leaves are prepared to make different teas. The white or pale green variety uses them almost raw, while black or red tea applies them more roasted or fermented. Tea can contain large amounts of caffeine in all forms, and commonly has been used in religious institutions to keep monks and nuns from falling asleep during meditation periods.

Chinese literature describes tea almost exclusively as bitter but sometimes also as sweet. Its medical benefits include the ability to increase blood flow, heighten awareness, speed elimination, prevent tooth decay, aid digestion, cleanse the skin, alleviate joint pain, and generally prolong life (Blofeld 1985, 144). It is also a way to ingest all five phases at once: earth through the bowl's ceramics, metal in the kettle, water as its base, wood in the plant, and fire in the heating. Western studies, too, have shown that especially green tea with low caffeine contains antioxidants which bind harmful free radicals. Drinking it regularly can prevent cell mutation in tumors, promote healthy arteries, reduce cholesterol, release toxins, aid digestion, increase metabolism, and control bacteria.

To sum up, food in traditional China as well as in Daoism has always a medical dimension to it. It is understood in terms of qualities and effects and used primarily to balance the *qi*-flow and temperature in the body. Food in general should be fresh and cooked, not raw or processed; it should be taken in moderation in conjunction with various teas and herbal drinks. It should also never be boring, using the variety of raw materials and ways of preparation to create enticing, tasty meals.

Chapter Two

Social Regulations

When working hard, do not eat; when eating, do not undertake physical activities. When you sweat, do not eat or drink. When you are enraged, do not eat; when eating, avoid getting angry or upset. In mourning do not eat; while eating do not entertain sad thoughts. (*Yangsheng yaoji* 6)

Food, as it is cultivated, prepared, and ingested, does not occur on the natural and personal levels alone. It is always also a social phenomenon that happens in specific community settings, expresses certain cultural values, and is bound by the limitations of society. As Mary Douglas points out, the human body is also an image of society and the passage of food in and out of the body in many ways equals social boundaries and their transgression (1973, 70). As a result, in addition to basic nutrition, societies use food to activate interpersonal relationships, determine social rank and status, express socio-religious ideas, help cope with stress and psychological needs (e.g., emotional eating), reward or punish certain behaviors, and treat or prevent illness and social deviations (Leininger 1970; Anderson and Anderson 1977, 366).

Food serves not only to create interpersonal connection but mirrors social organization and articulates distinctiveness (Counihan 1999, 6-7). It plays a key role in all societies, defined as integrated systems of functional unity where exchange of goods links people together (see Mauss 1967). Food is power in its most basic and tangible form; it is often a political factor in that hunger tends to be an instigation to rebellion or women use the avoidance of food as a form of self-assertion (see Bell 1985; Bynum 1987; Brumberg 1988). Class, caste, race, gender, status, and age all have to do with who has access to what kinds of food, leading to consumption patterns that are inherently social and political (Counihan 1999 8).

Food defines social context. Often family means the group of people who share the same hearth; feeding a stranger gives him the benefit of hospitality; and food offerings define the relationship between people and their gods (Counihan 1999, 15-17). The refusal of food in prolonged fasting, moreover, often serves to reject society while developing alternative social structures and conceptual realities. Food here, rather than being a form of physical sustenance, is seen negatively as a vehicle for mortality: its avoidance enables practitioners "to transcend their mundane and earthly selves in the quest for piety or perfection" (Counihan 1999, 98-99).

All these general observations also apply to Chinese and Daoist food. Consciously structured from antiquity, food in China signified social realities, and different sensory experiences were connected to moral realities (Sterckx 2005, 53). The emperor's body being a major conduit for the will of Heaven, nourishing it meant to support the proper governance of the world, enabled by the continuous vigilance of numerous court physicians and nutritionists (Lo 2005, 165-66). Different foodstuffs were employed in different contexts, changing over history as the economy developed and new items became accessible and fashionable. Also new settings unfolded (e.g., monasteries), and taboos of various sorts came to express newly arising fears and preferences.

In addition, social constructs of life cycles and expectancy as well as efforts to increase longevity had a distinct impact on the kinds of foods people were supposed to eat and combinations they better avoided. Some foodstuffs, notably things preserved by drying, pickling, or fermenting, as well as items that had an inherent toxicity, were prohibited or could only be taken under certain circumstances. Other social taboos include the consumption of certain animals considered dirty or of human flesh, although that taboo varied over the years.

The Chinese calendar, a complex mixture of solar and lunar features, moreover was important not only in defining the seasons but also the astrological connections of people and foodstuffs. Already formulated in Han-dynasty almanacs unearthed at Shuihudi (Loewe 1988; Lo 2005, 178), many of its regulations deal with the year of one's birth or that of one's parents as well as with certain kinds of food associated with the name of certain days. Thus, for example, shellfish was to be avoided on "crab" days, i.e., days that contained the cyclical sign *jia*, which means "crab," although as a cyclical sign the character does not have a specific meaning.

Antiquity and the Middle Ages

The earliest grains cultivated on Chinese soil, as documented in archaeological finds, were various forms of millet, known as *liang* 粱 and *shu* 黍, supplemented by less common specimens, such as wheat, hemp, barley, and rice, the latter being particular to the south (Chang 1977b, 26-27; Huang 2000, 19). The most important legumes were soybeans and peanuts, found together with various other kinds of beans, taro, and yams. Main vegetables included mallow, melon, gourd, turnip, leeks, lettuce, cattail, wormwood grasses, lotus root, as well as cabbage, garlic, scallions, water chestnuts, and bamboo shoots—thus representing many classic ingredients of Chinese dishes (Chang 1977b, 28; also Anderson 1988, 10).

Meats in prehistoric China came both from domesticated and wild species, such as pigs, dogs, and cattle, as well as the common deer and rabbit and the less frequently hunted wild boar, fox, panther, and tiger. Fowls included chicken, pullet, goose, quail, partridge, pheasant, sparrow, curlew, and others; fish was mainly carp and mullet, supplemented by various kinds of shellfish (Chang 1977b, 29-30; see also Huang 2000, 55-66). Even at the dawn of history, Chinese culture thus presented a rich dietetic environment that allowed the creative combination of many different kinds of food (Anderson 1988, 23).

Over the course of history, while the basic principles of Chinese diet remained constant, available and popular foodstuffs varied mainly due to technological and economic changes. That is to say, the different periods of Chinese history saw the emergence of new agricultural methods as well as improved infrastructure that allowed the cultivation, processing, and transport of both a wider variety and increased quantities of foods. The Chinese also tended to come into contact, both through trade and conquest, with various outside countries and cultures, and to the present day have continued to include new items into their traditional cookery.

Thus, in the Han dynasty, when the empire expanded well into what is today Afghanistan and noted travelers like Zhang Qian 張騫 journeyed through Central Asia into India, a number of important new foods became common (Anderson 1988, 34). They included grape, alfalfa, pomegranate, walnut, sesame, onion, caraway seeds, peas, coriander, and cucumber, as well as dragon fruit and litchi, fruits today typically associated with China (Yü 1977, 80). In terms of technology, it was under the Han that soybeans were boiled and pressed for the first time, creating the wide-spread soymilk and its derivative, tofu. They were also fermented and made into a kind of relish known as *shi* 豉, eaten both as a snack and used as a condiment. Another important change at this time involved the milling of grains into flour, probably based on technology imported from western Asia, which allowed the creation of various kinds of cakes and the earliest noodles, made mainly from wheat. Noodles (*mian* 麵) and steamed buns (*mantou* 饅頭) as well as baked cakes (*bing* 餅) became popular at the time (Yü 1977, 81; Huang 2000, 462-84).

The same trend continued in the Tang dynasty, when international contacts were intensified and technology advanced. In addition to millet and wheat, rice became more easily accessible, and barley was used more widely. New plant foods included rhubarb, water mallow, celery, nasturtiums, asparagus, parsley, shallots, as well as various kinds of algae and seaweeds. Exotic fruits imported from Central Asia and the tropical south were new varieties of peach as well as cherries, plums, apricots, pears, crabapple, quince, oranges, tangerines, bananas and many more. There were also the fruits of various palm trees, olives and various kinds of nuts and seeds, as well as numerous different types of animal products, consumed especially among the wealthier and noble classes (Schafer 1977, 89-99).

At the same time, preservation techniques advanced, including drying, smoking, and fermenting, as well as pickling in brine, salt, vinegar, bran, oil, chili, and various combinations thereof. Foods could be liquid-packed or dried, sealed or unsealed with various spices, strong in flavor or very mild. Grapes, for example, could be parched, crinkled, or dried and spiced to create a large variety of raisin-based dishes (Anderson 1988, 167; Schafer 1977, 113-16; Huang 2000, 379-429). Milk, especially from goats and horses but also from palms and almonds, became more widely available due to contact with northern Asian peoples. It was modified in many ways: curdled into cakes like tofu, fermented into kumis and yogurt, kaymak and clotted cream, as well as clarified butter (made from coagulated milk oils) (Schafer 1977, 106).

To make foods more palatable, Tang people employed sweeteners and spices. Sweeteners included various kinds of honey as well as sugarcane, sugar beets, raisin tree extracts, and maltose, "a kind of malt sugar derived from germinating grains" (Schafer 1977, 108). Among spices, hot pepper corns—the seeds of a plant known as fagara (jiao 椒)—were most popular. They came in various local varieties as well as in imported form from Persia, such as our black pepper, then known as "barbarian fagara" (hujiao 胡椒). Some Indian-style spices such as cardamom, nutmeg, and cumin too made their way to China, so that curry-like dishes became available (Schafer 1977, 110-11).

Unlike in the Han and Tang, when the main impact on the development of Chinese cuisine came from foreign contacts, the Song saw major changes in domestic economy and infrastructure. As the aristocratic elite was replaced by an educated bureaucracy and the merchant class grew in importance, agricultural technology transformed. Roads and waterways were expanded so more goods could pass more easily from one region to another. As a result, both rice and tea—prominent in southern China and delicacies for the upper classes before—became widespread all over the country while many local foods grew to national importance. As Michael Freeman says, "Song cooks were the beneficiaries of twin revolutions, in agriculture and in commerce, and enjoyed, especially in the two capitals [Kaifeng and Hangzhou], an unprecedented abundance that probably made city dwellers the best-fed mass population in world history up to that time" (1977, 143).

One major role in these changes was the import of a new, faster ripening and drought-resistant strain of rice from Champa, a Hindu kingdom in what is today Central Vietnam. It made double-cropping possible, greatly increased the yield of the fields, and supported the population explosion which led to an overall increase from 100 to 150 million in the course of the Song dynasty. In addition, sorghum (gaoliang 高粱) became available for the first time, useful as animal fodder and for distilling into hard liquor.

Another major transformation occurred through changes in infrastructure and the commercialization of food. Markets grew massively, so that Hangzhou alone had ten huge squares for trading. As Marco Polo notes, "on each of the said squares three days a week there is concourse of from forty to fifty thousand persons who come to market and bring everything you can desire for food, because there is always a great supply of victuals" (Moule and Pelliot 1938, 328; Freeman 1977, 149). Variety increased drastically and many different kinds of food became available to people from all walks of life. Both rich and poor ate pork, lamb, and kid as well as horse meat, beef, venison, and various kinds of game, poultry, fish, and shellfish. Vegetables, especially in the south, were fresh all year round and preserved in many ways for the colder regions. Fruit of an amazing variety was a common element in the Song diet and eaten at all times, before and after meals, in summer and in winter (Freeman 1977, 154-55). The restaurant culture flourished and both catering in family style and specialty cooking became widely available to satisfy social needs and pleasures.

At the same time, the Song dynasty also became the first major period that saw a wide-spread taboo against eating beef, partly due to religious or spiritual reasons—since it allowed people to belong to increasingly popular "vegetarian" sects yet accept social norms and still eat pork—but also to preserve the economically essential water buffalo (Goossaert 2005, 240-41). Daoists in particular tabooed beef together with the "three revolting animals" (*sanyan* 三厭: wild goose, dogs, and aquatic creatures like eels and turtles) and emphasized the power of these foods to invite demons and pestilence into one's life (Goossaert 2005, 243). For many centuries, until the anti-superstition campaign ended the popular temple culture in 1898, only ethnic non-Chinese, Muslims, vagrants, criminals, and Confucian fundamentalists consumed beef in China (Goossaert 2005, 245, 248).

Late Empire and Modernity

The Mongol conquest in the thirteenth century followed by the wars at the beginning of the Ming dynasty (1368-1644) led to a severe reduction in economic productivity and a shrinking population, which went back to about 100 million. While Chinese cuisine by and large remained stable and traditional, the foreign rulers introduced certain Mongolian and Middle Eastern ways of eating. These are documented in the *Yinshan zhengyao* 飲膳正要 (Principles of Correct Diet; dat. 1330) by Hu Sihui 忽思慧, which also details the medical uses of food (Buell and Anderson 2000; Sabban 1986). Another important document of the same period is the *Yinshi xuzhi* 飲食須知 (Essential Knowledge for Eating and Drinking; dat. 1368) by Jia Ming 賈銘, which presents detailed accounts of what kinds of food support life in what forms of preparation (Mote 1977, 225-33; Huang 2000, 137-38).

The Ming dynasty, preserving peace for several centuries, supported renewed growth and made inroads in technology and food availability. Major hydraulic projects prevented flooding in low-lying areas and created new lands for cultivation while contact with Western missionaries introduced new foods from the Americas, notably maize, potatoes, tomatoes, and peanuts (known earlier but popularized at this time). The court also supported major encyclopedic projects, which inspired Li Shizhen 李時珍 (1518-1593) to compile an encompassing handbook on herbal formulas and foodstuffs, the *Bencao gangmu* 本草綱目 (Systematic Materia Medica), whose 11,096 prescriptions still form an important resource today (Lo 2005, 175; also Unschuld 1986; Needham 1986; Métailié 2001).

These overall tendencies continued under the Qing, with the main difference that the population exploded once again, rising to 450 million by the mid-nineteenth century. This led to a vast increase in famines and rebellions—which of course further disrupted the food supply. More people lived on new crops of maize, potatoes, and sweet potatoes, while the share of rice dropped from 70 to 36 percent of overall food production (Spence 1977, 263, 271).

The modern age has brought a variety of food developments, mainly because of to political events. While Chinese food has spread all over the world due to increased emigration (see Wu and Cheung 2002; Roberts 2002), China itself underwent various periods of turbulence, notably in the early twentieth century, during the Japanese invasion, and in World War II, which lead to widespread shortages and famines. So did the Great Leap Forward in the late 1950s and early 1960s (Anderson and Anderson 1977, 351). At all other times China experienced an abundance of food and expansion of diet, both through foreign contact and advanced technology. Enhanced foreign trade brought various new and highly popular vegetables into the country, such as carrots from Europe, eggplants from India, okra from Africa, and cilantro from Mexico (Anderson and Anderson 1977, 331).

Advanced technology, while increasing food production and thus supporting yet another population explosion, especially under the Communists, has also had its downsides. The most obvious is the tendency to alter and denature foodstuffs, of which the most blatant example is the polishing of rice and bleaching of wheat flour that began in China in the late nineteenth century (Anderson and Anderson 1977, 345). Modern bio-engineering often reduces the nutritional value of basic staples and encourages the consumption of empty calories, thus leading to new and increased health problems, such as hypertension, diabetes, and obesity. Not immune to these development, Chinese eating habits have undergone a serious transformation especially in the last few decades. What Eugene and Marja Anderson note about Hong Kong in the 1970s holds very much true for China today:

> At an equal pace with improvement in quality and availability of food has been a pernicious sort of Westernization, involving low-extraction flour, highly polished rice, and above all white sugar in all its forms. . . . The tendency now is to eat less fruit and vegetables, more fat and flour and sugar. Soft drinks, candy, cookies, factory-made cakes (essentially unenriched flour, white sugar, and cheap cooking oil), and the like, have come to constitute a major part of diet. (1977, 353)

In many ways, therefore, not only Westerners but the Chinese themselves can benefit greatly from traditional dietetic wisdom to maintain health and reach vigorous longevity. One step in that direction is the increased popularity of Buddhist restaurants, which are strictly vegetarian and use more organic and whole foods, especially in Taiwan but increasingly also on the mainland. Another is the spread of medicinal restaurants serving medicated dishes (*yaoshan* 藥膳) that bolster and tonify *qi* as part of nutritional therapy (*shiliao* 食療) or personal self-care (*ziwo baojian* 自我保健) (Farquhar 2002, 51).

The aim of these medicated dishes is to balance yin and yang, strengthen the constitution, prevent and treat diseases, and lengthen life. Many of the specialized restaurants cater particularly to middle-aged men, helping them to supplement *qi*, prevent the depletion sexual essence, and generally improve the functioning of their organs, especially the kidneys. Dishes include regular foodstuffs, supplemented by *qi*-enhancing herbs, such as ginseng, astralagus, schisandra, chrysanthemum, fennel, hawthorn, and Asian cornelian cherry (Farquhar 2002, 60).

Life Cycles and Longevity

Chinese dietary recommendations literally extend from womb to tomb. Just as a child born in China is already a year old, so the influence of food on human life begins before birth (Despeux 2007, 25). To nourish the growing embryo, pregnant women must practice "fetal education" (*taijiao* 胎教), taking good care of themselves and their nutrition.

Already the Mawangdui manuscript *Taichan shu* 胎產書 (Book of Embryonic Generation) says:

> In the first month, it is called "flowing into the form." Food and drink must be the finest; the sour boiled dishes must be thoroughly cooked. Do not eat acrid or rank foods. This is called "internal fixture."
>
> In the second month, it first becomes lard. Do not eat acrid or stinking foods. The dwelling place must be still. For a boy, there must be no exertion, lest the hundred joints all ail. This is called "first deposition."
>
> In the third month, it first become suet and appears like a gourd. During this time, it does not have a fixed configuration and if exposed to things it transforms. For this reason, lords, sires, and great men must not employ dwarves. Do not observe monkeys. Do not eat onion and ginger. Do not eat a rabbit boiled dish. (Harper 1998, 378-79; Lo 2005, 180)

During pregnancy, *qi* tends to flow most strongly in the channels that run along the front and center of the torso—the earliest and most foundational vessels of the human body, from which the embryo grows. They are the Conception Vessel (*renmai* 任脈) and the Penetrating Vessel (*chongmai* 沖脈). Since all other channels are less active, there is a tendency toward a weakness of yin-*qi* and *xue* 血 (blood), especially in the first trimester. To off-set this tendency, pregnant women should enhance the liver and its related system by favoring soybeans, pine nuts, tomatoes, spinach, and eggs, and avoiding any overly yang foods, such as spicy, hot, and dry items as well as caffeine and alcohol. Also, they should moderate their intake of ginger, cinnamon, pepper, and game (Engelhardt and Nögel 2009, 39).

After giving birth, traditionally and still today, women are not allowed to do any work or exert themselves for an entire month. While largely feeding on chicken and chicken soup in all possible variations, they should also make sure that their *xue* (blood) does not stagnate by taking some leeks and adzuki beans. Breastfeeding, moreover, takes a lot of energy out of the body while nourishing the newborn baby. It is best to eat highly nourishing yet easily digestible foods for this purpose. Again, hot and spicy as well as cold, sour, and contracting foods are best avoided. The same goes also for cooling and raw foods, such as melons and bananas (Engelhardt and Nögel 2009, 39).

All these are rather ancient guidelines. Thus the fourth-century *Yangsheng yaoji* in its section on pregnancy, like the Mawangdui manuscripts, discourages the ingestion of intensely yang foods, such as meat and spicy dishes (including ginger, cinnamon, and sugar), as well as of very cold foods, such as ice-cold rice-soup, since they put increased pressure on the already weakened yin. Unlike modern sources, the text in addition connects foods with certain embryonic developments in a quasi-magical manner. For example, pregnant women should not eat the meat of the six domestic animals because their senses are not very keen and ingesting them might cause the child to suffer from reduced vision and hearing. They better not eat rabbit to avoid the potential development of a harelip; nor turtle to prevent the child having a very short neck. Raw ginger, which looks like a finger, is taboo lest the child grow an extra digit. Eating sparrows may cause intense, uncontrolled desires in the child, while alcoholic beverages may lead to mental confusion (Stein 1999, 208-09; also Despeux 2007, 26; Furth 1999).

Once children are weaned and eat on their own, other dietetic rules apply. Since their internal system is not fully developed and *qi* and *xue* are not completely stable, children tend to suffer easily from ailments of the center (spleen and stomach), tending toward nausea, constipation, and diarrhea. They should thus avoid all sorts of extremes in terms of both flavor and temperature, focusing on moderate and balancing foods. Anything very strong may burden the center and cause trouble (e.g., glutinous rice) as much as strongly cooling foods, such as cold milk, ice cream, raw foods, and yogurt. All these might increase dampness and a weakness in spleen-yang. Various grains, such as rice, millet, and wheat as well as gentle vegetables like carrots and potatoes, on the other hand, are highly recommended (Engelhardt and Nögel 2009, 38; Despeux 2007, 26). The *Yangsheng yaoji*, too, supports this understanding, suggesting the avoidance of heavy grains such as soybeans and roasted wheat as well as of cold drinks (Stein 1999, 212).

After reaching adulthood, people should match their nutrition with the seasons and adapt it to their individual constitution, avoiding specific food combinations and observing a plethora of temporal taboos (see below). They should take care to moderate food intake and avoid intoxication, engaging in regular exercise and aiding the digestion by moving gently after a meal. As already the *Yangsheng yaoji* says: "After a filling meal it is quite useless for the body to sit or lie down: much better to go out for a walk or work on a task at hand. Not doing that can lead to blockages and indigestion, or cause paralysis in the extremities and dark spots in face and eyes, in general diminishing life expectancy" (ch. 6; Stein 1999, 194; also *Yangxing yanming lu* 1.10a). It also insists that drinking water immediately after eating will disperse the grain-*qi* and cause ailments due to *qi*-congestion. Nor should one fast for a period, get very hungry, and then eat voraciously and fill up quickly (as in yo-yo dieting). This will lead to congestions in the heart area and cause harm in the long run (Stein 1999, 194).

When people grow old, their main dietary concern shifts toward the prevention of diseases and the enhancement of vitality. Since in older people *qi* and *xue* tend to become deplete while yin and yang grow weaker, foods should be easy to digest and enhancing. They best choose food for its balanced and neutral temperature and flavor, so that it may support the spleen and stomach in the center as well as the kidneys as the seat of vital essence. Especially cooked cereals, stews, and soups are recommended. It is also important to eat with care, avoiding the mixing of too many ingredients; to maintain regularity, staying away from odd hours and great variation in amounts; to preserve the center, focusing heavily on ground or flaked grains in various forms; to support the kidneys, using moderate amounts of lamb, chicken, eggs, milk, and seafood; and to enhance kidney function, seasoning food with walnuts, sesame, or other seeds (Engelhardt and Hempen 1997, 620-22; Engelhardt and Nögel 2009, 39-40).

Food Taboos

In addition to the variation over historical periods and the general guide-lines for different ages, Chinese dietitians also provided specific avoid-ances (see Huang 2007, 94-105). They fundamentally deal with substan-ces of a potentially poisonous nature, which need to be treated with care but are not to be avoided completely, since any toxin, if properly mas-tered, can combat disease and have a beneficial effect (Anderson 1988, 195). Examples of foods considered poisonous and handled with care include dominantly puffer fish (Fugu) and horsemeat as well as, to a lesser degree, garlic, cucumber, eggplant, pork, fox meat, as well as peach and apricot kernels (Despeux 2007, 24). While the inherent level of toxicity may vary with times and seasons, different methods of prepara-tion serve to eliminate or reduce it, notably cutting out the toxic part or thoroughly boiling and frying.

Another dimension of toxicity has to do with the freshness and quality of food. Many texts warn against consuming stale or old food, items that have been exposed to the elements or chewed by animals (Read 1931, 348; Lo 2005, 180), as well as—especially also in Daoist documents—things that have been preserved by drying, pickling, or fermenting. Certain signs, moreover, provide clear warnings: vegetables that are discolored, rabbits with their eyes shut, sheep's liver with holes, fruit or meat that has been on the ground, peaches and apricots with a double kernel, and any foodstuff that is being shunned by animals (Despeux 2007, 25).

Already Confucius already practiced appropriate avoidances:

> He did not object to having his grains finely cleaned, nor to having his minced meat cut up fine. He did not eat grain that had been injured by heat or damp and turned sour, nor fish or flesh that was gone. He did not eat what was off in color or smelled strange, nor anything that was not properly cooked or out of season. He did not eat meat that was not cut properly, nor what was served without its proper sauce.
>
> Even when there was meat in abundance he would not eat it in disproportionate amount over staple foods. Only in his ale he knew no measure, although he never got drunk. He did not partake of ale and dried meat bought in the market. When he had eaten his fill, he would not eat more, even if the ginger had not yet been cleared (*Lunyu* 10.8; Sterckx 2005, 50)

Daoists agree with these guidelines to a large degree. For example, the *Laozi shuo Fashi jinjie jing* on monastic eating prohibits the consumption of any food left behind by birds, beasts, worms, or fish; left over from offerings to spirits and demons at altars, shrines, or temples; as well as any rice or wheat cakes that are unclean or rotten; have moldy or damaged spots; are broken or burnt; were returned by children; or dirtied by flying birds. (#19-25; Kohn 2004b, 126-27)

Toxicity can also occur when food is taken that is unsuitable for the current constitution of the person, so that, for example, the very warming qualities of mutton can do serious harm to someone already suffering from a heat condition. More generally, certain combinations of food tend to create tendencies in the body that are harmful to wide ranges of the population regardless of personal constitution. The *Yangsheng yaoji* provides a rather lengthy list, indicating which foods combined with what will result in what potential harm (Stein 1999, 200-07):

Table 1

Harmful Food Combinations

Combination of	with	and/or with	Consequence
anything hot	cold		damage to *qi*
anything hot, fatty	vinegar		loss of voice
apricots	pork fat		death
celery	raw pork liver		flatulence
chestnuts	raw fish		swellings
dates	raw onions		pains
fish, raw	knotgrass		*qi*-obstructions
game	prawns	spiky vegs.	death
game	anchovies		death
game, raw	prawn broth		chest pains
garlic	malt syrup		harm
ginger, dried	rabbit		intestinal cramps
hollyhock	eggs		dull complexion
mallows	pork	millet	reduced *qi*
meat, raw	milk		parasites
millet, dried	pork	fatty dishes	digestive troubles
millet, white	honey		harm to organs
mussels, oysters	raw vegetables	plums	chest pains
mussels, oysters	fruits		chest pains
mustard	rabbit		diseases

oats	white honey		parasites
onion	cinnamon		diarrhea
onions, leeks	honey		diarrhea
onions, raw	chicken	meats	bleeding
onions, raw	carp	dates	ailments
pears	raw leeks		swellings
plums	pheasant		bleeding
plums	honey		harm to organs
plums, pickled	pork fat		harm
pork	fish		harm
pork liver	carp		emaciation
pork liver	caviar		harm
pork liver	small beans		reduced eyesight
poultry	eggs		harm
prawns	game	plums	chronic diseases
sweet soups	ginger		nausea, cramps
sweets	raw vegetables		chest pains
sweetwood	knotgrass		impotence
vegs., pungent	pork	raw fish	death
vegs., pungent	pungent vegs.		chest pains
vegs., raw	crab feet		harm
vegs., spiky	game	prawns	harm
wheat	oatmeal	alcohol	parched thirst
yogurt	vinegar		bloody urine
yogurt	ground fish		parasites
yogurt	rice soup		nausea

Seasonal Restrictions

By the same token, changes in the course of the seasons will require different nutritional preferences as well as behavioral adjustments. Sun Simiao in his *Sheyang lun* 攝養論 (On Preserving and Nourishing [Life], DZ 841) spells out specific guidelines for each month, presenting the overall pattern, general and specific dietary recommendations, and some behavioral taboos along the lines of a Farmer's Almanac.[1] For example,

---

[1] An early emphasis on seasonal adjustment of food and lifestyle is found in the *Yinshu* (Stretch Book), a manuscript on healing exercises unearthed from Zhangjiashan and dated to 186 B.C.E. For details, see Kohn 2008a, 41; Lo 2009. Similar guidelines also appear in the 6th-century *Qimin yaoshu* 齊民要術 (Essential

In the first month, kidney *qi* is susceptible to sickness, while lung *qi* wanes. It is best to reduce salty and sour flavors and increase spicy food. This will help the kidneys and supplement the lungs. To calm and nurture stomach *qi*, moreover, do not expose yourself to cold and frost nor get extremely warm and heated. Rise and retire early to relax body and spirit.

In terms of diet, avoid raw leeks, since they diminish fluids and blood. Do not eat raw pepper, which may lead to chronic conditions and can cause the face to attract wind. Do not partake of hibernating animals: this reduces human life expectancy. Nor should you eat the meat of wild beasts like tigers, panthers, and foxes—it may cause agitation in spirit and souls.

The 4th day of this month is good for plucking out white hairs. The 7th day is good for quieting thoughts and contemplating perfection, and doing retreats to increase good fortune. On the 8th day, take baths but avoid long journeys. (1a)

Each month in the course of the year has similar guidelines specifying foods that will match the changes of the five phases in the course of the year. They are still part of the medicated and Daoist diets today (see Despeux 2007, 26). The *Yangsheng yaoji*, too, has a pertinent list, providing comprehensive monthly taboos together with the dire consequences of their violation (Stein 1999, 189-93) (see Table 2).

Daoists, in broad agreement with this understanding of food avoidances, list similar taboos. The most detailed account appears in the *Lingshu ziwen xianji* 靈書紫文仙忌 (Immortals' Taboos According to the Purple Texts Inscribed by the Spirits, DZ 179).[2] According to this, Daoists should avoid giving offense to the spirits by relieving themselves or performing other acts of personal hygiene while facing north or developing a great

---

Arts for the People's Welfare), which contains 260 recipes. See Sabban 1996; Huang 2000, 123-24; Lo 2005, 166. For more classical works on seasonal adjustment, see Huang 2007, 70-73. For a modern perspective, see Engelhardt and Hempen 1997, 617-20.

[2] The text formed part of the Highest Clarity (Shangqing) revelations in the mid-fourth century and in its present form probably dates from the fifth century (Robinet 1984, 2:412-15; Kleeman 1991, 176). Its taboos also appear in *Zhen'gao* 真誥 (Declarations of the Perfected, DZ 1016); *Zhenzhong ji* 枕中記 (Pillowbook Record, DZ 836) 5a-6a; *Shangqing xiuxing jingjue* 上清修行經訣 (Scriptural Instructions on Shangqing Cultivation, DZ 427), 22b-25a; and in *Yunji qiqian* 雲笈七籤 (Seven Tablets in a Cloudy Satchel, DZ 1032; abbr. YJQQ), 33.6a, 40.11b-12a.

rage against the celestial forces. In terms of diet, they should eschew "the meat of armored [shelled] animals like turtles or dragons on the days of Six Armored Gods [Liujia]." Also, they should avoid pheasant on *bingwu* days; the meat of black animals on *bingzi* days; getting drunk on *yimao* days; and sexual relations or sleeping in the same bed with their spouse on *gengjia* days (Bokenkamp 1997, 365)—all taboos that have to do with the cosmic significance of the cyclical signs for the days and years that form part of the sexagenary cycle, a central part of the Chinese calendar since the Shang dynasty (also Despeux 2007, 27).

Table 2

Monthly Taboos

Mo	Avoid eating	Otherwise	And also
1	food chewed by rats	rat bumps on head	mouth cankers
	raw onions	latent diseases	
	liver	damage of *hun* soul	mental confusion
2	spring water	malaria	spleen damage, phlegm
3	pickled meat /vegs.	summer heat ills	hepatitis
4	garlic	harm in five organs	
	heart	damage of spirit	emotions: fear, sadness
5	unripe fruit	abscesses and boils	hepatitis, colds, diarrhea
	mixed vegetables	extreme cold	cold yang, short breath
6	soft turtle	turtle-shaped boils	
	fruit after dropping	fistulas	
7	honey	diarrhea	intestinal cramps
	lungs	damage of *po* soul	impulsiveness
8	pig's lungs, vinegar	cough in winter	
9	frozen herbs	colds in winter	nausea
	ginger	ills of *hun* soul	
10	frozen raw vegs.	dull complexion	chest and abdominal aches
	pepper	*qi* weakness	
	kidneys	damage of will	restlessness
11	dried, old meat	kidney damage	numbness
12	dog-chewed food	heart fistulas	throat infections

More specific monthly taboos include not to eat fish on 2/9 or vegetable hearts on 4/8. Beyond the mere dietary guidelines, they also include behavioral prohibitions, so that Daoists should not look at blood on 5/5, dig the earth on 6/6, think of evil things on 7/7, sell or buy footwear on 8/4, sleep on a high bed or thick mat on 9/9, punish offenders on 10/5, and bathe on 11/11. On the other hand, they should remain aware of the Dao at all times and specifically on the last three days of the 12th month prepare for the New Year by fasting, burning incense, and being mindful of the immortals (3ab).

Besides incurring straightforward physical harm by disobeying dietary and other taboos, Daoists believed that people are closely supervised by the celestial administration. As the *Lingshu ziwen xianji* notes: "All these taboos are the great prohibitions of the celestials. The Three Offices [of Heaven, Earth, and Water] report and examine them, counting them among the gravest sins. As punishments they order people's three spirit souls (*hun*) to be sick and make their seven material souls (*po*) engage in fighting" (3b; Bokenkamp 1997, 365). Eating as well as various other forms of social interaction thus formed an important aspect in the Chinese and Daoist way of being in the world.

To conclude, in addition to incorporating the same overall principles and food classifications as the traditional Chinese medicated diet, Daoist dietetics is also subject to the same social, political, and historical circumstances. Both share ideas about age-related eating and have many food taboos in common. Both are subject to change over time, seeing new food stuffs arrive and integrating them into their established patterns. Thus in Daoist kitchens even today, one may find bread with stir fries alongside rice, and it is probably only a matter of time until tofu burgers, bacon, and hot dogs make their debut in Chinese vegetarian kitchens. The question remains open whether one should look forward to or dread the arrival of Daoist fast food—following the footsteps of the buffet-style Buddhist eateries and the medicinal restaurants already widespread in Chinese communities the world over.

Chapter Three

Dietary Therapy

> People of antiquity cured diseases by creating internal harmony with sweet spring [saliva] and moistening themselves with primordial *qi*. Their medicines were neither astringent nor bitter; they tasted sweet and were full of flavor. They would take their nourishment and pass it through their five inner organs, then tie it into their hearts and lungs. Thus their entire bodies would be free from afflictions. (*Luoshu baozi ming* in *Yangxing yanming lu* 1.5a)

While the ultimate goal of both Chinese and Daoist dietetics is to eat like the people of antiquity, in such a way that food nourishes the five organs and spreads harmonious *qi* throughout the body, the fact remains that people suffer from a wide variety of ailments, which in many cases are food related or can at least be alleviated by dietetic means. Given this situation, nutrition plays a major role in all forms of Chinese healing, and few treatments will be without dietary recommendations.

In addition, food is also used as medicine by itself, in a practice known as dietary therapy, described variously as food cures (*shiliao* 食療), nutritional therapy (*shizhi* 食治), and medicated foods (*yao'er* 藥餌) (Engelhardt and Hempen 1997, 1; Lo 2005, 163). It means selecting food stuffs and forms of preparation in the conscious attempt to balance *qi* and alleviate or cure medical conditions. Paying attention to food qualities as expressed in color and inherent temperature, making sure of the proper saturation with flavor, and seeing to the addition of *qi*-modifying ingredients in accordance with the organs and *qi*-flow of the body are all factors which distinguish the medical from the culinary (Lo 2005, 176).

Dietary therapy in China is closely connected to the traditional under-standing of the body which, as much as the world in general and food in particular, essentially consists of *qi*. The body as *qi* is a complex system of different forms of energy, absorbed from outside sources and trans-formed variously into yin and yang aspects, such as defensive and nutri-tive *qi* and different kinds of body fluids. All these are managed in the body's storage centers and transport channels, described in terms of in-ner organs and *qi*-channels.

Unlike in Western biomedicine, organs here are entire complexes or functional systems that include a series of other physical aspects, such as senses, body tissue, emotions, and the like. They connect to each other in subtle ways and combine in an intricate webwork of rise and fall, so that action in one complex will have an effect on the condition of another and affect the whole. The most essential organ-system is the spleen-stomach complex in the body's center. Any ingested item goes there first, before being transformed into useable *qi* and transmitted to the others. Beyond having the basic characteristics of temperature and activity as described earlier, each food thus also works through these organs, enhancing or diminishing their yin and yang aspects, and thereby allowing for a highly specific and detailed application of food therapy.

Each organ-complex, moreover, tends toward specific forms of imbal-ance, described typically in terms of yin (moisturizing, stable) and yang (drying, active) as well as depletion and excess, sinking and rising, cool-ing and heating, so that particular patterns of pathologies unfold. They tend to range from the more elementary to the highly complex, increas-ing in symptoms and intensity if weaknesses go unchecked. For each case, dietary recommendations allow patients to modify their food in-take toward optimal organ functioning.

To determine which dietary measure should be taken for what condition is the task of traditional Chinese diagnostics. It works less with concrete and measurably data, such as blood pressure, temperature, and pulse rate. Instead physicians analyze the state of the patient's *qi*-flow, using—besides obvious immediate impressions and questions about symptoms and case history—tongue inspection, pulse analysis, and abdominal pal-pation. Also, in contrast to Western medicine, they do not wait for large, intense, and obvious conditions to occur, but pay close attention to even minor signs of imbalance and discomfort, hoping—often with dietary measures—to prevent their growth into serious symptoms and, worst of all, pervasive syndromes.

Medical dietetics or nutritional therapy, then, works with the qualities of food described earlier and treats all kinds of conditions. Examples include cases of all different ages, genders, and pathologies; remedies involve specific recipes as much as dietary patterns and overall lifestyle recommendations. The goal is, as much in medicine as in Daoism, to create a way of eating that matches time and place and is perfectly suited to the individual's needs.

The Body As Qi

The body as *qi* has both primordial and postnatal aspects. Primordial *qi*, received at birth from Heaven and Earth through the parents, is centered in the kidney area, from where it manifests as vital essence (*jing*). Postnatal *qi* is derived from food, air, and water. The postnatal metabolism utilizes especially the spleen and lungs and their associated channels to convert worldly materials into useable *qi* as well as into *xue* 血 (blood), the yin counterpart of *qi* and a more internal force.

Thus, the lungs receive breath from the nose. While drawn in through the nose, this is called pure *qi* (*qingqi* 清氣), but once it reaches the lungs it is known as empty *qi* (*kongqi* 空氣). From the lungs, it descends to the kidneys. At the same time, the stomach grinds up food after ingestion through the mouth, preparing it for the spleen to extract its *qi*. Known as grain *qi* (*guqi* 穀氣) this ascends to the chest area where the fire of the heart, driven by the essence of the kidneys (which is enhanced by empty *qi*) and assisted by the Upper Heater transforms it into ancestral *qi* (*zongqi* 宗氣).

Ancestral *qi* next combines with the primordial *qi* already stored in the depth of the person to form perfect *qi* (*zhenqi* 真氣). This in turn divides and moves on to return again, in its new form, to the spleen and lungs. In the lungs, it divides into channel *qi* (*maiqi* 脈氣), i.e., the *qi* in the channels of the body, and defensive or protective *qi* (*weiqi* 衛氣) which circulates close to the body's surface. In the spleen, it transforms into nutritive or constructive *qi* (*yingqi* 營氣) which flows in the deeper interstices and transports the *xue*, also distilled in the spleen and stored in the liver (Jackowicz 2006, 71; Kaptchuk 1983, 46-55).

Defensive and nutritive *qi* pulsate through the body at different levels to defend and nurture it. Defensive *qi* is yang in quality; it moves next to the channels and travels widely around the body, nourishing and strengthening the skin. It regulates the sweat glands, moistens the skin and hair, nourishes the tissues, and controls the opening and closing of the skin's pores. Forming a defense against harmful outside influences and pathogenic stress, it maintains the stability of the body, not unlike the immune system in Western medicine.

Nutritive *qi* is yin in nature and associated with *xue*. Situated more deeply inside, it nourishes the muscles and organs and ensures that the body's tissues remain strong. The two form a complementary pair, like *qi* and *xue*. They are characterized similarly in that their yin aspect is thicker and heavier and stays deep within the body, while its yang counterpart is thinner and lighter and moves at the surface of the body, interfacing with the outside world.

The same also holds true for the body fluids (*jinye* 津液). They are defined as nutritive substances, formed when food in the digestive process is subjected to the functions of the stomach, spleen, lungs, and so on. Among them, *jin* are yang in nature. They appear as light, clear fluids that come to the body's surface due to internal processes. Examples include saliva (associated with the kidneys), tears (liver), sweat (heart), nasal mucus (lungs), and oral mucus (spleen). They lubricate the skin and the flesh. *Ye*, on the other hand, are yin. They are heavy, thick fluids diffused internally due to body movement, as for example lymph and internal mucus. They lubricate the joints and tendons, protect the brain, and fill the spine. The fluids, when produced in their appropriate amounts, serve as protectors and lubricants of the body. When they are deficient or excessive, however, they can be useful diagnostic tools. (Kohn 2005, 32-33; Kaptchuk 1983, 66-67).

The body as *qi* in its various forms is managed by the five organ-complexes, which—in close link with their related cosmic and bodily forces—maintain it in a constant flow of movement and exchange. To describe them individually, the "spleen" (*pi* 脾) is not just one organ but part of the phase earth and all the cosmic connections that implies: the color yellow, the season of late or Indian summer, the direction of the center, and in general with stability and centeredness.

Further connected with muscles and sinews, mouth and lips, the sense of taste, and the body fluid of oral mucus, its key emotion is worry, which includes thoughtfulness, planning, and overanalyzing, leading to the fact that many brain-workers tend toward spleen issues. Among virtues, it represents the honesty: trust in oneself and others, faithfulness, and confidence. Most closely associated with *qi*, together with its yang partner, the stomach, it is "the primary organ of digestion, the crucial link by which food is transformed into *qi* and *xue*-blood" (Kaptchuk 1983, 79). As the *Huangdi neijing suwen* notes: "The stomach is the residence of the granary administration: the various kinds of taste originate here" (3.1a).

The spleen is the root of the person's acquired constitution, the seat of nutritive *qi*, and the place where both *qi* and *xue* originate. It distributes active fluids throughout the body, firms up the tissues, and stabilizes the internal fluid system. Its main function is to divide clear from turbid *qi* after food and drink have been ingested through the mouth, its associated sense of taste providing a first indication of what to expect energetically. The spleen has two major aspects, an active dimension known as spleen *qi* and a warming power called spleen yang (fire). Both have warming and drying powers needed in food processing to eliminate extraneous liquids. Should these aspects go astray, some liquids are not processed but remain as a kind of slush to create condition known as "dampness" which eventually may grow into phlegm and lead to serious obstructions (Engelhardt and Hempen 1997, 421).

Symptoms of a depletion of spleen *qi* include fatigue, lack of appetite, belching, a weak digestion, loose stools, a bloated abdomen, and a pale or white tongue. Depletion of spleen yang is indicated by the same signs, plus a pervasive feeling of cold, especially also in the hands and feet, and a strong desire for warm drinks. Spleen dampness, finally, may also come with feelings of fullness, lack of thirst, nausea, numbness, as well as a general sense of weakness (Engelhardt and Hempen 1997, 424).

Aside from treating these conditions by stimulating the spleen channel (which runs along the inside of the leg and through the abdomen) with acupuncture, moxibustion, acupressure, or qigong, herbal and dietary remedies are highly effective. The latter work particularly with the two flavors associated with the spleen: sweet and neutral. Most foods of all the different food groups reflect these flavors, especially all kinds of grain, sweet tasting vegetables (carrots, cabbage, potatoes, squash), non-citrus fruits, as well as an extensive selection of meat, poultry, fish, and dairy. It is best to select those that are warming and have a draining effect on dampness, as is the case particularly with fish and beans. They should be well cooked and eaten warm (fruits, for example, as compote), preferably in a calm setting. Any fatty, heavy, and sticky foods should be avoided, as much as any form of cooking that adds oil, strong spices, and excessive sweetness (Engelhardt and Hempen 1997, 425-35).

The spleen's matching yang organ is the "stomach" (fu 腹). It serves as an intermediate and balancing center in food processing, taking care to properly cool and moisturize the various substances. Its channel runs across the face, through the torso, and along the outside of the leg to end on the medial side of the second toe. Its favored flavors are neutral and slightly sour, while its desired temperature is cooling rather than warming. Pathologies include an excess in stomach heat which manifests in an increase of appetite and thirst, as well as pain in the upper abdomen, heartburn, swollen gums, a general itchiness, and a rather red tongue; and a depletion of stomach yin, which is apparent in a tendency toward constipation, a dry mouth, and a feeling of heat or fever (Engelhardt and Hempen 1997, 439-40).

To remedy these conditions, the dietary recommendation is for cooling and slightly sour foods, which include especially wheat, buckwheat, and sweet potato among grains, as well as cucumbers, tomatoes, celery, bamboo shoots, bean sprouts, eggplant, spinach, and napa cabbage among vegetables, plus all citrus fruits, tofu, fish, and some dairy (Engelhardt and Hempen 1997, 441-43).

As far as dietary therapy is concerned, all other conditions and organs are secondary to the spleen-stomach system. All food cures essentially begin by stabilizing the middle, making sure that the center is strong and well balanced. They establish a firm digestive and transforming pole which in turn will help stabilize the qi in all the other organs.

Extended Application

The first organ affected by the center is the "lungs" (fei 肺), the organ associated with the phase metal: fall, white, and west. It is also linked with the large intestine as its yang partner and in charge of the skin as main body part. This explains why people with chronic digestive dysfunction often develop asthma and skin problems, which—in reversal of the disease's unfolding—tend to clear up with a lung-supportive diet.

The lungs are in charge of transforming air into ancestral *qi* by mixing empty *qi* with the grain *qi* of the spleen. They then distribute it all over the body through the exterior (*jin*) body fluids and the defensive *qi*. Their related sense organ is the nose, matching the body fluid of nasal mucus and connecting them to the common cold. In general, the lungs are easily harmed by cold and wind, favoring warms and dryness, which connects to their flavor of pungent, spicy (Engelhardt and Hempen 1997, 455-56).

The emotion of the lungs is sadness, i.e., pensiveness, melancholy, and reluctance to let go, while its virtue is righteousness, impartial justice or integrity, the ability to accept gain and loss, success and failure as they come (Kaptchuk 1983, 91). As the *Huangdi neijing suwen* says: "The lungs are the residence of the high ministers of state: order and division originate here" (1.3b). Their related *qi*-channel starts in the chest, moves through the armpit and along the inner side of the arm, and ends at the top of the thumb. It has eleven acupuncture points, used to treat symptoms of colds and cough as well as cases of shoulder and back pain (Kaptchuk 1983, 112; Kohn 2995, 53).

The main pathology is depletion of lung *qi*, which manifests in shortness of breath (lack of active *qi*), cough (inability of *qi* to move downward), a tendency to perspire (*qi* cannot close the pores properly, connection to the skin), getting cold easily (lack of defensive *qi*), as well as a weak voice, fatigue, and a pale complexion (all indicative of *qi* weakness). Closely connected to depletion of spleen yang, the same warming and stabilizing foods are recommended here. It is important to build up the middle before any major impact on the lungs can be seen.

Another potential problem is the depletion of lung yin, which means that there are insufficient body fluids, accompanied by an overall sense of dryness (dry mouth, dry skin, dry cough), night sweats and interrupted sleep, burning palms, hoarseness, as well as a general feeling of heat. This is very similar to depletion of stomach yin and accordingly requires cooling and moisturizing foods. Again, building up the middle is key (Engelhardt and Hempen 1997, 458-60).

In terms of excess, the lungs may suffer from wind, which essentially means all the symptoms of the acute common cold and comes with a closure of the body's surface. Warming and especially spicy foods are highly recommended, using the prime flavor of the lungs. Spicy foods avoid grains, fruit, and meat, and rely on certain select vegetables: onions, garlic, ginger, radish, fennel, and bell pepper, plus all kinds of spices (Engelhardt and Hempen 1997, 415). Aside from aiding the lungs, these foods also tend to be heating and yang-strengthening, which is why many of them are eschewed by religious practitioners.

Another possible condition is lung dampness: a chronic cough, bronchitis, or asthma, which means a build-up of phlegm and a white complexion. Not unlike spleen dampness in nature, it can be treated with similar foods: warming and sweet with a tendency to drain. Beyond this, however, citrus fruits and ginger, as well as fresh juices, especially of radish and pear, are recommended here, while sticky rice and dairy should be avoided (Engelhardt and Hempen 1997, 471-72).

Receiving ancestral *qi* from the lungs and transporting it into the body's channels, next, is the "heart" (*xin* 心) the organ linked with the phase fire, the color red, the season of the summer, and the direction of the south. It also manages the constructive *qi*, which transports *xue*, and the workings of the blood vessels. Among senses, it corresponds to touch, among body fluids it connects to sweat (a precious entity that contains many important substances), among emotions it relates to joy (enthusiasm, euphoria, or hatred), while its virtue is propriety, i.e., appropriate behavior, timely interactions, and behaving suitably in a given context.

The heart is also the seat of the spirit, ensuring that internal consciousness, awareness, thought, and reflection intersect properly with the world of time and space (Kaptchuk 1983, 88). It is very much in charge of the person in general and takes care of its proper rest by providing sufficient sleep. As already the *Suwen* says: "The heart is the residence of the ruler: spirit and clarity originate here." Its channel begins in the armpit and, with an internal branch connecting to the heart itself, passes through the chest and lungs. After moving along the side of the throat and through the inner side of the arm, it ends at the tip of the little finger (Kaptchuk 1983, 118; Kohn 2005, 54).

A depletion of heart yang or *qi* is indicated by cold and listlessness, combined with fatigue and irregularities in the heart beat. It is best treated with stimulants, such as limited doses of coffee and cocoa as well as with the matching animal organ (Engelhardt and Hempen 1997, 276-77). A depletion of heart yin or *xue*, on the other hand, is a nervous heat condition, which means sleeplessness, forgetfulness, numbness, vertigo, and eruptions of heat in different parts of the body. Since it is caused by de-

pletion rather than excess, the remedy is a support of yin through warming sweet or neutral foods, very much like those used for depletion of
spleen *qi*. In addition, spicy foods that aid the lungs may also be helpful
as well as bitter foods—the flavor associated with the heart: not found in
grain or fruits, it appears in a variety of leafy greens, such as lettuce, endives, chicory, celery, and dandelion, plus pig's or hare's liver among
meats, and tea, cocoa, and coffee among liquids (Engelhardt and
Hempen 1997, 413; 516-18).

The matching yang organs of the lungs and the heart are the large and
small intestines, whose channels run along the outer arms, connecting
the hands to the torso. Typical pathologies are excess heat and depletion
of *qi*, manifest in tendencies toward constipation and diarrhea, as well as
invasion by parasites. For excess heat, cooling and soothing substances
are helpful, notably nuts and seeds as well as soft fruits, vegetables, and
dairy. For depletion, take *qi*-enhancing foods, such as grains and warming vegetables, fried with chilies, pepper, nutmeg, and ginger. Parasites,
finally, can be driven out by garlic and scallions as well as other kinds of
onions combined with grains and beans (Engelhardt and Hempen 1997,
525-32).

Complementing the heart in the scheme of the five phases is the kidney
complex (*shen* 腎) which belongs to the phase water, the season winter,
and the color black. The most yin among organs, it is also the most potent, being in charge of essence (*jing*), a core form of concentrated *qi* that
forms bones, teeth, and brain, and is key to hard work, endurance, and
perseverance. Essence also rules birth, development, and maturation and
is the primordial seat of the life process, often associated with sexuality
and procreation (Kaptchuk 1983, 83-84).

The body fluid of the kidneys is the saliva; their related sense organ are
the ears—described in Daoist literature as the "Dark Towers," the name
also given to the kidneys. The related emotion is fear (caution, anxiety,
panic), counteracted effectively by the virtue of wisdom, a sense of life
and its unfolding, the intuitive knowledge when to move and when to
rest. The *Suwen* notes: "The kidneys are the residence of the business
men: activity and care originate here" (3.1b). The related channel begins
at Bubbling Well (Yongquan 湧泉) in the center of the sole, then runs
through the instep, circles around the medial ankle, moves up the inner
leg and through the abdomen to the chest (Kaptchuk 1983, 122-23; Kohn
2005, 55).

The kidney system warms the center and supplies *qi* to the heart as well as running the entire water-system of the body. Its flavor is salty, which means no fruit at all and only selected other foodstuffs: millet among grains; seaweed among vegetables; octopus, crab, oysters, and abalone among seafood; duck, pigeon, and pork among animal flesh (Engelhardt and Hempen 1997, 413). The kidneys being so important to the overall functioning of the body, and salt being essential to life, these foods play a relatively large role in food preparation. It also explains the ubiquity of soy sauce, the great all-spice of Chinese cooking.

Pathologies tend to be in the form of depletion: of kidney yang and *qi* as well as of kidney yin. Yang and *qi* depletions are cold conditions, involving breathlessness, cold hands and feet, frequent urination, discharge of sexual fluids, ear problems (infections, loss of hearing, tinnitus), joint pains, head aches, and hair loss. Spicy, warming foods are best: leeks, walnuts, fennel, grapes, as well as chicken and game. Kidney yin depletion comes with increased thirst, dark urine, night sweats, constipation, dry mouth, vertigo, numbness, as well as back pain. Sweet, neutral and warming foods, such as chicken, will benefit here; so will the kidneys of animals (Engelhardt and Hempen 1997, 500-04).

Its matching yang partner is the bladder (*pang* 膀) with the longest of the channels that runs down the back in two parallel lines as well as across the head and along the outside of the legs. Its main task is to transform body fluids and lead them toward elimination. It is very sensitive to cold and dampness, which lead to symptoms commonly associated with bladder infections. The best dietary therapy involves neutral, lightly salty as well as bitter foods (Engelhardt and Hempen 1997, 509).

Finally, the last of the five organ systems is the "liver" (*gan* 肝), associated with the phase wood: spring, east, and green. The moderator of the entire system, its main task is to control the overall flow of *qi* and to store the *xue*. In terms of its wider associations, it is linked with the working of joints and tendons and corresponds to the sense of vision and the eyes (Porkert 1974, 117-19). Among body fluids, liver means tears, among emotions it relates to anger (aggression, courage, or lack thereof), while in the virtues it matches benevolence or kindness.

The liver is also indicative of the repetitive cycles of human life, curtailing extremes and ensuring the smooth movement of *qi* (Kaptchuk 1983, 81-82). The *Huangdi neijing suwen* describes it as "the residence of the strategists: planning and organization originate here" (3.1a). Its channel begins at the tip of the big toe, then moves up the instep to the inner side of the leg, crosses the pubic region, lower abdomen, liver, and lungs to end in the rib cage. An internal branch ends at the liver. Its most important point is Too Fast (Taichong 太衝; Li-3) on the top of the foot near the ankle. It is a strong point for moving *qi* and helps with numerous ailments (Kaptchuk 1983, 128; Kohn 2005, 57).

The most common pathology of the liver is an excess of *qi*, which manifests in a blockage that can lead to internal heat and wind. Symptoms include abdominal or chest tension, nausea, constipation, and PMS, as well as a continued sense of frustration or even depression. Cooling and moisturizing foods are best; however, shrimp should be avoided since they increase energetic mobility, and alcohol is bad because it produces too much heat (Engelhardt and Hempen 1997, 480).

A depletion of liver yin or *xue*, on the other hand, leads to rising liver yang (fire), which causes insomnia, vision problems (blurring, dizziness, night blindness, dry eyes), vertigo, numbness, dry nails, paleness, and menstrual inhibition. Neutral, lightly cooling foods as well as some sweet and sour items are best—not unlike the diet recommended for depletion of spleen *qi*. In addition, soybeans, nuts, and seeds are good as well as the liver of animals, especially chickens. Eggs and pork may also be used, but in limited amounts (Engelhardt and Hempen 1997, 483-86). Other than that, special liver foods are helpful, which means those of sour flavor: adzuki beans, tomatoes, pheasant, yogurt, and anything spiced with vinegar, as well as most fruits, notably all kinds of citrus, but also apples, apricots, pears, kiwis, peaches, mango, plums, pineapple, and star fruit (Engelhardt and Hempen 1997, 413).

The matching yang organ is the gall bladder (*dan* 膽), the main recipient of fluids from the liver and provider of *qi* for the stomach. Also associated with decision making, courage, and initiative, it suffers mostly from dampness which manifests in nausea, fever, yellow complexion, dark urine, and a bitter taste in the mouth as well as in frustration and emotional tension. Sweet and cooling foods are helpful, as notably buckwheat, yellow soybean sprouts, dandelions, and tea (Engelhardt and Hempen 1997, 492-93).

Diagnostics

To find out which organ needs to be treated most urgently, what kind of food should be taken, and what lifestyle changes might be indicated, practitioners have to correctly diagnose where the current imbalances of *qi* are located and find where exactly excesses, obstructions, or depletions are present. To do so, they examine the patient on several levels.

They begin by questioning—notably with regard to ten classical areas of health and lifestyle: appetite, digestion, elimination, activity, sweat, sleep, menstruation, sexual health, reproduction, and demeanor. The range of questions is fairly broad and includes also, and importantly, concerns about diet (Kaptchuk 1983, 187-94). For example, too much raw food can cause dampness, while lots of hot, greasy food can create internal heat. A life-style that involves too much caffeine, alcohol, processed foods, irregular meals, or stressful eating may contribute significantly to the symptoms. Any digestive and dietary imbalance needs accordingly to be addressed with food therapy and possible lifestyle changes, while specific symptoms may be treated in a variety of other ways, such as with acupuncture and herbs.

The second diagnostic step is visual. The practitioner notes the overall presentation of the patient, gaining an impression of his or her disposition as overall bouncy or sluggish, positive or depressed. This provides a general indication of the patient's attitude and general energy, allowing a basic prognosis of success or failure. Next, each person is classified according to body type, again in terms of the five phases. For example, if the patient is fleshy and round, she may be an earth body type; if wiry and tall, he is likely to be wood type—in either case indicating general tendencies that provide a backdrop for understanding the pathology.

Third, and most importantly, Chinese clinicians examine the tongue, considered a mirror of the body, which contains reflections of all inner organs, and an accurate indicator of the body's internal balance (see Kaptchuk 1983, 181-86). More specifically, they look

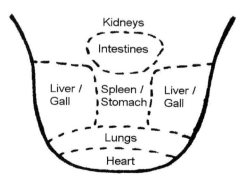

at the tongue's coating, shape, and color. The coating or "moss" of the tongue indicates the relative state of body fluids in a continuum from no coat through thick coat to peeled coat, with multiple variations in between. The absence of a coat may indicate a lack of the stomach fluids necessary to generate a coat. The thickness of a coat indicates the relative thickness of the body fluids. A thin white coat is considered normal and indicative of a relative fluid balance. If the coat is thin and clear, fluids are depleted and the body lacks the ability to lubricate its membranes.

The shape of the tongue is evaluated for whether it is short or long, swollen or thin, cracked or smooth, and for the presence or absence of visible veins. A swollen tongue seems too large for the mouth. Often the sides of the tongue appear wavy in a pattern known as "teeth marks" or "scalloping." This is caused by the swelling between the ligaments which hold the tongue together and cause it to flare out at its lateral edges. Mechanically the swollen tongue is indicative of a relative imbalance between interstitial fluid and blood fluid volumes; essentially the tissues are water logged. The swollen tongue is clinically related to weak spleen yang which is responsible for transformation of the fluids. This presentation often also evidences edema in the joints as well as a puffy appearance. When the tongue is thin, it indicates a depletion in the blood which should fill the tongue. This is considered a precursor to yin depletion, evidenced by dry signs on the mucus membrane as well as insomnia, irritability, hot flashes, and amenorrhea.

Cracks in the tongue indicate a long-standing disharmony of the organs matching specific areas of the tongue. Finally, the underside of the tongue is inspected for the visibility of veins. If the veins are dark and visible, the overall circulatory system is inefficient—like the hands of an arthritic patient who develops darker veins due to the poor circulation. The color of the body of the tongue is the last parameter inspected. If the tongue is pale and washed out, the qi is deplete. If the tongue is dark, black, or purple, the blood is stagnant. These colors can be general to the tongue body or they can be local to a given correspondence area.

After visual inspection comes touching, which may involve palpating painful areas and examining the abdomen. Most essentially, however, it means pulse diagnosis. Physicians take the radial pulse, subdividing into three positions from the wrist crease up and feeling it at three levels of depth. This creates eighteen positions that are cross-referenced to twenty-eight possible quality assessments, eventually resulting in a diagnostic pattern. The pulse is always taken in three positions on both sides, by applying three different pressures—superficial, medium, and deep—each matching the quality of *qi* in two of the twelve key organs:

1. left: heart/small intestine	1. right: lungs/large intestine
2. left: liver/gall bladder	2. right: spleen/stomach
3. left: kidney/bladder	3. right: pericardium/triple heater

The twenty-eight types of pulses, then, consist of eighteen classes distinguished according to depth (2), speed (2), width (2), strength (2), shape (4), length (2), rhythm (3), and balance (1); plus ten types, i.e., flooding, minute, frail, soggy, leathery, hidden, confined, spinning, hollow, and scattered. The most desirable pulse is moderate, regular, medium, strong, and even. When taking the patient's pulse, variants due to seasons, time of day, and gender must be taken into consideration. All other abnormalities indicate weakness or excess of the *qi* in specific organs. Typical indications include (see Kaptchuk 1983, 194-210 and 323-49):

superficial	easily palpable but weak	beginning disease
deep	felt only with pressure	internal syndromes
slow	less than four beats	cold syndromes
rapid	more than five beats	heat syndromes
taut	forceful and tight	yang hyperactivity
wry	rolling or flowing	excessive phlegm
thready	rather fine pulse	depleted *qi*/blood
short	uneven, missing beats	*qi*/blood-stagnation
knotted	slow, irregular misses	endogenous cold
intermittent	slow, regular misses	impairment of *qi*

Using the information gathered from these examinations, the clinician classifies the information in terms of two systems: the main changes of the condition and its main characteristics.

The main changes are described in terms of the so-called six pathogenic patterns (*liuxie* 六邪), classified generally into yin and yang and more specifically divided into two aspects: external (those that invade the body) and internal (those generated in the body).

The three yang patterns are:

> 1. Wind (*feng* 風, *ventus*), i.e., fast change or movement, associated with the liver. Externally generated through wind, draft, air conditioning, changes in temperature. Manifests first on the body surface, may appear as pain, skin erup-

tions, colds, fever, and fear of drafts. It can also be an internally generated, chronic liver problem.

2. Heat (*re* 熱, *calor*), i.e., acceleration or dilation of *qi*, linked
with the heart. Externally created from exposure to heat or
internally due to conditions related to the heart. Symptoms
include red skin, swellings, inflammation, yellow secretions,
dry tongue, thirst, rapid pulse, perspiration, red face, fever,
and swollen throat. The patient appears agitated and talka-
tive, thirsty, and constipated.

3. Dryness (*zao* 燥, *ariditas*), i.e., withering or shriveling tendency, related to the lungs. Developed due to chronic dehydration and blockages in fluid movement. Manifests as
asthma, phlegm, fever, body aches, dry nostrils, tongue, or
skin, and lack of urination. It indicates an internal loss of
fluids and often comes with irritation, weakness, or anemia.

The three yin patterns are:

4. Cold (*han* 寒, *algor*), i.e., contracting or slowing *qi*, linked
with the kidneys. Due externally to exposure to cold. Patient appears pale, cold, contracted, with clear secretions.
He may have a fever but no sweat, and tends to feel cold,
stiff, crampy, or sleepy; appears shrinking and clenching, is
quiet and unwilling to talk, shows a lack of thirst, and
tends toward diarrhea.

5. Dampness (*shi* 濕, *humor*), i.e., sinking or accumulating, related to the spleen. Generated by exposure to damp conditions and the ingestion of sticky, cooling foods (dairy, ice
cream). Produces turbid, sticky, or cloudy secretions, feelings of nausea, swellings, a greasy tongue, as well as heavy
or sore limbs. Patients often have oily skin and indigestion.

6. Summer heat (*shu* 暑 *aestus*), i.e., drying out, linked with the
pericardium. Caused by exposure to extreme heat, it creates
exhaustion, depletion of fluids, sweating, and bursts of
high fever. (Kaptchuk 1983, 146-57; Engelhardt and
Hempen 1997, 540-65; Kohn 2005, 70-71)

In addition to understanding the main pathogenic pattern, clinicians also
evaluate their findings in terms of the dominant characteristics of the
condition, described in terms of the eight key criteria (*bagang* 八綱),
which answer four questions. The first is the general nature of the condition: is it yin or yang? Second comes its degree of penetration: is it exter-

nal (*biao* 表) or internal (*li* 裏), acute or chronic? Third is its fundamental dynamic: is it cooling (*han* 寒) or heating (*re* 熱) in nature, tending toward sluggish or enhanced movement? And fourth is its general state: is it deplete/empty (*xu* 虛) or excessive/full (*shi* 實), indicating weakness or intensity?

Usually the picture presented by the patient is a mixture of these indications, from which physicians discern a pattern. For example, the presence of an obstruction of *qi* could be caused by cold or by heat. If it is cold-induced, there will be a pale skin and complexion, a white coat on the tongue, and a dislike of cold. Such an obstruction tends to be long-term or chronic; it comes from an insufficient flow of *qi* to the area in question. A heat-induced obstruction, on the other hand, shows an overflow of *qi* that is moving fast in different directions and thus creates blockages. This is more acute. The patient shows redness and swelling, and express a strong liking for coolness and cold substances. The treatment various accordingly: cooling herbs and foods as well as drainage for the heat-induced disorder; warming compresses, teas, and medicines, as well as enhancement of *qi* through acupuncture for the cold condition.

The Practice

To activate the principles of dietary therapy in practice, all symptoms and conditions need first to be translated into the Chinese diagnostic system, related to specific organs and channels as well as to qualities and movements. Only then can specific recommendations be made and food therapy begin. For example, in case of pain in the joints and muscles, the first question is whether it is due to *qi* obstruction, cold, or wind, leading to a recommendation to increase foods that support energetic movement, warmth, or calm. In cases of nervousness and insomnia, the question is whether it is caused by worry (a spleen-related condition) or the depletion of liver energies. In the first case, the center needs to be stabilized with foods related to spleen and stomach; in the second, anything that supports liver *qi* is helpful, such as celery, water chestnuts, mung beans, peanuts, and shrimps (Engelhardt and Hempen 1997, 574-603). It is not possible to list all the different variations in these pages, but here are a few pertinent case examples.

In one case, a mother brings her three-year old son into the clinic because he tends toward colds. After a normal pregnancy and birth, he began having feverish ear infections at six months. At the moment he is not sick, but the mother worries that entry into preschool and exposure to multiple germs will create difficulties and would like to see the child strengthened.

Upon questioning it emerges that the boy gets cold easily and has a tendency toward phlegm. He often complains of belly aches and tends to have soft stools. He likes warm foods and drinks, however, he eats corn flakes with cold milk for breakfast. He has three main meals plus two snacks in the course of a day. To make sure he gets sufficient vitamins, the mother also provides him with fresh fruit, juices, and some salads.

Looking at the patient, the child appears normal for his age, but has a pale complexion and dark rings under the eyes. The tongue is light in color and soft. Pulse diagnosis shows a slow and wry pattern, indicative of cold and dampness. In terms of the six pathogenic patterns, the boy matches the "cold" syndrome; in terms of the eight key criteria, his condition is more yin than yang, internal and chronic rather than external, matches a cold rather than hot pattern, and shows a depleted rather than excessive mode.

The final question is which inner organs are most involved in the condition. In this case, they are the kidneys, spleen, and lungs. The weakening of the kidneys, the seat of central life energy, is evident from the pale complexion and the dark rings under the eyes; another indication is the tendency toward ear infections—the ears being the sense organ associated with the kidneys. The reduced function of the spleen, with the stomach responsible for digestion and the production of inner warmth, is made clear from the belly aches, the soft stools, the low appetite, and the tendency to feel cold. The affect on the lungs, finally, connected to breathing, nose, and defensive *qi*, is apparent from his tendency toward colds and feverish infections.

Altogether, the diagnosis is that the boy suffers from a depletion of the kidney, spleen, and lung complexes, indicated dominantly in a pervasive pattern of cold. The therapeutic principle is accordingly a warming and strengthening of the *qi* in these three organs. This can be achieved through acupuncture and moxibustion (the burning of the moxa herb on selected acupuncture points) as well as massages or acupressure. Qigong, physical movement that encourages energy flow in the specific areas, is also a good measure. More importantly, though, is the ingestion of herbal remedies and a lasting change in diet.

As regards dietary measures, the boy should take his meals regularly and eat slowly to avoid upsetting the stomach. He should avoid anything cold, oily, or heavy, which may place a burden on the lungs and kidneys. In the mornings, rather than cold corn flakes he should eat a warm breakfast, preferably a cooked cereal with nuts and dried fruit and maybe some ginger. During the day, his meals should consist of cooked foods and soups, including as much as possible warming elements, such as chicken and various kinds of onions. Rather than having fresh fruit and salads, for the time being it is better if he eats compotes and cooked or fried vegetables (Engelhardt and Nögel 2009, 40-43).

Another example is the case of a 53-year-old woman who has trouble with menopause. Her periods having ceased several years ago, she stopped hormone replacement therapy due to serious side effects and is now suffering from irregular sleep patterns, hot flashes, and overall irritability. She also complains about a recurring tendency toward acid reflux or heartburn, which was diagnosed by Western doctors as an inflammation of the esophagus. She takes medication to reduce stomach acid, and has a tendency toward constipation.

Visual examination reveals a tongue with deep cracks, while pulse diagnosis shows flooding and rapid patterns in the upper regions of the body, while those related to the lower half are hollow and thready. In terms of the eight key criteria, her condition consists of an internal overproduction of heat (yang), connected to a weakness or depletion of yin. The cracked tongue and the hollow pulse as well as the nightly intensification of hot flashes and agitation also indicate an overall yin weakness. The constellation of symptoms and patterns, moreover, is typical for women undergoing menopause.

Upon questioning, the dominant pathogenic patterns emerge. The patient tends to eat irregularly and with haste, she likes to drink red wine at night and takes a rather heavy dinner late in the evening. All these are heat-creating patterns: red wine is classified as very warming while irregular, hasty, and especially late meals tend to weaken moist, cool, yin energies. In addition, her nervousness and exhaustion are intensified by professional stress and the fact that she is the main caretaker of an invalid mother—both depleting inner resources and weakening yin.

Among the inner organs, the one under most pressure is the kidneys, which through *jing*-essence is responsible for the sexual maturation and development of the person, and thus also in charge of the menopausal transition. In her case, the yin qualities of the kidneys are diminished, causing normally harmonious and balanced yang potencies to become overbearing and rise into the heart. The heart, connected to psychological aspects of the person, represents the outward personality of the individual. In this case, the affect on the heart is evident in the patient's irritability, nervousness, insomnia, and hot flashes. Her tendency toward constipation and acid reflux, finally, indicate heat in the stomach, exhausting nurturing fluids and using up necessary yin energies.

Her diagnosis is a depletion of yin in the kidneys, stomach, and heart. This has caused the development of heat, which is further intensified by various nutritional errors. The main therapeutic principle is accordingly to support and moisturize yin, combined with a cooling and calming of the heart. Again, acupuncture, qigong, and herbs will be helpful. In terms of dietetics, the patient should eat regularly and in a calm setting, taking a light evening meal early without wine. She should avoid anything spicy, hot, or warming in nature, focusing instead on cooked cereals with raisins and nuts, and consume relatively more pork, squid, and tofu with gentle and cooling vegetables such as avocados, seaweeds, and tomatoes, as well as fresh, cooling fruits, such as dragon fruit and water melon (Engelhardt and Nögel 2009, 43-45).

Chinese dietary therapy, to sum up, works with the fundamental principles of the Chinese diet and is closely connected to the social realities and food apperception in Chinese culture. It allows for general patterns and overall guidelines but is also strongly linked to the individual, modifying its prescriptions on the basis of personalized diagnosis and the recognition of unique energetic patterns. Daoists fully conform to this fundamental Chinese dietary system and follow its guidelines in many respects. On the other hand, Daoists also go beyond medicinal diets, adding their own suggestions and methods and matching them to the specific social setting and cultivation goals of individual practitioners.

Part Two

Daoist Food

Chapter Four

What Daoists Eat

> Now, mentally float in emptiness and stillness, let go of worries, rest in nonaction, absorb primordial *qi* after midnight, practice healing exercises in a calm setting, support and nourish life without fail, take healthy food and efficacious herbs—if you do all this, then a hundred years of vigorous longevity are your proper due. (*Yangxing yanming lu* 1.1a)

In many ways, the way Daoists eat is a continuation and adaptation of the Chinese medicated diet. They strive to be conscious of seasonal change, aware of the needs of their bodies, focused on how best to nurture their organs, and alert to cosmic and social taboos. Within this framework, however, Daoists also aim to set themselves apart from ordinary society, creating communities that are clearly distinct. Choices about dress, attire, personal items, daily routines, and—very importantly—food selection, preparation, and consumption all serve as markers of a community set above and beyond normative society.[1] Rather than one dominant form of such community, moreover, there are several distinct kinds of Daoists who live, eat, and work in different social settings, thus creating a variety of lifestyles and eating habits.

Already the ancient *Taiping jing* notes different levels of practitioners. As cited in the sixth-century *Sandong zhunang*, it says

---

[1] For detailed studies about such communities, see Goffman 1961; Kanter 1972; Kohn 2003a; Turner 1969.

[As regards the highest level] Heaven is distant and knows no
bounds. If one does not eat wind and *qi*, how can one travel
fast enough to go along fully with the course of Heaven? Thus,
to work alongside the spirit-envoys and be associated with
them, one must live largely on wind and *qi*.

On the next level, one matches the essences of Earth in
one's powers, harmonizes the five types of soil, looks down on
mountains and rivers, follows high ridges and enters waterways. One has commerce with the changing patterns of Earth
and eats and works together with others. To do so one cannot
eat grains. One drinks water and uses herbs and medicinal
formulas.

On the third level, eating in moderation is the way. Although one does not firmly establish one's form, one eats less
than ordinary people and is slightly different from them.
Therefore, even those who merely ingest little that passes
through their intestines are people who are in the process of attaining Dao. (4. 3a; see Campany 2005, 109; Huang 2007, 18).

This defines three levels: high-level practitioners at one with Heaven
who float freely along with the celestial bodies and live only on pure *qi*,
essentially not eating at all; middle-level adepts on par with Earth who
match mountains and rivers and have given up ordinary food, replacing
it with vegetal, herbal, and mineral substances; and a third kind who are
still part of the world and eat ordinary food but do so with awareness
and in moderation.

Reversing this order, most Daoists today and in history belong to the
third level. Lay followers and married priests, so-called fire-dwelling
Daoists (*huoju daoshi* 火居道士), mostly of the Celestial Masters school,
continue to reside in ordinary society and observe its rules. Obliged socially to eat with other people, they consume essentially everything but,
as the *Taiping jing* notes, try to be moderate and conscious about it
(Huang 2007, 2). A subcategory of this group, next, consists of priests
during preparation for major rituals and Daoists living in monastic institutions. They usually observe a series of avoidances, most notably of
meat, alcohol, and the five strong vegetables (onions, garlic, etc.). They
also try to cultivate a more conscious attitude toward food and, in their
sacrificial banquets and ceremonial meals, make a point of relating the
food to the cosmos at large and sharing it with gods, ancestors, and all
beings.

The second group (matching the middle level of the *Taiping jing* description) consists largely of hermits, traditionally associated with mountains and caves but also found in the subtemples and hermitages of monastic complexes and, more recently, in the anonymity of the cities. Going beyond the basic avoidances of ritually pure Daoists, they have given up ordinary food to a large extent and live increasingly on herbal, vegetal, or mineral substances, like walnuts, cinnamon, or mica. Combining this diet with breathing techniques, healing exercises, and meditations, they refine their bodies to a subtler level and thus attain a closeness to the universal flow that goes beyond ordinary living.

The highest among the practitioners, finally, live only on *qi*. A select subgroup of hermits, they practice what is known formally as *bigu* 辟穀, which literally means "avoiding grain" but in fact implies a complete transformation and reorganization of the *qi*-body from a postnatal to a prenatal or primordial constitution. Daoists at this level are furthest removed from ordinary life. They undergo a strict regimen of cutting out ordinary food, sometimes with the help of specific formulas or concoctions, while also training intensely in breathing and *qi*-guiding exercises to reach a point where they become like embryos, being nurtured completely and without any outside materials by the Great Dao, the cosmic equivalent of the gestating female.

Lifestyle and Attitude

The lifestyle embraced by Daoists and their fundamental attitude toward food in many respects resembles the teaching and methods of macrobiotics, a modern Japanese adaptation of traditional Chinese dietary therapy. Its founder, George Ohsawa (1893-1966), contracted tuberculosis in 1909 and was told that he would die soon. Trying to avoid this, he studied a book by Sagen Ishizuka called *The Curative Method of Diet* and began to eat accordingly. He consumed only natural foods and beverages and made whole grains the backbone of his diet. After he cured himself, he taught the method to others. His main disciples were Herman Aikawa and Michio Kushi. In 1949, the latter brought the practice to the U.S. where he gave lectures, conducted workshops, wrote books, and founded centers in Boston and San Francisco. He educated wide segments of the population on the relationship between diet, lifestyle, and disease, and with his whole-food nutrition method was successful in curing numerous degenerative diseases, including terminal cases (see www.macrobiotics.org).

Macrobiotics is based on the cosmology of yin and yang in relationship to Dao, which here is described as Infinity. Infinity manifests itself in the complementary forces yin and yang, which are endless in change and transformation. Yin represents centrifugality; yang represents centripetality. Together they produce *qi* and thus all phenomena. They attract and repel each other and constantly change into one another. Nothing ever is solely yin or solely yang, and—as Chinese and Daoist dieticians would easily agree—one has to maintain the proper balance between them for continued health and prosperity.

To find this balance, one should eat organically grown, whole, and local foods that are in season and, Daoists would add, picked or harvested at the right time in the proper alignment with Heaven and Earth. One should listen to the body, undertake regular exercise—including breathing, stretches, and meditations—and keep stress levels low. Macrobiotic followers further specify that meals should contain one part yang to five parts yin, a ratio found naturally in whole grains, especially in brown rice, which should make up half of the diet. The other half should consist of organic vegetables plus beans, seaweed, condiments/pickles, soups, and beverages (Kushi and Esko 1993).

Daoists do not have any specifications of this sort, rather encouraging people to find the balance between grain, vegetables, and other food-stuffs that is best suited to their individual constitution, plus matching the seasons and social context. They also do not emphasize whole grains nearly as much, allowing the use of white rice, bread, and noodles (Saso 1994, xix; Peng 2006a-e). As traditional manuals point out, all foods of the different groups should be prepared so they are neither too hot or too cold, too spicy or too bland, or contain any harmful substances (*Yaoxiu keyi* 9.14b). Food overall should "harmonize the blood and body fluids, preserve and nourish the body and spirit, calm the spirit soul and settle the will, and in general expel all wind and dampness, thus greatly enhancing life and extending old age" (*Fashi jinjie jing*, l. 17-18).

Like macrobiotic practitioners, dedicated Daoists ideally avoid meat, alcohol, sugar, and caffeine; anything cold, canned, frozen, and irradiated; as well as all artificially colored, preserved, sprayed, or chemically treated foods (such as sodas). Medieval monastic kitchens also prohibited materials imported from far-away places as well as those coming from families with a recent birth or death, from robbers or lascivious people. Monks and nuns avoided anything left behind by birds, beasts, worms, or fish; any food offered to popular (and thus impure) spirits and demons at altars, shrines, or temples; anything unclean, rotten, moldy, broken, burnt, or defiled; as well as any foodstuffs that children had touched and returned to their mothers (*Fashi jinjie jing*, #14-25). If any donor came to the monastery offering food of this type, it was considered nonritual (*feifa* 非法) and not accepted. "If someone among the faithful demands nonritual food, quietly send him away and do not allow him to come again" (*Qianzhen ke* 14a; *Yaoxiu keyi* 9.9b).

Beyond being careful about selecting the food, both macrobiotic and Daoist practitioners place a great deal of emphasis on its proper treatment and careful preparation (Saso 1994, xvii; Huang 2007, 108). Kitchens should be light and airy, comfortable rooms that create a happy work environment. The design should match the rules of traditional Feng Shui and apportion light, water, and fire in the proper manner (Miles 1998, 35). All base materials and utensils, moreover, should match the requirements of naturalness and clarity. Thus macrobiotic cooks prefer natural oils, rice paste, or bean paste as bases and use only natural utensils such as unglazed pottery or earthenware, wooden spatulas and strainers (Kushi and Jack 1985).

Both also agree that the mind of the cook is essential to its efficacy and wholeness, a feature emphasized also in Zen Buddhism.[2] All kitchen staff should cultivate a calm, meditative, and cosmically aware attitude. Already the sixth-century *Badi jing* 八帝經 (Scripture of the Eight Emperors, DZ 640), a key text of the Three Sovereigns (Sanhuang 三皇) school, emphasizes the importance of personal integrity, both in society and in relation to food. It insists that Daoists should by all means avoid:

1. exhibiting vulgarity because it drains life away;
2. eating a lot because it clogs the conduits of *qi*;
3. drinking a lot because it weakens the bladder;

---

[2] The most famous incident in this regard is the meeting of Dōgen (1200-1253) and the cook. In 1223, the Japanese master traveled to China to study meditation. Still on the ship, he was received by a senior envoy of his host monastery who turned out to be the cook—a traditionally lowly role that yet was essential for the functioning of the whole and also showed the importance of activating the teaching in mundane reality. See LaFleur 1985; Dumoulin 1988.

4. getting very warm because it dissolves the bone marrow;
5. getting very cold because it harms the flesh;
6. eating cold food because it causes illnesses;
7. crying and spitting because it drains the body's juices;
8. watching things for a long time because it dims the eyesight;
9. listening for a long time because it clogs the perception;
10. crying for a long time because it saddens the spirit;
11. shouting suddenly because it startles the souls;
12. thinking complex thoughts because it obscures the will;
13. becoming angry because it makes the spirit unhappy. (13ab)

Medieval monastic rules echo these guidelines. As the *Guanxing jing* 觀行經 (Scripture of Behavioral Observations; Dunhuang manuscript P. 2410; S. 3140) specifies, all kitchen work should be done with great circumspection, exhibiting tolerance, humility, and obedience (l. 244-46). Workers should be the first to rise and the last to bed, serving the community with dedication and always striving to avoid the noisy banging of pots and pans or shouting of orders. Responsible for communal health, they must never waste supplies by, for example, cutting the roots off vegetables or taking firewood from growing trees (l. 246-54). They should always measure the proper amounts while carefully picking grasses, alien seeds, and animal droppings out of the grain and washing it in a sturdy container with clean water for at least five times (l. 278-83).

In the same spirit, meals in traditional settings as well as among modern Daoists and macrobiotics are holy and treated with awe and respect. While eating, the focus is entirely on the food and its sharing with the gods and all beings. Although there may be the recitation of a sacred text, in all cases idle chatter or business talk are suspended, all chewing is patient and conscious, and a portion of the stomach, as much as a third, remains empty. Ideally, one takes a short walk after the meal or does some other movement that supports digestion (Huang 2007, 44, 113).

Both Daoist eating and macrobiotics have further in common that they create healing, increase vigor, and enhance longevity. As has been shown in some detail for macrobiotics, the diet detoxifies the body, supports its self-healing abilities, and strengthens the immune system by increasing the functioning of the organs and aiding natural stabilization. It is important in this context that neither macrobiotics nor the Daoist way of eating are merely a diet but involve a complete change in lifestyle, spending more time preparing and eating food and becoming more conscious of one's relationship to nature and Dao or Infinity

Modern Monastics

The modern school of Daoist monasticism, Complete Perfection (Quanzhen 全真), has continued the medieval tradition in many ways. Its initial ordination text is the *Chuzhen jie* 初真戒 (Precepts of Initial Perfection, (JY 278, 292; ZW 404; [3] trl. Hackmann 1920). It represents the first step in a three-level ordination system, standardized by Wang Changyue 王常月 (*zi* Kunyang 崑陽, d. 1680), who served as the leader of the dominant Longmen 龍門 subsect and abbot of its headquarters at the Baiyun guan 白雲觀 (White Cloud Temple) in Beijing (Esposito 2000, 629).

The text begins by requiring ordinands to take refuge in the Dao, the scriptures, and the masters, then swear to obey sets of five and ten precepts. The latter specify, among others, that they should not "be lascivious or lose perfection, defile or insult the numinous *qi*." They should abstain from "drinking wine beyond measure or eating meat in violation of the prohibitions" (22a). A complementary work, the *Qinggui xuanmiao* 清規玄妙 (Pure Rules, Mysterious and Marvelous, ZW 361), [4] similarly prohibits the consumption of wine and fancy foods, such as luscious mushrooms and meat, and punishes violations of this rule by caning and expulsion (see Yoshioka 1979; Kohn 2003b).

Food was precious and important. Monastics partook of it in formal meal-time ceremonies and, like Buddhists, obtained some of it by begging. Using the begging bowl and eating from it was a highly ritualized activity, performed with great care. As the *Chuzhen jie* says:

---

[3] The abbreviation "JY" stands for *Daozang jiyao* 道藏輯要 or "Collected Essentials of the Daoist Canon," a collection of texts from the early nineteenth century. "ZW" indicates *Zangwai daoshu* 藏外道書, "Daoist Texts Outside the Canon," a recent compilation. Both are numbered according to Komjathy 2002.

[4] The text was collected in manuscript form by the German missionary Heinrich Hackmann in 1910-11. It originally appeared in the *Gu shuyinlou cangshu* 古書陰樓藏書 (Library of Hidden Books in the Ancient Pavilion) by Min Yide 閔一德 (1758-1836), the eleventh patriarch of the Longmen 龍門 branch of the Complete Perfection school on Mount Jin'gai. See Kohn 2003b.

> The begging bowl should have the shape of the eight trigrams. Only the opening for the lid should be round. It should be kept in a special bowl bag and taken out only when it is time to eat.
>
> After concluding the incantation [at meals], mentally gather your *qi* and visualize the spirit, then eat without opening your mouth widely or making any sucking noises. Use the spoon when appropriate. After food has been taken, wash the bowl and return it to its bag. Every time you go against this, it will count as one transgression. (30a)

These rules applied both to men and women, however, the latter also received a set of twelve special precepts, listed in the nineteenth-century manual *Nü jindan* 女金丹 (*Women's Golden Elixir*, ZW 871, 878; Tao 1989, 57-122). Rules here emphasize the mental state women needed to cultivate, encouraging them to "restrain the recurrence of inappropriate thoughts;" to "cut off lust and sexual indulgence;" to avoid "flying into rages" or giving in to anger, fear, or anxiety; as well as to curb tendencies toward curiosity, gossip, stinginess, and scorn. Women were not supposed to "kill or harm any living being" and had to "avoid excess in eating meat" (1.4a-5a; Despeux and Kohn 2003, 165).

Most Complete Perfection followers today undergo initial ordination simultaneously with that into the second level, which involves taking the 300 precepts listed in the *Zhongji jie* 中極戒 (Precepts of Medium Ultimate, JY 293, ZW 405; trl. Hackmann 1931). Closely patterned on the medieval *Guanshen dajie* 觀身大戒 (Great Precepts of Self-Observation, DZ 1364; trl. Kohn 2004a, 204-29), this contains three groups of rules: a set of 180 socially oriented prohibitions that frequently follow the rules of the *Laojun shuo Yibai bashi jie* 老君說一百八十戒 (180 Precepts Revealed by Lord Lao, DZ 786) a fourth-century collection of Celestial Masters' precepts (Hendrischke and Penny 1998, 22; Schipper 2001; Kohn 2004a, 73-74, 136-44); thirty-six admonitions that specify forms of monastic behavior, and eighty-four altruistic resolutions.

With regard to food, the text prohibits killing for nourishment (no. 1), taking the five strong vegetables (no. 4), wasting food (no. 70), throwing it into water or fire (no. 41), and touching it with bare hands (no. 154). It emphasizes that one should live on a vegetarian diet (no. 217), be content with taking coarse and tasteless bits (no. 188), and "wish that the donor may attain good fortune and be always full and satisfied" when given a morsel during begging rounds (no. 195) (see Kohn 2004a, 53-54; Huang 2007, 16-17).

Modern Daoists also tend to stay away from eggs and dairy and drink a lot of tea, selecting the particular kind that best matches the individual's constitution, time, temperature, and place. It may sound difficult and expensive at first to eat in this manner, but it is in fact quite affordable, since the amount of food one consumes is considerably less than in a diet that relies on processed foods. The body, after all, eats *until* it gets the nourishment it needs: the more one consumes calories without nutrients, the longer and the more one has to eat.

Vegetarianism

Vegetarianism is the conscious and intentional avoidance of animal products in one's diet. It comes in three distinct forms (Brownlie 2002, 4-5). The most common is the avoidance of meat, i.e., the flesh of butchered, caught, or otherwise dead animals, summarized in the simple rule: "If it has eyes, don't eat it." Vegetarians of this kind will usually consume eggs (preferably unfertilized) and dairy products as well as honey and other foods that are based on animals but do not involve killing. They are technically called ovo-lactarians. Subgroups include those that eat eggs but no dairy, and vice versa (Fox 1999, 55).

Another kind of vegetarianism, less radical and found among some Hindus and certain groups in the West, is the avoidance of all "red" meat, i.e., the flesh of mammals, but allowing the consumption of poultry and fish on the grounds that their nervous systems are too different from the human constitution to make a difference. It might be called semi-vegetarian. A third kind, more radical and increasingly popular in the West, is the so-called vegan diet, whose followers eschew all kinds of animal products, even eggs, dairy, and the like. This often also involves the avoidance of other animal-based objects, such as silk and leather. Subgroups here include macrobiotics who eat mainly whole grains and sea vegetables, natural hygienists who also propose periods of fasting, and raw food eaters (Fox 1999, 55).

The motivation for vegetarian eating, too, is threefold: physiological, psychological, and ecological. The most common reason in the modern West is ecological: an ethical sense of responsibility for the world that includes compassion for the suffering of animals and the understanding that world hunger and ecological destruction could be easily stopped if so much grain and vegetables were not used in raising animals for slaughter (see Inglis 1993; Young 1999; Roth 2009; Fox 1999, chs. 5-6). While animal welfare as an aspect of humanitarianism emerged only in the 1870s (Spencer 1993, 266), vegetarian eating for world community reasons has forerunners in ancient Egypt, Greece, and India. Most important in the West was the thought of Pythagoras (ca. 570-495 B.C.E.), after whom vegetarianism was called the Pythagorean diet until 1847 when the Vegetarian Society was founded at Northwood Villa in Ramsgate, England (Spencer 1993, 238; Stuart 2006, 422).

Already the ancient Egyptians considered plants and animals to be gifts of the gods that had to be honored and not killed (Darby et al. 1977), a teaching that Pythagoras adopted after being trained as a priest in Diospolis (Spencer 1993, 44-45). Besides being a stellar mathematician and natural observer, he believed in reincarnation and espoused a radical philosophy of cosmic integration and non-violence. His academy trained numerous disciples in rigorous self-cultivation, requiring ascetic practices and a five-year vow of silence (Spencer 1993, 46). His thinking and practices may have been influenced by India, home of the foremost vegetarian culture on the planet and a definite sponsor of Western vegetarianism after the Renaissance.

Indian thinkers adopted an ecological position due to the doctrine of reincarnation or metempsychosis, which means that all living beings are interconnected and the killing of one affects all others (Spencer 1993, 74). The beef taboo in China, too, is a manifestation of this. It began in the Tang-Song transition and continued until the late nineteenth century. The taboo arose due to economic necessity, the slaughter of water buffalos causing a potential shortness of draft animals, then expanded into broader views of animal welfare (see Goossaert 2005; 2009). Numerous stories in Song-dynasty literature tell of butchers being converted to vegetarianism by a slaughtered ox appearing to them in a dream and telling them just how badly they felt and how much they suffered, in some cases swearing revenge on them and their family (see Lavoix 2002; Kieschnick 2005, 195).

The psychological motivation for vegetarianism is that conscious eating creates subtler awareness in the mind (Adams 2000, 43; Fox 1999, ch. 7). It is also at the root of the Buddhist position: the mind is essential in creating reality and continuing karma, and animal consumption adds to the store of negative emotions. It does so through two factors. First, according to Buddhist understanding, in order to kill anyone or anything, one has to generate violent aggression in the form of either hatred or greed, either detesting the being or person or strongly desiring their possession, such as in robbery or butchering.

The second factor is that any animal, however "humanely" slaughtered, dies a sudden and violent death. At the moment of death, it inevitably is terrified and—as has also been shown in scientific studies—releases large amounts of stress hormones throughout its entire body, which remain in the meat. As a result, anyone consuming animal flesh is subject to the karmic emanations of both the killer and the victim, absorbing certain amounts of greed and fear, a condition Buddhists describe as "secondary karma." Since the entire Buddhist enterprise is geared to the lessening and eventual dissolution of karma, adding to one's store is counterproductive and should be avoided.

At the same time, early Buddhists were not strict vegetarians, nor are contemporary practitioners in Japan, Tibet, or Southeast Asia. The Buddha, himself allegedly dying from eating spoiled pork, supported the eating of meat for medicinal uses and specified only that one should not consume elephant or horse meat because they were the ruler's animals, serpents because they were holy, and dogs because they were lowly and filthy (Kieschnick 2005, 188).

The problem was that "beggars can't be choosers." In other words, being strict vegetarians would make mendicant monks pick and choose from among the alms they collected, creating a sense of entitlement and strong ego, which is karmically even worse than traces of secondary karma (Spencer 1993, 81). Devadatta, a senior disciple of the Buddha, accordingly criticized vegetarians for ostentation and even called it a form of extremism that went against the Middle Way (Kieschnick 2005, 189). The original rule in the ancient Buddhists texts was, therefore, that monks could eat meat and use animals for other things, such as milk products, silk, shells, and leather, but that the animal should under no circumstances be killed specially for them and that they should, as much as possible, take the meat out of dishes (Kieschnick 2005, 190).

As Richard Mather has shown (1981), this changed in China where begging was frowned upon and the sangha could grow its on food on land donated by wealthy aristocrats and the imperial court. Having control over food production eliminated the need to accept meat in any form. Strict vegetarianism grew. Emperor Wu of the Liang (r. 502-549), a devout Buddhist, was also a dedicated vegetarian and did much to spread the practice, including the promotion of gluten as a meat substitute (Huang 2000, 497-98). His "Essay on the Renunciation of Meat" argued against the traditional medical position that consuming only vegetables would create too much cold in the body and thus impede health, emphasizing that meat could also deplete qi and that the gods were repelled by the acrid smell of burning flesh (Kieschnick 2005, 198-99; Despeux 2007, 30). [5]

His influence made a big difference and the new standard gradually spread, also into Daoist circles. It was aided greatly by increased pressure of the laity who liked to see their clergy pure and otherworldly, not showing off wealth or engaging in sensory entertainments such as eating meat (Kieschnick 2005, 201). Faux meat, such as fish, duck, or pork made from tofu became popular in the tenth century, allowing religious representatives to save face at formal banquets and be active participants in various social situations (Huang 2000, 299; Kieschnick 2005, 186). The full practice of Chinese religious vegetarianism that also involved the abstention from garlic, onions, and eggs, has been in place since the thirteenth century and is still actively pursued today (Kieschnick 2005, 187).

Another dimension of the Buddhist objection to meat eating is the overall Indian notion that, due to the ongoing rebirth process, the cow, pig, or chicken one is consuming might possibly be a relative reborn in animal form. Both Indian and Chinese texts describe various heinous deeds leading to rebirth in nasty situations and as animals. For example, the *Bala-pandita-sutta* (Discourse on Fools and the Wise) says that sinful people are first made to suffer in the Niraya Hell, then come back as animals, including not only worms and insects but also horses, cattle, sheep, deer, chickens, pigs, and dogs (Horner 1967, 3:213-14; Kohn 1998a, 4). Anyone consuming such an animal would, therefore, be potentially guilty of cannibalism, prohibited widely in traditional cultures and also in China (Despeux 2007, 30).

---

[5] His writing was as influential in China as the 4-volume *Abstinence from Animal Food* by the Phoenician thinker Porphyry (ca. 232-305) was in the West. It, too, made arguments in terms of health and sacrifice. See Spencer 1993, 103-05.

The Daoist Position

Daoists adopted both the Buddhist practice of vegetarian eating and the arguments for it, especially since much of their ethical and philosophical teaching developed under Buddhist influence (see Zürcher 1980; Bokenkamp 2007). However, their main take on meat avoidance is physiological rather than psychological. That is to say, they object to the consumption of animal flesh not so much because of strong emotions and karmic implications but because of what it does to the body, to a certain degree matching modern health concerns (Fox 1999, 66-72). There are, however, two more specific aspects in the Daoist case. For one, meat is impure and offends the pure celestial gods who reside both in the body and the stars. Unlike the popular deities of the masses, they consist of subtle cosmic *qi*, are opposed to killing in any form, and find the preparation and consumption of meat repulsive (Kleeman 2005, 149).

For another, Daoists follow Chinese medical lore and see animal flesh as yang in quality, pulling the person toward life and materiality, and thus increasing internal heat. Just as traditional physicians would recommend the consumption of a matching part (brain to enhance brain power, lungs to aid lung capacity, penis for greater sexual stamina, etc.) and warriors would eat the flesh of their enemies to absorb them and their inherent power or *mana* (Despeux 2007, 30), so Daoists do *not* eat meat because it would make the person more like a beast. As the Daoist diet aids refinement and physical purification, practitioners work more and more with subtle forms of *qi* and thus avoid strong, aggressive substances (Huang 2007, 4-5).

Vegetarianism is part of Daoist codes from the beginning. Already the fourth-century *Laojun shuo Yibai bashi jie* has a series of related precepts:

> 172. If someone kills birds and beasts, fish or other living beings for you, do not eat them.
> 173. If something has been killed for food, do not eat it.
> 176. To be able to cut out all meat of living beings and the six domestic animals is best.
> 177. To be able to eat only vegetables is most excellent; should it be impossible, match [your food to] the ruling constellation. (Kohn 2004a, 145)

Matching the "ruling constellation" means to avoid offending the spirits associated with certain days and celestial patterns. More details appear in the fifth-century *Lingshu ziwen xianji*:

> Do not eat the flesh of animals associated with your parent's birthday.
> Do not eat the flesh of animals associated with your birthday.
> Do not eat the flesh of the six domestic animals.
> Do not eat the meat of armored [shelled] animals like turtles or dragons on the days of Six Armored Gods [Liujia 六甲].
> Do not eat pheasant on bingwu days.
> Do not eat the meat of black animals on bingzi days.
> Do not eat fish on the ninth day of the second month. (2ab; Bokenkamp 1997, 365)

Here meat is allowed but in controlled limits and in correlation with the cosmic constellation of the adept's birth date and that of his parents, as well as with various astrological constellations in the course of the year. The text also says that followers should "not get drunk on *yimao* days" (2b), implying that it was acceptable to partake of wine on other days of the cycle.

The Daoist tendency toward self-refinement and otherworldliness through vegetarian eating is also borne out by modern physiological research which shows that the refusal of meat and heavy foods is a common characteristic of the natural dying process. About six weeks before death, the dying person will want lighter food, taking only vegetables, fruits, and juices, and gradually, reducing food intake to nothing. This allows the body to shut its digestive system down and eliminates all waste in the bowels, preventing involuntary defecation at death. Similarly, the kidneys stop working and shut down the body's water system. Like Daoists on a radical *bigu* regimen, patients at the very end of life will not take either food or water. With both digestive tract and kidneys out of commission, any nourishment given would be stored in the skin and cause painful swelling (see Callahan and Kelly 1992; Mims 1999). Vegetarian eating combined with heightened internal awareness and deeper breathing, whether spontaneously at the end of life or consciously in Daoist practice, thus serves as a preparation for radical transformation, be it toward death or its ultimate overcoming.

The Five Strong Vegetables

The same energetic argument is also made with regard to the so-called five strong vegetables (*wuxin* 五辛), which are various kinds of onions and garlic, all plants in the genus *Allium*. They include:

—*Allium cepa* (*hucong* 胡葱), the common onion, a plant of globular shape that consists of multiple layers, originated in Spain and Portugal, and today grows mainly in the south of China and in Indochina. Often described as the "poor man's meat" (Stuart 1976, 26), it plays a key role in the Chinese diet, commonly eaten with rice, millet, or bread and other vegetables. Medicinally, it stabilizes various conditions, being administered in cases of fever, headache, diarrhea, urinary infections, and rheumatic disorders. It has an upward moving tendency, so that onion tea may excite vomiting and skin conditions are covered with bulbs or anointed with its juice (also Huang 2000, 38-39).

—*Allium fistulosum* (*cong* 葱), the green onion or scallion, a northern plant, is much like the common onion, except that it does not form a bulb. Its medical uses are similar and it, too, has an energizing, warming, and stabilizing effect (Stuart 1976, 26).

—*Allium ascalonicum* (*xie* 薤), the garden shallot, is also known as the "bunching or Welch onion" (Anderson and Anderson 1977, 328). Its bulbs (*xiebai* 薤白) are pickled for medicinal use, having tonic, nutrient, and astringent properties.

—*Allium odorum* (*jiu* 韭), a small version of leek, is indigenous to Siberia, Mongolia, and China. Already used in ancestral sacrifices under the Zhou dynasty, it has strengthening properties, nourishing and purifying the blood and efficacious in case of poisonous bites (Stuart 1976, 27).

—*Allium sativum* (*suan* 蒜), garlic, is one of the oldest and most common Chinese herbs, used in cooking and for healing. Now called *xiaosuan* 小蒜 (small garlic) in distinction to *dasuan* 大蒜 (*Allium scorodoprasum*), the rocambole which has a deleterious effect (Stuart 1976, 28), it came originally from Central Asia and today is grown everywhere. Available in fresh bulbs, as oil-based extracts, dried powders, and pills, it kills internal parasites and is known as the "poor man's antibiotic." It contains many natural antioxidants, anti-clotting agents, and detoxifiers, released as the phytochemical allicin when a clove is crushed or cooked.

Also containing various sulfur compounds which inhibit platelets in the blood from adhering to one another, garlic has been shown to lower cholesterol, protect the heart, and serve as an anti-inflammatory and pain-relieving remedy. It is good for colds, asthma, diabetes, yeast infections, and many other ailments. It has also, for many years, been known to reduce the risk of cancer, especially of the breast, colon, larynx, and stomach. On the negative side, garlic can lead to blood thinning and should be avoided before or after surgery. Very high doses will also irritate the intestines, not to mention other people (see www.acupuncture.com/herbology/herbind.htm; Fulder 1993; Rister 1999).

From an early date, these five were prohibited in Daoist communities, as is made clear in the *Laojun shuo Yibai bashi jie*. It states categorically: "Do not eat garlic or any other of the five strong vegetables" (#10). In its wake, Daoist monastics of the late Six Dynasties and early Tang frowned on the strong vegetables because their consumption diminished purity in the inner organs and caused bad breath which impacted on Daoist discipline, community cohesion, and respect among outside supporters. Bad breath, the manuals insist, is especially harmful when one attends Daoist services, sends a petition to the gods, or lectures to a group of commoners (*Daoxue keyi* 1.4b-5a). Another dimension of the five strong vegetables that makes them unsuitable in a monastic setting is their medicinal power, heating the blood and raising the fires of yang, which is associated with an increased tendency to violate the precepts against tolerance and abstinence (Kieschnick 1997, 24).

The most detailed formulation of the Daoist objection appears in the *Yinyuan jing* 因緣經 (Scripture of Karmic Retribution, DZ 336), a Buddho-Daoist work dated to the late sixth century. It links them specifically to the drinking of alcohol and the eating of meat and notes that they cause either a stuffy nose that prevents the person from "smelling either fragrances or odors" or a lascivious and uncontrolled nature, which will create karmic problems. Also, eating these vegetables may result in death by drowning or in rebirth in an unclean and foul-smelling body, be it human or animal. At the worst, approaching the Three Treasures (Dao, scriptures, and teachers) after having partaken of these noxious foods, will cause one to be reborn as a flea or a wood-louse (Kohn 1998a).

Buddhists also supported the prohibition, as is first documented in the *Fanwang jing* 梵網經 (*Brahmajāla sūtra*, T. 1484, 24.997c), an apocryphon dated to around the year 450 (DeGroot 1969, 42; see also Groner 1990). It mentions the five vegetables in its secondary commandments, emphasizing the bad smell they cause (Kieschnick 2005, 191). Next, they appear in the *Shoulengyan jing* 首楞嚴經 (*Suramgama sūtra*, T.945, 19.141c), compiled under the Tang around the year 700. Rather than because of their smelly nature, the text rejects them due to their aphrodisiac and anger-inducing qualities (19.141c; Ch'en 1973, 98; Kieschnick 2005, 202). Buddhists did not allow any practitioner who had eaten garlic or other unclean substances to enter the lecture, worship, or meditation halls or any other monastic spaces for seven days (Kieschnick 2005, 192). Both Daoist and Buddhist institutions, as well as regulations to prepare for sacrifices among lay priests, still prohibit their use to the present day (see Welch 1967; Hackmann 1931, 8).

Beverages

Just as the five strong vegetables create an effect that may increase passions and lead to impure forms of behavior, so is alcohol a potentially destructive substance that is prohibited both in Daoist and Buddhist communities. While this includes all kinds of alcoholic beverages today, in ancient times the generic word *jiu* 酒 referred primarily to "a brew made from fermented grain with added yeast, close to modern beer" (Sterckx 2005, 35; see also Poo 1997). However, it is not really beer, either, since it does not involve hops or malt, but a fermenting additive made from cooked grain and known as *qu* 麴, variously translated as "barm," "leaven," "yeast," and "starter" (Huang 2000, 154).

In contrast, wine made from grapes and other fruits which was known in the West since antiquity arrived in China from Ferghana under the Han but did not play a significant role until recently, its local production essentially a modern phenomenon (Huang 2000, 239-40). The social role of *jiu* being close to wine in Western societies, however, the translation "wine" is not completely inappropriate (Huang 2000, 150). To complicate matters even further, in texts of the middle ages, *jiu* might also indicate hard liquor, again made from various fermented grains but with a much higher alcohol content.

Daoist monastic codes object to alcohol consumption, setting up rules against intoxication that are mainly precautions against the development of uncontrolled behavior. Such behavior includes sloth and torpor, violence and killing, eating meat, consuming the five strong vegetables, and disregarding taboos or the ritual schedule. These offend the celestial officers, sicken the spirit and material souls, bring nightmares and bad fortune, and cause bad karma and rebirth (*Daoxue keyi* 2.5a).

More specifically, as the fifth-century *Taishang Laojun jiejing* (Precepts of the Highest Lord Lao, DZ 784), specifies, alcohol consumption leads to an entire chain of negative events that lead from intoxication to loss of control and the breaking of precepts. It says:

> Dead drunk, people get into disputes and quarrels, bringing misfortune to their lives and shame on themselves. Lying and cheating, they lose all guidelines they could follow. Stealing even from their six relations, they grab from all, not just from strangers. Killing off a host of living beings, they are only interested in giving satisfaction to their mouths and stomachs. (17b-18a; Kohn 1994, 206)

Not only in this life, they will also experience negative consequences in future rebirths. Being born among non-Chinese peoples and barbarians, they will have a husband or wife who is ugly and cruel. "Poor and destitute, cold and exposed, they will find no peace anywhere they live; whatever wealth and livestock they may acquire will be stolen by others; whatever they say, nobody will believe them" (18b). In general, their minds will be dull and blocked, and they will be objects of contempt.

A similar list of consequences also appears in the *Shier shangpin quanjie* 十二上品權戒 (Twelve Highest Precepts of Admonition, DZ 182), a Numinous Treasure (Lingbao 靈寶) collection of the sixth century. It says:

> People who drink wine may expect three kinds of retribution for their sins:
> 1. In this world they hinder or lose all goodness and connection to the divine law. In future lives, they will be born with a dark and obtuse spirit.
> 2. They are crazy and confused in their minds, lacking clarity and radiance. Later they will fall among the bats, lizards, and similar creatures.
> 3. Even if they attain human birth again, their conscious minds and inner natures will be mad and deluded, full of evil and folly. (9b-10a)

On whichever level of the rebirth process, people who indulge in alcohol are likely to be deluded and subject to bouts of madness. This connection between madness and drinking is also pronounced in the Buddhist *Bao-*

ying jing 報應經 (Retribution Sūtra, T. 747, 17.562b-63b), translated in the mid-fifth century, and the Daoist *Yinyuan jing* (Kohn 1998a, 19). The latter text links it to a lack of respect for the scriptures, which causes one to be reborn as a fish. Fish, as everyone knows, drink, so in one's next life one comes back into the world as an alcoholic. This alcoholism leads to madness and a rebirth in mud and filth, as a result of which one may again show disrespect for the scriptures and come back once more as a fish. The only way to avoid this vicious circle is to be careful in one's consumption of wine—and also of meat, which medieval texts commonly link with becoming the victim of violence and being reborn as a wild animal (Kohn 1998a, 30-31).

Alcohol is further blamed for ten kinds of problems or evils, including unfilial, offensive, and belligerent behavior, sexual hankerings and rule violations, as well as riding accidents and getting lost on the road. Its consumption leads to the creation of bad karma, mainly due to the desire to eat meat and kill living beings. It will eventually result in the loss of the good-will of masters, family, friends, and companions (*Daoxue keyi* 1.3b-4a). It harms all forms of social interaction and leads to violence and aggression; also, its production is a perfect waste of thousands of pounds of good grain that could feed the people (*Yaoxiu keyi* 14.1ab). It is, therefore, best to stay away from alcohol completely and instead create one's own inner liquor from refined saliva and *qi* (*Qianzhen ke* 15a).

In contrast, traditional manuals as well as modern Daoists much encourage the consumption of tea, especially green tea. Mentioned already in texts that go back to around 800 B.C.E., tea was first used medicinally then became a mainstay of Chinese culture. It began to replace alcohol as a social drink in the eighth century under the Tang, promoted vigorously in the popular *Chajing* 茶經 (Book of Tea) by the scholar Lu Yu 陸羽 (733-804), who later came to be venerated as the God of Tea (Benn 2005, 213-14; Huang 2000, 515-17).

Botanically a member of the *Camellia* family, tea grows as various shrubs that can reach fifty feet in height and commonly bear shiny leaves whose ends form pointed, spear-like tips. Picked and dried or roasted, and occasionally mixed with blossoms or flowers, the leaves are prepared to make different teas. The white or pale green variety uses them merely withered and dried, green teas use them fired, rolled, and then dried, while black or red tea applies them withered, rolled, and then roasted or fermented before drying (Huang 2000, 552). Tea can contain large amounts of caffeine in all forms, and commonly has been used in religious institutions to keep monks and nuns from falling asleep during meditation periods.

Medical literature describes tea almost exclusively as bitter, but also links it with the sweet flavor. Its benefits include the potential to increase blood flow, heighten awareness, speed elimination, prevent tooth decay, aid digestion, cleanse the skin, alleviate joint pain, and generally prolong life (Blofeld 1985, 144). It is also a way to ingest all five phases in one fell swoop: earth through the bowl's ceramics, metal in the kettle, water as its base, wood in the plant from which it grew, and fire in the heating. Western studies, too, have shown that especially green tea with low caffeine contains antioxidants which bind harmful free radicals. Drinking it regularly can prevent cell mutation in tumors, promote healthy arteries, reduce cholesterol, release toxins, aid digestion, increase metabolism, and control bacteria.

Daoists of all kinds and levels are very fond of tea. Many temples and monasteries grow their own crops, sell different varieties, and often offer samples to visitors, so they can choose the right kind. Teas come in endless variation, from very simple and cheap to extensively complex and costly. Conscious of the seasons, the time of day, and their particular constitution, Daoists choose and pick teas carefully, and modern Daoist-run clinics and spas often have special tea-shops to cater to their clients.[6]

Prominent kinds of tea today include so-called brick tea from Hunan, packaged in small, medium, and large blocks that open up into vast amounts of leaves, frequently served to visitors; Pu'er 普爾 tea from Yunnan with a cooling effect that is best used in hot climates; Gongfu 功夫 or "leisure" tea from Fujian and Guangdong, a gourmet form of the half-green and half-black Wulong 烏龍 tea, which releases strain and relaxes; Maoshan green tea from Jiangsu which is a light summer drink often served at banquets; Longjing 龍井 (Dragon Well) tea from the Hangzhou area in central eastern China which refreshes and revitalizes; ginger root and ginseng tea from the northeast with warming and strengthening properties; as well as cinnamon and lemon black tea from Yunnan which helps with infections and discomforts (Saso 1994, 113-26).

---

6 Examples include the Shaolong guan 紹龍觀 (Intertwined Dragon Temple) in the southwestern metropolis of Chongqing and the Daoist Long Life Center in the Qingzhi yuan 青芷園 (Blue Iris Garden) condominium complex in Beijing

Immortal Nutrition

Once a Daoist decides to move beyond the basic level of adjusting to Dao and enhancing internal purity, he or she changes the diet and starts to take increasing amounts of specific herbal and mineral substances which not only enhance health and vitality but also aid the body in the transformation of *qi* into subtler and more spiritual forms (Poo 2005, 130; Campany 2005, 113). Refining *qi* to purer levels, Daoist strive to become immortals, etheric beings who, according to legendary accounts, can be feathery or sometimes hairy, have no need to eat or drink, and are completely invulnerable to heat and cold, fire and water.

Light as ether, they can appear and vanish in an instant, and despite their advanced years look young, fresh, and radiant. Subjectively feeling detached from their environment, light in body yet immeasurably strong, and always comfortably warm, immortals supposed also have a wondrously light and radiant complexion as well as vastly improved eyesight to the point of being able to see in the dark and discern ghosts and spirits (Poo 2005, 131-34; see also Huang 2007, 163-75).

Many historical and hagiographical records describe practitioners experimenting with individual substances and formulas. The *Liexian zhuan* 列仙傳 (Immortals Biographies, DZ 294) of the early Han dynasty already mentions numerous items, including first and foremost various pine products, such as seeds, nuts, resin, sap, bark, and roots, but also

> —plants: cinnamon, peach, citrus peel, chrysanthemum flowers, calamus, pine, cedar, sesame, angelica, persimmons, lotus root, and mushrooms;
> —animals: turtle shells, deer antlers;
> —minerals: mica, hematite, aconite, saltpeter, mercury, and cinnabar. (Kaltenmark 1953; Huang 2007, 55-62; 2008a, 100-63)

One example is Chang Rong 昌容 who lived in the mountains and ate only ash raspberry roots, thereby maintaining the complexion of a twenty-year old for several centuries (*Liexian zhuan* 2.5b; Kaltenmark 1953, 152-53). Even more famous is Yu Jiang 玉姜, better known as Maonü 毛女, the Hairy Woman. A palace woman under the First Emperor of Qin, she saw the collapse of the dynasty approach and took refuge on Mount Hua. There she met the immortal Gu Chun 谷春, who taught her how to eat pine needles and survive in the wilderness—thus gaining the ability to live without solid food and become immune to cold and heat (2.7b-8a; Kaltenmark 1953, 159-60). Several hundred years later, she was discovered by a group of hunters, who saw a naked person with black hair. After chasing her for a while, they eventually captured her:

Calculations showed that this woman, having been the concubine of Prince Ying of Qin, was more than two hundred years old. When she was brought back to court to be fed grains, their odor nauseated her for several days, but then she got used to them. After about two years of this diet, her body lost its hair, and she turned old and died. (*Baopuzi* 11; Ware 1966, 194; Reed 1987, 174; Campany 2005, 110-11)

Maonü in due course became a highly venerated and respected immortal. She is typically shown in a leafy gown and with hairy legs. To the present day, there is still a temple dedicated to her on the northern slope of Mount Hua, the Maonü Grotto (Porter 1993, 69).

Other traditional figures include: Master Wen of Nanyang 南陽文 whose great-grandfather fled into the mountains at the end of the Han, ate thistles to alleviate hunger and became younger and radiant and could walk on ice and snow without feeling cold; Han Zhong 韓終 who lived on sweet flag for thirteen years, grew hairs on his body, did not feel cold; Zhao Tuozi 趙他子 who ate cinnamon for twenty years, grew strong and developed great stamina; Yimenzi 移門子 who fed on schisandra for sixteen years and developed the complexion of a young girl plus invulnerability to water and fire; and Prince Wen of Chu 楚文子, an eater of yellow dock for eight years, who developed a radiant complexion.

In addition, there were Du Ziwei 杜子微 who ate only asparagus and had eighty concubines and sired 130 sons; Ren Ziji 任子季 who lived on truffles for eighteen years and was healed of all scars while able to make himself invisible and to converse with immortals; Zizhong of Lingyang 陵陽子中 who only fed on bitter milkwort for twenty years, begat thirty-seven sons, and had exceptional memory; as well as Zhao Qu 趙瞿 who was abandoned due to sickness, received herbal formulas from immortals, then lived only on pine resin for many years and developed great strength and lightness in his body, living to the age of 170 without showing any signs of aging (*Baopuzi* 11, Ware 1966, 194-96; see also Poo 2005).

In more recent years, Bill Porter, searching for Chinese hermits, found various isolated figures on remote mountains who lived on very little food and/or specialized in certain kinds of diet. Most prominent is the Walnut Lady, a woman practitioner who took care of a walnut grove, selling the nuts for simple necessities and living mostly on them herself (1993). Not only in China, ancient Greece, too, had similar phenomena. The Cretan seer Epimenides of the sixth-century B.C.E., for example, lived on pills made from mallow and asphodel, attained great vitality, and lived to over 200 years (Spencer 1993, 53).

Cultural Implications

The tendency toward fresh vegetarian and raw food typical for the ancient immortal diet means a return to natural simplicity and the way humans were originally supposed to eat (Campany 2005, 116). Carnivores typically have a short bowel to allow the expulsion of toxins; they have long, sharp teeth and retractable claws to tear the meat from the bone; their jaws open straight up and down, unable to move side to side or in a circular pattern; and they keep cool by rapid breathing and the extrusion of the tongue (Spencer 1993, 19-20). None of these characteristics applies to humans or other herbivores.

Culturally the adoption of a vegetarian or raw food diet means the rejection of mainstream values, both in terms of time and space. For Daoists, this means that, in terms of time, they go back to the period of the great sage rulers before the domestication of fire and animals, thus recovering a more primitive and more primordial state in the development of humanity and social culture (see Lévi 1983). In terms of space, it means that they join the barbarians and other primitive people on the fringes of the Chinese empire, rejecting the hallmarks of civilization and proper Chineseness found in cooking food and eating grain and meat (Chang 1977b, 42; Huang 2000, 28; Campany 2005, 98).

The Daoist position is not unique but seems to reflect a common planetary memory. As Colin Spencer says:

> Common to all religions is the idea of the Golden Age, the paradise before the Fall. This period of peaceful co-existence between early humankind and the other creatures of the earth would have been non-violent and vegetarian, so there must have been within the race memory of early humans a knowledge of their herbivore past when no blood was shed, a distant memory of peace and plenty. (1993, 25)

Indeed, upon examination of human history on the planet it becomes evident that hunting animals for meat came very late in evolution. "If you imagine the lifetime of a seventy-year-old group, then it was only nine days before they were seventy that meat eating began and another two and a half days before they ate it cooked" (Spencer 1993, 20).

While meat eating may have started out of necessity during the Ice Age when so much fertile ground was under glaciers, once vegetables were available again its consumption became a sign of social superiority. By the same token, the domestication of animals around 6,500 B.C.E. was closely linked to power and social hierarchies, "a logical extension of the dominance of humans" (1993, 33; Fox 1999, 26-28). It also meant the end of diversity: "The hunter gatherers of the early Mesolithic used at least 120 seed foods, but by the end of Neolithic, the farmers used only 5 seeds, 3 cereals, and 2 pulses" (1993, 35). By taking up a vegetable-based and herb-centered diet, Daoists as much as other religious adepts on the planet thus seek to recover a saner, calmer, more peaceful, and egalitarian way of life.

In addition, eating Paleolithic-style and focusing on raw and organic plant-based food has been related to health benefits not unlike those claimed by immortality seekers. Its medical effects were studied particularly by the Swiss physician Maximilian Bircher-Benner (1867-1939), best known for the invention of *Müsli*, the forerunner of granola, and author of several important books on healing diets that focus on raw food (Spencer 1993, 281-82). In his wake, proponents of raw food today argue that cooking or preserving food eliminates large amounts of vitamins and minerals and that any food heated to over 116 degrees Fahrenheit loses all enzymes and protein structure, so that ingesting it actually takes beneficial agents out of the body. Pasteurizing milk destroys three quarters of the milk protein; altered, partially hydrogenated fats can become lethal compounds—in contrast to whole fats, as found in nuts, virgin olive oil, and flaxseed oil.

The positive effects of a raw food diet are numerous. Adherents claim that it boosts lymphocyte production, empowers the immune system, and contains enzymes that aid digestion. It also delays the aging process, increases oxygen consumption, and leads to more vitality and athletic ability. Beyond that, it heightens the senses, increases sensitivity to alcohol, tobacco, and drugs, and improves sexuality and aesthetic sensibility. It aids weight loss, eases allergies (often caused by food toxins), helps cure addictions, can reduce tumors, and helps in cancer recovery. It provides all eight of the twenty-two essential amino acids that must come from outside sources (especially through green leafy vegetables, pumpkin seeds, almonds, and fruits), increases flexibility and brain function through essential vegetable fats, and prevents diseases caused by pathogenic bacteria in meat and dairy (see Kenton and Kenton 1984).

While the adoption of a vegetarian diet thus signals a separation from and possible rejection of mainstream society, many effects found true by modern raw-food eaters match the results claimed for ancient immortals and herbal practitioners throughout history, leading credence to the Daoist claim that a radical change in diet not only creates different social structures but has a serious transformative effect on the body.

Chapter Five

Food in Ritual

In all the fields of blessedness,
Donating food is by far the best.
In the present it spreads pure happiness,
After this life it gives rebirth in heaven
And a future residence in the Pure Land
Where all food and clothing arrive spontaneously.
Therefore we present this offering today,
Spreading it equally to the various heavens.
(*Shishi weiyi* 10a; *Fengdao kejie* 6.6a)[1]

Just as the medicated diet goes beyond individual bodies and has a lot to do with social structures and historical developments, so Daoist eating takes place in various organizational settings and changes over the centuries. Eating and offering food are sacred activities that connect the practitioner to the divine and enhance the cosmic link of communities and institutions. Adapting ancient ritual structures, Daoists practice purifications by abstaining from food, have sacrificial offerings as part of daily and seasonal rituals, celebrate feasts at special occasions, and transform the monastic noon meal into a ceremonial occasion. In all these situations they use food differently from people in the ordinary world, relating to self, environment, and the cosmos in their own unique way.

In ordinary society, food tends to serve the establishment and maintenance of harmony—bodily, social, and cosmological—through balancing

---

[1] Texts on Daoist monasticism from the 7th century: *Shishi weiyi* 十事威儀 (Ten Items of Dignified Observances, DZ 792); *Fengdao kejie* (Rules and Precepts for Worshiping the Dao, DZ 1125).

qi and interactive connections (Anderson and Anderson 1977, 367; Douglas 1973, 70). In contrast, the religious importance of food has to do with liminality. Liminality is the state of ritual transition, defined first by Arnold van Gennep in his study of the rites of passage (1909). The concept was later developed by Victor Turner in his work, *The Ritual Process*. He describes it as the "threshold" phase, when a person, undergoing a passage from one social or religious status to another, is no longer in one and has not yet reached the next, being "between positions assigned by law, custom, convention, and ceremonial" (1969, 95; 1977, 37).

In other words, the bride going down the aisle is no longer a daughter and not yet a wife; the woman in labor is no longer pregnant and not yet a mother; the boy at initiation is no longer a child and not yet a man; the nun in her convent is no longer of this world and not yet fully of the next. Liminal transitions, and thus most religious rituals, are formalized in three phases: the separation, the "threshold" phase, and the reaggregation, structuring the passages that lead people into and out of liminal states.

Within this context, food tends to come in two major forms: as holy fast and as holy feast (see Bynum 1987), and is often practiced in a combination of the two. Thus, priests preparing for sacrifice or hermits in social isolation eschew ordinary foodstuffs and eat only very limited, prescribed diets or fast completely for a period. At the same time, the fruits, viands, and delicacies offered to the gods and ancestors—who partake of their vapor (Spencer 1993, 37)—are usually consumed afterwards by priests and the community in an extensive, often lavish feast that sets aside common rules of abstinence and control. Just as fast, therefore, creates a deliberate separation and distance from society, setting up a special realm of religious or spiritual attainment, so feast encourages union and communion, symbolizing the reaggregation stage and the joining of different levels of the supernatural and natural worlds.

Types of Rites

From the earliest times and still in Confucian and popular temples today, Chinese ritual has followed a tripartite division into purification (*zhai* 齋), sacrifice (*ji* 祭), and thanksgiving or offering (*jiao* 醮). Purification is the fasting or separation part of the ritual: it involves a set of preparatory measures undertaken before conducting or joining the sacrifice as well as before extended meditation practice, including abstention from all or

specific foods, avoidance of contact with blood and dirt, sexual abstinence, and taking baths in fragrant waters. This phase may last from one
to seven days. As the *Lüshi chunqiu* 呂氏春秋 (Mr. Lü's Spring and Au-
tumn Annals, 3rd c. B.C.E.) describes it:

> A gentleman fasts and observes vigils, makes sure to stay deep
> inside his house, and keeps his body utterly still. He refrains
> from music and sex, eschews associations with his wife, main-
> tains a sparse diet, and avoids the use of piquant condiments.
> He settles his mind's *qi*, maintains quietude in his organs, and
> engages in no rash undertaking. (5.42; Knoblock and Riegel
> 2000, 135; Lo 2005, 166)

The central part of the ceremony, the sacrifice in the liminal phase,
means the presentation of ritually prepared foods such as wine, tea, rice,
sweets, fruits, and animal carcasses to the gods and ancestors. It might
also play out as a sacrificial banquet, during which the honored ancestor
was fed through an impersonator. Either way, the rite suspends ordinary
divisions, while serving to create a formal hierarchy among the dead and
the living, aiming at "making ancestors," thereby transforming supernatural powers and domesticating potentially harmful forces (Keightley
2004; Puett 2002, 78; 2005, 80).

The third part, the thanksgiving or reaggregation, consisted of a great
communal feast, during which ordinary food restrictions were loosened
and the various offerings consumed. As sacrifices in ancient China were
often connected to ancestor worship, the mortuary feast at the tomb or
temple was major occasion to reactivate family connections and enhance
social ties (Cook 2005, 11). In all three parts, therefore, the proper presentation and sharing of food were essential for the ritual's overall success.

In Daoism, all three aspects of classic Chinese ritual underwent significant changes. The purification part was expanded into monastic meals,
retreats, and communal festivals, the word *zhai* taking on a slew of new
and more complex meanings. The sacrifice part changed into audience
rites, which placed less emphasis on the offering of food and material
objects—although they were and still are placed on altars to the gods—
than on the presentation of written documents. The thanksgiving part
first became so-called kitchen-feasts and later evolved into the festival of
cosmic renewal, the most elaborate and extensive Daoist rite and still a
great community celebration today.

Daoist Ritual

Zhai. Originally "preparatory purification," under the influence of Buddhism and in imitation of Hindu *pūja*, *zhai* in the early middle ages began to refer to an integral part of the ritual. Indicating the offering of pure food to the deities and the sharing of food among humans and gods, lay donors and recluses, *zhai* was used to translate *upavasatha*, "fast," a technical term for the main meal according to Buddhist regulations, which was to be taken before noon. The food was vegetarian and simple, provided by donors who gained merit through their generosity. *Zhai* as a result no longer meant "fast" but came to indicate "vegetarian feast," either offered to the gods or shared among the religious community (Mollier 2000, 46; Stein 1971, 437; Kohn 2003a, 124).

Adapting this usage, monastic Daoists in the sixth century began to use *zhai* as the word for the ceremonial meal or midday ceremony, a most formal occasion that—like its Buddhist counterpart—occurred in the hour before noon and involved extensive chantings and food offerings as well as a communal feeding. A host of related terms appeared, so that we now translate *zhaishi* 齋食 as "ceremonial food," *zhaitang* 齋堂 as "refectory," *zhaiqi* 齋器 as "ceremonial dishes," and *jianzhai* 監齋 as "meal supervisor." *Zhaiguan* 齋官, moreover, was the "leader of the ceremony," and *zhaizhu* 齋主 the "donor of the feast" (Kohn 2004c, 59-60).

In addition, Buddhists used the word *zhai* to indicate "temporary renunciation." Going back to the Indian monastic practice of bimonthly confession and chanting of precepts (see Prebish 1975), these *zhai* were opportunities for lay followers to behave with increased purity, taking eight precepts instead of the ordinary five and participating in the monastic routine. Commonly known as *zhaijie* 齋戒 (lit. purification and precepts), this happened in sets of six, eight, or ten days per month, centered around the new and full moon. The six *zhai* days were the 1st, 8th, 14th, 15th, 28th, and 29th of every month. The eight *zhai* days added the 23rd and 24th; and the group of ten days, known as the "ten days of uprightness" (*shizhi* 十直), involved practice also on the 18th and 28th (see Soymié 1977; Kohn 2003a, 183; Despeux 2007, 30). Daoists also adopted this system, matching the dates to the times when cosmic administrators inspected their earthly charges. As outlined in the Tang ritual manual *Yaoxiu keyi* 要修科 儀 (Essential Rules and Observances, DZ 463), practitioners would take serious precepts and offer prayers for atonement and good fortune to various administrative deities, notably the Great One (Taiyi 太一) and the Northern Dipper (Beidou 北斗) (8.4a; see Kohn 2003a, 182).

Above and beyond these meanings, *zhai* in Daoism—and especially in the Numinous Treasure school as it flourished in the fifth century—also came to indicate "rite of purgation" or "festival," a major ritual event usually dedicated to the expiation of sins or the blessing of ancestors and the emperor, held at regular intervals throughout the year (see Malek 1985; Yamada 1999). An intensification of the days of temporary renunciation and continuation of early Daoist community events, these were important Daoist rites during which the officiating priest became a celestial officer and transmitted prayers and confessions to the celestial administration (Benn 2000, 332-35; Eskildsen 1998, 117-21; Huang 2007, 11-14).

Most important were the gods of the Three Primes (Sanyuan 三元), the celestial bureaus of Heaven, Earth, and Water who exerted most power over human life and destiny and had been central to Daoism since the early Celestial Masters. They updated their records on the fifteenth of the first, seventh, and tenth months, and were greatly honored with large-scale ceremonies on those dates (*Yaoxiu keyi* 8.2a; Kohn 2003a, 182). Another important group of *zhai* were the purgations of the Eight Nodes (*bajie* 八節), the beginnings and high points of the four seasons, already celebrated in ancient China as made clear in the description of "monthly commandments" (*Yueling* 月令) in the Zhou-dynasty *Liji* 禮記 (Book of Rites; Legge 1968, 1:249) and the Han eclectic work *Huainanzi* 淮南子 (Book of the Prince of Huainan, DZ 1184; Major 1993).

Today *zhai* still means both preparatory purification and purgation festival, the latter indicating rites geared to the saving the souls of the dead, while rituals of cosmic renewal (*jiao*) are used to elicit blessings for the living. Both involve confession of sins and prayers for forgiveness as well as the formal offering of wine, food, and other objects in an act of blessing and thanksgiving, which was originally part of the *jiao* (Asano 2002, 274-75).

Chao. From the early Celestial Masters onward, Daoists merged the structure of traditional sacrifices with the court rituals of ancient China, which governed the formal interaction of the emperor with his ministers and local representatives. At audiences, which were known as *chao* 朝, literally, "sunrise" because they occurred in the very early morning, officials lined up before the throne to present reports and requests in written announcements, petitions, and memorials. They were dressed in formal court garb and held special tablets and seals of personal identification.

Adopting this system, early Daoists no longer offered bloody carcasses, which the pure gods of the Dao found repulsive since they had no corporeal substance and accordingly no need for solid, material sustenance (Kleeman 2005, 149). Instead offerings included flowers, valuables, and vegetarian foods, as well as, in accordance with the new "audience" nature of the rite, written documents: announcements, petitions, memorials, and mandates (see Maruyama 2002). In a monastic setting, moreover, Daoists since the middle ages have celebrated daily services or "regular audiences" (changchao 常朝) at dawn and dusk. Like the ceremonial meal at noon, they involve the formal assembly of all recluses in the central sanctuary, the presentation of offerings, and the extensive recitation of prayers and scriptures.

These morning and evening services, in addition to combining sacrificial and court ritual, can also be traced back to the morning and evening audiences with the parents that were prescribed for all filial children as early as the Zhou dynasty. As outlined in the Liji, a devoted son and daughter-in-law had to purify themselves, don formal dress, then:

> go to their parents and parents-in-law. On getting to where they are, with bated breath and gentle voice, they should ask if their clothes are (too) warm or (too) cold, whether they are ill or pained, or uncomfortable in any part; and if they be so, they should proceed reverently to stroke and scratch the place. . . .
> They will ask whether they want anything, and then respectfully bring it. All this they will do with an appearance of pleasure to make their parents feel at ease. [They should bring] thick or thin porridge, spirits or ale, soup with vegetables, beans, wheat, spinach, rice, millet, maize, or glutinous millet— whatever they wish, in fact. (10/1.4; Legge 1968, 1:450-51; Kohn 2003a, 175-76)

This "offering [food] and nurturing" (gongyang 供養) of the parents matches the presentation of food to support the gods in the Daoist audience rite and is called by the same phrase, now rendered "presentation of offerings." The term, moreover, is also prominent among Buddhists who use it to translate pūja, the ceremony of hosting the deity. Daoists, who have left their native families for the Dao, regard the celestial gods as their true father and mother and venerate them accordingly (see Mugitani 2004). At the same time they also recognize their high standing in the celestial administration and pay political-style homage, combining the traditional Confucian virtues of loyalty and filial piety in a new, cosmic dimension.

Food plays an essential part in these rites as offerings made on the altar. A full presentation includes:

—incense, fresh flowers, and red candles, presented every time;

—tea, wine, and other liquids, such as four-fruit tea or licorice soup, offered specifically to Three Pure Ones, and talisman water (*fushui* 符水), created when the ashes of a burned talisman are dissolved in water, frequently used to purity the altar and specifically used during the noon sacrifice (*wugong* 午供) (Asano 2002, 275; see also Huang 2007, 60; 2008a, 164-69);

—fruit and grain, the latter either whole or ground: uncooked grain to feed ghosts and demons, cooked rice or millet for ancestors and local gods, rice balls (*zongzi* 粽子) and other non-ground grain products for the overall pantheon, as well as various cakes, buns, and pastries, some of which have auspicious characters written on them (Asano 2002, 276);

—other foods, including candies in creative shapes, vegetables in various sized bowls, dried foods, and traditional cookies, as well as delicacies from the sea and the mountains (sugar, salt, ginger, and peas);

—valuables, i.e., money and jewelry that are placed on the altar for a period, spirit money in different colors and types which is burnt to satisfy the otherworldly needs of ghosts, gods, and ancestors, and silver pieces that may be thrown among the faithful (Asano 2002, 278; see also McCreery 1990);

—writing utensils, such as paper, ink-stones, black and red ink sticks, and brushes, which symbolize the transmission of written documents and are placed on wooden buckets and set up in the five directions of the altar area, as well as "dragon cards," papers printed with a dragon design that signify the activation of dragons as divine messengers, a con-

tinuation of the old rite of "throwing dragons" (*toulong* 投龍; see Chavannes 1919) (Asano 2002, 278-79; 288-90).[2]

Jiao. The last phase of the traditional ritual was a merit-assuring rite after the successful sacrifice with the goal of inducing the gods to give
their blessings to humanity. In Daoism, this was first transformed into
great communal banquets known as "kitchen-feasts" (*chu* 廚), when the
community would gather together and enjoy the fruits of their labor as
well as unifying deities, humans, and the creative powers of the cosmos.

In the Song dynasty, the terminology changed back to *jiao* 醮, and the
thanksgiving became central to Daoist practice, integrating and replacing
both early banquets and medieval purgations. The key function of the
jiao is to guide multiplicity back to original formlessness and recreate the
world in a "rite of cosmic renewal" (Saso 1972). An elaborate event that
can last from three to seven days, it is ideally celebrated jointly by various communities once in every sixty-year cycle. It typically involves
elaborate settings, numerous officiants, and nonstop rituals over many
days, and attracts much outside attention and support (Kohn 2008c).

The celebration typically begins with a one-month purification period,
during which participating priests practice abstinence and purity, including mental cleansing by repenting sins and thinking of the gods.
Next they prepare the sacred space, usually a large, multi-level platform
in or near the temple. Next, in a rite of formal invitation, they summon
the guests of the ceremony—gods, ancestors, and people—each visual-
ized by the officiating priest. He directs Daoist gods to sit the north, so
they can face south as did the emperor of old; places popular deities to
the south, heavenly bureaucrats of yang quality and dragon spirits, are
in the east; yin administrators who rule the dead, water, and tiger spirits
in the west; people in the southeast; and the various other types of spirits
are in the remaining corners.

---

[2] Daoists today, in adaptation of popular rites, may also offer meat: raw for
gods of lesser standing (e.g., pork chops for a paper tiger); cooked or in tofu rep-
licas to medium-level deities; and as whohle sacrificial animals (pigs, goats) for
higher ranking officers of the popular pantheon. See Asano 2002, 280-86.

Three major types of rites are performed. Secret ceremonies are held behind locked doors in the temple to establish a close relationship between humanity and the gods. Semi-public rites of merit and repentance include the reading of relevant texts and the offering of prayers for the forgiveness of sins, healing of diseases, and mending of social disharmonies. Fully public rites are highly dramatic and include the enactment of Daoist myths of creation and renewal. The ritual ends with a large banquet, joined by everyone—friends and foes alike—to celebrate the successful cosmic invigoration of the community (see Saso 1972; Lagerwey 1987; Dean 2000).

Kitchen Feasts

The earliest documented use of food in Daoist ceremonies is found in a unique form of the sacrificial banquet which the early Celestial Masters called "kitchen-feasts," held at essential community celebrations, such as the festivals of the Three Primes. These were times of general assemblies and tax management: in the first month, the tax was set according to the number of people in the household; in the seventh and tenth months, it was collected as the harvest was brought in (see Kleeman 1998). The group was tightly structured and followers in ordinary times obeyed precepts that encouraged frugality and simplicity as formulated in the *Xianger Commentary* 想爾註 to the *Daode jing* (see Bokenkamp 1997, 49-50; Kohn 2004a, 58-60). At festival times, on the other hand, kitchen-feasts, like rites for the sun god in antiquity, involved great banquets with rich food and wine as well as offerings of matching morsels to the gods (Stein 1971, 489; 1972, 491; Mollier 2000, 46; Kleeman 2005, 151).

The sources do not provide any details about the exact nature and arrangement of the feasts among the early Celestial Masters. On the other hand, there is some documentation about later practices, notably under the Daoist theocracy in fifth-century North China and among the southern Celestial Masters in the sixth-century.

The Daoist theocracy began with Kou Qianzhi 寇謙之 (365-448), the son of a Celestial Masters family in the Chang'an. Living under the foreign Toba-Wei rulers, he deplored the disarray of Daoist communities and hoped to contribute to their renewal. He duly withdrew to find solitary inspiration on Mount Song in Henan and—as detailed in the *Weishu* 魏書 (History of the Wei Dynasty, ch. 114; trl. Ware 1933)—received several revelations from Lord Lao. The main document that resulted from these revelations was the *Yunzhong yinsong xinke jiejing* 雲中音誦新科戒經 (Precepts of the New Code, Recited in the Clouds, DZ 785), a text containing a set of thirty-six precepts for the renewed community, usually called the "New Code" (see Yang 1956).

In 424, Kou took his inspiration to court, where he was welcomed by Emperor Taiwu and found the support of the prime minister Cui Hao 崔浩 (381-450), a Confucian fond of mathematics, astrology, and magic, as well as the author of a book on diet (Huang 2000, 125), who like Kou envisioned a renewed and purified society. Together they convinced the ruler to put the "New Code" into practice, creating an administrative system for the foreign dynasty that made Kou as Celestial Master a central power broker in the capital while Daoist institutions and priests served throughout the state as agents of tax collection, law enforcement, and seasonal relief. Cui Hao in the meantime masterminded various military successes and worked on the compilation of a national history, rising higher in rank and honor. The pinnacle of the theocracy arrived in 440, when the emperor underwent Daoist investiture rites and changed the reign title to "Perfect Lord of Great Peace." The experiment flourished for another decade, then came to a rather rapid end after Kou's death in 448 and Cui's execution in 450, to be replaced by a Buddhist-sponsored system known as sangha-households.[3]

A key aspect of the theocracy was the celebration of regular communal rites of the so-called Dao people (*daomin* 道民). They were geared to create a land of perfect peace, where harmony prevailed and everybody, as in the Confucian ideal, was restrained by rules of ritual behavior. People had to observe daily, seasonal, and special rites, the latter two usually involving communal meetings and kitchen-feasts. There were grand, medium, and lesser feasts, lasting seven, five, or three days respectively (Ware 1933, 233).

To prepare for a feast—also called "fortunate feedings" (*fushi* 福食) or "rice for the wise" (*fanxian* 飯賢; see Mollier 2000, 46)—members had to purify themselves by abstaining from meat and the five strong vegetables as well as from sexual relations and contact with impure substances (no. 11; 8a). A typical banquet, then, consisted of three courses—a vege-

---

[3] For more on the theocracy, see Tsukamoto 1961; Mather 1979; Kohn 2000.

tarian meal, wine, and rice—but those who could not afford all three could resort to having just wine, up to a maximum of five pints (no. 12). The ritual activity during feasts (no. 20) as well as during daily services (no. 19) and ancestral worship (no. 23) involved a series of bows and prostrations as well as the burning of incense and offering of a prayer or petition, which had to follow a specific formula (no. 19). There were to be no blood sacrifices, lascivious practices, or ritualized intercourse as in the "harmonization of *qi*" (*heqi* 合氣; see Raz 2008) undertaken by the early Celestial Masters (no. 4; 2a; Mather 1979, 113).

Similar guidelines also applied among the southern Celestial Masters as documented in the sixth-century collection of organizational rules, *Xuandu lüwen* 玄都律文 (Statutes of Mystery Metropolis, DZ 188). The text, too, divides kitchen-feasts into grand, medium, and lesser, specifying that the so-called Three Assemblies (*sanhui* 三會), i.e., the festivals of the Three Primes, as well as the birth of a male child qualified for a grand feast. The birth of a female child and the ceremonial prevention of diseases and avoidance of dangers necessitated the arrangement of a medium event, while a death in the family or other potentially life-changing event was reason for a lesser kitchen (12a; Kohn 2004b, 39).

In each case, the feasts were formally arranged by the community leader who, in the beginning of every year and under consideration of recent demographic changes, would organize the populace into groups of ten. Within each group, one member would provide the feast materials for another in mutual sharing, not entirely unlike potlucks today, but distinctly avoiding the use of any animal products that might necessitate killing (12ab; Kohn 2004b, 39). The "Statutes" further specify that during a grand feast, each participant should "receive five pints of wine and 300 cash; during a medium feast, four pints of wine, 200 cash, and five coins; and during a lesser feast, three pints of wine, 100 cash, and 100 coins" (13b-14a; Kohn 2004b, 40)

In addition, the feast came with the presentation of presents and pledges to the central priestly administration and the Daoist gods, thus ensuring protection and good fortune. As the text has:

> When a male child is born, set up a kitchen-feast for ten people.
> In the midst of the feast, present 100 pages of petition paper,
> one set of brushes, one ball of ink, and one writing knife. When
> a female child is born, set up a kitchen-feast for five and offer

one seating mat, one dust pan, and one broom. [13a] Deliver these taxes one month after the child's birth.

Anyone going against this statute and law will be punished by a two-period reduction in reckoning.[4] The child will similarly suffer a reduction in reckoning and will not be able to grow up in a parish of the Celestial Masters. His *qi* will be tied by demons and he will undergo harm to the point of not even being able to reside in the underworld. On the other hand, if treated properly, the child can bring fame to family and self. All these are potentially grave sins that lead to loss of life. (12b-13a; Kohn 2004b, 39-40)

The proper performance of the feasts and their various related activities thus had a major impact on the social role and fate of the participants.

In terms of concrete procedures, the text reaffirms the traditional requirement of initial purification and the need for proper attire and formality during the ceremony. It says:

When the time has come for male and female officers, register disciples, and Daoist followers to participate in a kitchen-feast, in each group of ten the head of the family should undergo fasting and restraint. On the eve of the feast, he should invite the guests, speak the proper words, and encourage them to come in.

All this is to be done with dignity and seriousness, not allowing any disturbance or defilement. All sweat should be washed off in a bath, all clothes should be changed—robe and skirt, cap and gown, leggings and breeches. Do not wear a plain skirt or let it show from under your robe, but be of utmost seriousness in your attire. (13b; Kohn 2004b, 40)

The kitchen-feasts continued even after Daoism was integrated into one organizational and doctrinal structure in the early Tang dynasty, as the *Yaoxiu keyi* documents. It too recognizes three levels of feasts and distinguishes various types, such as seasonal (Three Assemblies), situational (birth, sickness, death), and occasional (repentance, liberation) (Kleeman

---

[4] This refers to the belief that the celestial authorities would keep track of people's good and bad deeds and adjust their life-expectancy accordingly. For details, see Kohn 1998b. Depending on the text, a "period" can vary between a hundred days, three hundred days and as many as twelve years (see Yoshioka 1970, 190).

2005, 152). Part of organized religion rather than performed in a closed millenarian group, the feasts would be arranged by sponsor or donor and run by professionals. They included most importantly the "kitchen supervisor" (jianchu 監廚) who examined the food, balanced raw and cooked materials, managed flavors, and decided on the order of dishes; and the "group regulator" (jiezhong 節眾) who checked the time, sounded the chimes for each new phase, and in general kept people in line (Kleeman 2005, 154). The feast would be joined by local people who served as secondary participants and appreciative audience. They would receive the distribution of leftovers, particularly grains, after the event (9.11b), a practice much like the sharing of offerings after rituals of universal deliverance (pudu 普渡), requiem services (gongde 功德), and other ceremonies today (see Dean 2000).

In accordance with traditional structures, each feast came with a three-day preparation period that involved the confession of sins and purification (qingzhai 清齋) for all major players and was followed by a thanks-giving rite known as the "statement of merit" (yangong 言功) (Kleeman 2005, 153). Throughout, purity had to be maintained by sticking to vegetarian substances, and there should not even be the verbal acknowledgment of destructive actions such as killing, hunting, fishing, or trapping (12.2a Kleeman 2005, 154).

Ceremonial Meals

The same holds also true for the "noon purgation" (zhongzhai 中齋) at Daoist monastic institutions, i.e., the main meal of the day that was—in adaptation of Buddhist patterns—usually held around 11 a.m. as part of a major ceremony that also included scripture readings and the formal sharing of food and merits with the donors and all beings. As described in the *Shishi weiyi*, it typically involved four phases:[5]

(1) preparation [separation]: donning vestments, cleaning hands and face, picking up dishes, and entering the refectory;

---

[5] The events are also described in *Zhengyi weiyi jing* 正一威儀經 (Scripture of Dignified Observances of Orthodox Unity, DZ 791) 9b-10b, 15ab; *Qianzhen ke* 千真科 (Rules for a Thousand Perfected, DZ 1410) 5ab, 29ab; and *Fengdao kejie* 6.4a-7a (sect. 16; trl. Kohn 2004c). The following is a summary of the more detailed account in Kohn 2003a, 123-32.

(2) initial formalities [liminal phase 1]: rites to the Dao and dedication of the food to the gods, ancestors, and all beings, accompanied by also burning incense and chanting invocations, as well as the correct placement of dishes and the taking of seats;

(3) the actual meal [liminal phase 2]: rice gruel, rice, and several different dishes, each announced and handed around by serving monks, as ritual verses are chanted;

(4) concluding formalities [reaggregation]: repentance of all rule violations during the meal, obeisance to the Three Treasures, stacking of bowls, and exiting the hall (9b-12a).

To begin the meal supervisor ascertains the correct time and rings the bell. Daoists don their vestments and wash their hands, then pick up their dishes plus chopsticks and a spoon (lacquer or copper in the old days, metal or plastic today) from special racks. Dishes consist of three bowls of different sizes, made from metal, lacquer, earthenware, or porcelain, depending on the wealth of the institution.[6] In addition, in the middle ages Daoists had two cloths, one wrapped around the bundle of dishes, which were stacked inside one another, the other folded inside it. Both cloths were used during the meal and had to be kept perfectly clean, never used for wiping off sweat or blowing one's nose (8b).

Once cleaned, garbed, and ready, Daoists file into the refectory and find their proper place. They put their bundle of dishes on the table, but remain standing to perform the initial formalities—burning incense, bowing, and reciting a verse of praise to the Heavenly Worthies (9b). They sit down—on chairs today, on cushions at low tables in the middle ages—and open the cloth that wraps their dishes, straightening it to serve as a place mat. They unpack their dishes in the proper order and place the second cloth over their knees to be used as a napkin. They rinse their dishes with clear water that is handed around (9b). Thus readied, they offer the prayer-at-meals, a sequence of good wishes for the donor's benefit, the empire, the ancestors, and all beings.

The meal itself begins with the serving of grain, followed by a number of different vegetarian dishes, made up of the five classical food groups. Substances avoided include the five strong vegetables as well as any-

---

[6] For a discussion of traditional Chinese eating utensils with numerous illustrations, see Huang 2000, 75-89, 104-09.

thing processed or nonritual. The preparation, moreover, ensures that the food is well balanced, enhancing health and vitality (*Yaoxiu keyi* 9.14b).

Each dish is announced with its name either by the supervisor or by the servers. As the first steaming bowls arrive at the tables, the medieval liturgy requires the chanting of an incantation that praises the selfless giving of the donor, known as the "Incantation for Receiving Food" (see above, p. 96). It links food with great merit for everyone who engages in its donation, a charitable act which leads to happiness now and a good rebirth later. Daoists participate in this merit by not keeping the food for themselves but passing it on ritually to the celestials and all beings, ensuring the widest possible spread of merit and reaffirming their role as intermediaries between the cosmic realms.

As more food is passed around, a further chant is sung which again establishes the celestial connection of the meal and offers it to all beings. It runs:

> This fragrant feast and wondrous offering
> Above we give to the Heavenly Worthies,
> In the middle to the perfected and sages,
> Below to the host of living beings.
> May all be equally full and satisfied,
> While good fortune flows to our [generous] donor
> Like rivers pouring into the sea. (10a; *Fengdao kejie* 6.6a)

As the community eats, each member internally visualizes the Three Ones and other gods in the body, thus again raising the mundane activity to a heavenly level. Everyone is to eat his or her fill and can get as many as three helpings, but there is to be no overeating and no scorning of dishes as not being fancy enough. Whenever a dish is announced, raise your bowl to receive it. If you prefer not to partake of it, simply raise a finger and let the server pass by. While being served, if you desire more, advance the bowl a little; if you prefer less, withdraw it slightly. There is, however, to be no speech on the subject. Noises in general should be kept to a minimum, avoiding all slurping, sucking, and gulping, and not clattering with bowls and chopsticks. Speech is not prohibited but should be controlled and calm, avoiding all exclamations or shouts. Exceptions to this rule are emergency situations, such as a military incident, a flood, a fire, a robbery, or a sudden death (10b-11a).

The act of eating in a traditional monastery, therefore, is less a way of fulfilling bodily needs than an active nourishing of the gods and all beings, a way of joining Dao. The physical control of food intake, body movements, and speech aids recluses in thinking with compassion and sharing with all beings. Anything touched during the meal is sanctified and even leftovers are not wasted or thrown out but given to servants, beggars, sick people, or farm animals—always with the wish: "May all thus giving attain good fortune! May all thus eating be free from suffering!" (11a; *Fengdao kejie* 6.6b).

After everyone has eaten their fill, the concluding formalities begin. Here, too, the pervasive importance of purity is made clear. After all have finished eating, they fold the cloth on their knees, rinse their dishes with clear water, stack them back into one pile, and wrap them in the place mat cloth (11a). Then they undergo a rite of repentance, chanting the following verse:

> To the Highest Worthies of the ten directions!
> Respectfully see here before you
> This great crowd of disciples.
> Today, during the presentation of food,
> We fear that
> Our hands were smudgy and not clean,
> Our garb was not properly purified,
> Our utensils were not pure,
> Our rice and millet were not sifted,
> And all manner of things and acts
> Were not as prescribed by the divine law.
> May the Three Treasures spread their mercy upon us
> And widely give us joy and good cheer. (*Fengdao kejie* 6.6a)

Following this, they chant a pledge on behalf of the donor to make further efforts toward the Dao and formally share the rite's merits with the donor and all beings by chanting two additional stanzas. This concluded, the recluses pick up their dishes and file out of the refectory in an orderly manner, to assemble at the water basin for washing dishes and cleaning teeth. The final rule regarding the ceremonial meal, then, is that while leaving and cleaning up, all should maintain strict discipline and return to their quarters silently, not standing about chatting idly (12a).

Similar rules and structures also apply in Daoist monasteries of the late imperial period and, by extension, today. They are described in the Qing document *Qinggui xuanmiao* and reported by Yoshioka Yoshitoyo in the 1940s (Yoshioka 1979). As in the middle ages, so in modern times meals begin and end with formal prayers and chantings. Monastics should avoid speech and laughter or limit themselves to a few soft words. If you do not like the meal, do not complain; after it ends, do not sit around and chat idly but collect bowl and chopsticks quietly. During the meal, do not pick your teeth, wipe your mouth with the sleeves of your robe, make smacking noises, click the tongue, scratch the head, or put something already chewed back into the bowl. Should you discover that the rice has a stone or some alien grain in it, take it out and place it softly on the table, not hurl it on the floor. If there are bugs in the food, remove them silently. Generally, avoid causing trouble or making a stir, never rejecting what is offered or craving fancy dishes that are not there (ZW 361; 10.603).

Whether in the middle ages or today, monastic meals are highly ritualized affairs that—on a smaller scale and with greater routine—continue the sacrifices and feasts of old. They follow the classical pattern of preparation, main rite, and conclusion; they place their participants in a liminal sphere and allow them to reach for a higher level of spiritual awareness and celestial connection. Not merely giving food to their bodies, Daoists in the ritual meal share food and kindness with the gods and all beings, thereby making the entire universe holier and purer. The standards of good conduct, moreover, express the self-consciousness Daoists are encouraged to acquire just as the way they consume food reveals their reality as including the larger realm of the cosmos and the entirety of living beings.

Cosmic Catering

A yet different variant of ritual food in Daoism appears in a procedure of meditative self-cultivation that involves visualizations and incantations as well as taking certain herbal substances and guiding *qi* through the body. Already the *Zhuangzi* describes a perfected being who lives on heavenly nectar and celestial manna and to whom food and clothes appear spontaneously (ch. 5; Mollier 2000, 67).

In its wake, Ge Hong mentions that immortals, able to control fire and water, could also cause celestial delicacies to arrive at a moment's notice. He calls this practice "traveling kitchen" (*xingchu* 行廚), an "imaginary cornucopia of wondrous drugs and foods" served by luscious jade maidens that could feed sixty or seventy people at the drop of a hat (*Baopuzi* 16; Kleeman 2005, 149; Stein 1971, 490). He also lists a *Xingchu jing* 行廚經 as well as a text called *Riyue chushi jing* 日月廚食經 (Sun and Moon Cooking; ch. 19) that presumably referred to preparing and absorbing the essences of the sun and the moon (Mollier 2000, 66).

Practitioners of Highest Clarity in due course adopted the practice and added the application of talismans, the visualization of specific deities, and methods to exert control over the gods—both in the body and the stars (Robinet 1984, 1:31-33). The best description survives from a Song text called *Daodian lun* 道典論 (Daoist Records and Discourses, DZ 1130; 4.10b-11b), which in content may well go back to the Han (Stein 1972, 491-92). It describes a practice called "Absorbing Yellow *Qi*" (*fu huangqi* 服黃氣) which consists of taking vegetal and mineral substances (such as cinnabar, fungi, herbs), envisioning the pure yellow energy of the spleen, then making deities bring a feast in golden dishes, the imaginary consumption of which prevents all feelings of hunger and thirst (Mollier 2000, 67).

Buddhists, too, took on the technique from an early age, the idea of a celestial kitchen (*tianchu* 天廚) already mentioned in the *Zhong benqi jing* 中本起經 (Sutra of Central Origins and Deeds, T. 196; 3.13), translated in 207 (Mollier 2000, 68). Later sources mention that to avoid feelings of hunger, one should practice deep meditation and visualize deities bringing heavenly nectar. The color of the divine potage depended on the practitioner's merit: if it was low, it would appear dark green; if medium, red; if superior, white. Whichever form it took, adepts should take it in the mouth, feel it merge with their saliva, then swallow it. It would feel like spontaneously cooked food and have a great celestial fragrance (Mollier 2000, 69).

The most extensive Buddhist kitchen ritual, as allegedly revealed by the Buddha at the time of entering nirvana, appears in the *Sanchu jing* 三廚經 (Sutra of the Three Kitchens), a Tang manuscript discovered at Dunhuang (S. 2673, S. 2680). It is further supplemented by the *Tingchu jing* 停廚經 (Sutra of the Pavilion Kitchens, in P. 2637), a medical compendium which includes drug recipes that help to eliminate hunger (Mollier 2000, 52-62.

According to this, one needed three fundamental conditions before practicing the rite, which would lead to freedom from hunger, clarity of spirit, and extended long life: devotion to the Three Treasures of buddha, dharma, and sangha; family and community support; and consistent practice of the Six Perfections (Mollier 2000, 53). One should then withdraw to a solitary retreat in the mountains, well protected from nosy interlopers, where one could keep the method secret, since any doubt—like in traditional alchemy—would compromise its efficacy. The actual practice involved the silent chanting of a sacred verse (*gātha*) to the five directions, each associated with a specific boon and a set number of recitations:

east	wood	attainment of long life	90 times
south	fire	invulnerable to heat	30 times
center	earth	freedom from hunger	20 times
west	metal	invulnerable to cold	70 times
north	water	freedom from thirst	50 times

If done daily, preferably at the *yin* hour (3-5 a.m.), while assembling and swallowing saliva, and especially in combination with strong seated meditation and the persistent visualization of Amitābha, this would free adepts from all needs of sustenance (Mollier 2000, 54-55). The text describes effects much like those Daoists claim for the practice of *bigu*, i.e., certain symptoms of dehydration in the early days, then a great sense of vigor, followed by support from celestial envoys and the attainment of perfection.

The Buddhist method represents a certain degree of internalization of the practice. Rather than visualizing the delectable viands being produced through heavenly spontaneity and presented by celestial messengers, practitioners see the central kitchen as located in their own bodies. The stomach serving as the great storehouse (*taicang* 太倉), they bring forth internal transformation while calling upon gods and cosmic powers for active support. An even more internalized version appears in the Daoist *Laozi shuo Wuchu jing* 老子說五廚經 (Scripture of the Five Kitchens as Revealed by Laozi, DZ 763). Edited and commented by Yin Yin 尹愔 (*zi* Sizhenzi 思貞子), imperial counselor under Xuanzong of the Tang and abbot of the Suming guan 肅明觀 (Monastery of Majestic Brightness), this goes back to the eighth century (Mollier 2000, 62) and is part of the meditation circle around Sima Chengzhen.[7]

The text is a highly abstract mystical poem in twenty verses which guides adepts toward a mental state of detachment, nonthinking, and equanimous perception by cultivating the energy of universal oneness (yiqi 一氣) and merging with cosmic peace and harmony (taihe 泰和). This will lead to complete physical satisfaction: "The five organs are abundant and full; the five spirits are tranquil and upright." This in turn, means that all sensory experiences are calmed and all cravings and desires eliminated—including those for food and drink (1a).

The work strongly emphasizes mental restructuring over bodily practices, in fact saying that "accumulating cultivation will not get you to detachment" (l. 14, 4b) and that methods of ingestion are ultimately useless. As the commentary to "All food combines into qi" (l. 17) says:

> We receive solidity from earth, coagulate moisture from water, are endowed with warmth by fire, and rely on wind for our breath. These four conditioning factors combine and dissolve constantly, none having any part in the wondrous underlying solidity [of the universe]. Therefore they muddle and obscure the energy of universal oneness, confuse and disturb cosmic peace and harmony, and cause the arising of delusory perception. They stir up nothing but corruption and pollution. (5b)

On the other hand, the recitation of the scripture is beneficial, especially if combined with intellectual, mental, and ethical practices:

> Bow your head and recite the five stanzas of this scripture, and you will easily get the true essentials of cultivating the personal body and protecting life. To complete harmony and encompass universal oneness: penetrate [ultimate] meaning, so you can enter into spirit, sit in oblivion, and let go of brilliance; bring peace to the body, so you can venerate virtue, investigate sensory experience, and nourish yourself forever. (pref. 1b)

---

[7] A variant version appears in YJQQ 61.5b-10b: Wuchu jing qifa 五廚經氣法 (Energetic Methods of the Scripture of the Five Kitchens). The methods are also advocated in Sima Chengzheng's Fuqi jingyi lun (see p. 131), notably in the YJQQ edition (57.10-11b). A short summary also appears in its DZ version (9b-10a). See Mollier 2000, 65. For a complete translation and discussion in a meditation context, see Kohn 2010.

From the abstention from food during preparatory purification through extensive offerings at holy Daoist altars and communal sharing during festive banquets and meal-time ceremonies, the ritual practice of food has thus come full circle to culminate again in a form of abstention, but predicated in meditative vision and ritual recitation. Throughout, Daoists adopt concepts and practices from mainstream rites and Buddhist organizations, yet—as always—create their own unique system and develop their methods in unprecedented ways.

Chapter Six

Living on Qi

> Boundless and far, I am trembling with dread,
> Sharing primordial fear with spirit:
> I start absorbing essence and florescence,
> Replacing food and drink.
> The Dark Warrior sways beneath me as my mount,
> The Jade Equalizer serving as my wheels.
> Above and below without limits,
> I enter and leave the timeless [spheres].
> The hundred ailments leave, and I am healed,
> Spirit and *qi* alone uphold me.
> (*Xuandu liiwen* 4ab)

The ultimate and most advanced level of Daoist dietetics is the complete avoidance of ordinary food while living on pure *qi*, being upheld by spirit and transforming into an immortal. Already the *Zhuangzi* describes the wondrous man of Gushe Mountain:

> With skin like ice or snow, he is gentle and shy like a young girl. He does not eat the five grains but sucks the wind, drinks the dew, climbs up on the clouds and mist, rides a flying dragon, and wanders beyond the four seas. (ch. 1, Watson 1968, 33; Campany 2005, 105)

The first technical manuals on how to stop ingesting ordinary foods survive among the Mawangdui medical manuscripts (dat. 168 B.C.E.), notably the *Quegu shiqi* 卻穀食氣 (Giving Up Grain and Eating *Qi*), which outlines scheduled procedures and describes how to use the herb pyrrosia for best effects (Harper 1998, 305-09; Engelhardt 2000, 86; Campany 2005, 106). Soon after this, the *Heshang gong zhangju* 河上公章句 (Verses and Sayings of the Master on the River, DZ 682), the *Daode jing* commentary by the legendary Master on the River (see Chan 1991), describes the five *qi* of the inner organs and emphasizes their connection to the spirit and material souls, the yang and yin parts of the person. The transformation into an immortal means the refinement and purification of the yin parts into increasingly yang patterns, moving from solid, earth-bound energies to subtler, more spirit-oriented levels. Since there is ultimately only one *qi*, this is not a change in substance but in nature, a transfiguration toward finer energies that vibrate and oscillate at a much faster rate.

Daoists of the early middle ages expanded this notion by adding a mythological dimension to medical energetics. The word *shen* 神 (spirit) no longer just meant "configurative force" (Porkert 1974), the power that connects a person to Heaven and original destiny, nor was it just the vague power of spirit, which works through the human heart and signifies the psychological dimension of the individual (Kaptchuk 1983, 58). Rather, *shen* came to mean body gods, a multiplicity of divine entities that reside both in the body and in the stars, inhabiting halls and palaces and keeping the energy lines open (Kohn 1991; Kroll 1996).

To modify nutrition from Earth-bound food to Heaven-centered *qi*, practitioners accordingly also had to replace yin-deities with yang-gods. Daoists expressed this in guidelines on how to eliminate the so-called Three Worms or Deathbringers, noxious parasites that report flaws and failures to the celestial administration, and instead maintain a firm presence of the Three Ones, pure gods of Dao, in the body's energy centers.

The procedures for doing so, as much as the formal elimination of grain from the diet (*bigu* 辟穀), involve a multiplicity of practices, most importantly dietary changes, herbal formulas, breath control, and the conscious guiding of *qi*, as well as various forms of meditation, such as the visualization of deities and the absorption of directional energies. In addition, there are two major dimensions to the practice: the replacing of ordinary food with *qi* which maintains the digestive and inner-organ system while refining it to subtler levels; and the ultimate transformation of nutrition toward pure *qi* which reverts the structure toward a primordial level before creation. In other words, eliminating grains either by eating *qi* (*shiqi* 食氣) or by learning to absorb it (*fuqi* 服氣).

Souls of Yin and Yang

Already the medical classics emphasize that the five inner organs are not only the seat of specific body fluids but also have a psychological and spiritual dimension to them (see Porkert 1974, 184-85; Ishida 1989, 52; Kaptchuk 2000, 59-62). The *Huangdi neijing suwen* says:

> Blood is stored in the liver—the residence of the spirit soul.
> Nutritive *qi* is stored in the spleen—the residence of the intention.
> The pulse is stored in the heart—the residence of the spirit.
> *Qi* is stored in the lungs—the residence of the material soul.
> Essence is stored in the kidneys—the residence of the will. (ch. 2)

Among the psychological aspects, spirit is the most potent and most fundamental, associated with the heart, the leader of the organs and seat of the ruler (Ishida 1989, 53); it is the representative of pure Dao. Next are two types of souls, sets of psychological forces that link the person to Heaven and Earth and are described as spirit powers supporting the person yet working in opposite directions.

The spirit or cloud soul (*hun* 魂) connects people to Heaven, is yang in nature, and resides in the liver, the organ related to aggression and benevolence. It governs the person's overall attitude to the outside world and supports intellectual, artistic, and spiritual endeavors. At death it returns to Heaven, transforming into the ancestral spirit that is worshiped on the family altar.[1] The material or white soul (*po* 魄) connects the person to Earth, is yin in quality, and resides in the lungs, the seat of material exchange with the world (Jarrett 2006, 30). It controls basic survival instincts, such as the need for food, sleep, and sex, and in general manages the physical aspect of the individual. At death it returns to Earth by staying with the corpse; it is nurtured in proper burial sites and procedures as well as through sacrifices at the tomb.

---

[1] It is also the agent that is called back in the death ritual known as "Summoning the Soul" (*chaohun* 招魂). A shaman or priest climbs to the roof of the house and calls out in all directions to the departed soul to return, depicting each region as dreary and dangerous. The rite, as much as the three-day delay of the burial, makes sure that the soul is not just on temporary leave or the person in a state of suspended animation. For original chants, see Hawkes 1959. For Han beliefs, see Yü 1987. For modern Hong Kong, see Chan and Chow 2006.

As the *Heshang gong zhangju* says, commenting on the phrase, "This is called the mysterious [and the] female:"

> Heaven feeds people with the five *qi*, which enter the organs through the nose and settle in the heart. The five *qi* are pure and subtle, they cause people to have sentience and spirituality, intelligence and perception, sound and voice, as well as the five kinds of inner nature. They are represented in the spirit soul, which is male and leaves and enters the human body through the nose in order to interact with heaven. Therefore, the nose is "the mysterious."
>
> Earth feeds people with the five tastes, which enter the organs through the mouth and settle in the stomach. The five tastes are turbid and heavy, they cause people to have body and skeleton, bones and flesh, blood and pulses, and the six kinds of emotional passions. The are represented in the material soul, which is female and leaves and enters the human body through the mouth in order to interact with Earth. Therefore the mouth is "the female." (ch. 6; see Kohn 2009, 163-64)

Beyond the souls, there are two further mental forces, called will (*zhi* 志; yin) and intention (*yi* 意; yang) which function in close relation to the kidneys and spleen. They are specific aspects of the mind, i.e., the general power of thinking and planning in the intention and the more focused determination directed toward a specific objective in the will. All these aspects of the mind are in constant interaction and change, so that consciousness is the integrated flux of various forces and energies.

The spirit, then, is the most primordial aspect of the mind as it is received from Heaven and Earth. The two kinds of souls are its moving and active dimensions that determine human attitudes, thoughts, and desires, while will and intention are its concrete everyday functions. In general, the yin aspects are more body-oriented, material, and linked with Earth, while the yang aspects are more spirit-oriented, ethereal, and connected to Heaven. Thus, the intention can be described as the thinking mind, while the will is the thinking body. The entirety of both, however different they may be in vibrational frequency and orientation, makes up human consciousness.

The transformation into an immortal begins with controlling the will and intention, which are set radically toward otherworldly goals and cut off from earthly ideals. Next, the souls are reformed, calming the instinctual and materially-centered desires of the material soul while enhancing the spiritual orientation and energetic purity of the spirit soul. Again, the Master on the River:

> People sustain the two kinds of souls and thereby obtain life. They should love and nurture them, realizing that joy and hatred cause the spirit soul to vanish while haste and alarm make the material soul leave. The spirit soul resides in the liver, the material soul in the lungs. Indulging in wine and sweet delicacies harms the liver and lungs. Instead people should keep the spirit soul tranquil so that their will can be set on the Dao, and they will be free from trouble. They should maintain the material soul in a state of peace so that they attain long life and can extend their years. (ch. 6)

Medieval Daoists expanded this idea by multiplying the numbers of the souls to three spirit and seven material entities, envisioning them as body gods, and prescribing certain techniques to deal with them (see Eskildsen 1998, 49). Thus the *Baosheng jing* 保生經 (Scripture on Preserving Life, DZ 871) of the ninth century says:

> The three spirit [yang] souls are located beneath the liver. They look like human beings and all wear green robes with yellow inner garments. Every month on the third, thirteenth, and twenty-third day, they leave the body in the evening to go wandering about.
>
> At this time, lie down with your feet up, your head supported by a pillow, and your legs stretched out straight. Fold your hands over your heart, close your eyes, and hold your breath. Click your teeth three times. (1b)

The names of these positive aspects of human existence are "Spiritual Guidance," "Inner Radiance," and "Dark Essence" (1a). As shown in the text, they look noble and appear human in shape and are dressed in courtly garb. To support them in their beneficent activities, the text recommends physical exercises, breathing practices, as well as meditations and incantations. Treated in this manner, the three spirit souls will bring out the best in people and take care that "there is no disaster or affliction [to the person], and all evil demons are subdued. The body at peace, you attain Dao. Then there is no more suffering or pain" (2a; Ishida 1987, 86).

Their yin counterparts are the material or yin souls, nasty and evil. They are beastly in shape and quite disastrous in their activities.:

> The seven material souls consist of the energy of yin and of
> evil. They are basically demons. They can make a person
> commit deadly evils, be stingy and greedy, jealous and full of
> envy. They give people bad dreams and make them clench
> their teeth, incite them to say "yes" when they think "no."
>   They cause people to lose their vital essence in sexual pas-
> sion, dissipate it by hankering after luxury and ease. Through
> them, people waste their original purity and simplicity. (2a)

These souls, far from looking like human beings, are strangely formed
devils, having birds' heads, only one leg, tails, abominable outgrowths,
and the like. Their names are accordingly nasty: Corpse Dog, Arrow in
Ambush, Bird Darkness, Devouring Robber, Flying Poison, Massive Pollution, and Stinky Lungs (3ab).

Where the three yang souls, the representatives of Heaven, therefore
guide people toward greater goodness and spiritual transformation, the
seven yin souls, essential material aspects necessary for physical survival,
pull them toward worldliness, tension, and conflict. While following the
latter leads to loss of vital energy, illness, and death, cultivating the former brings about a transformation toward purity, health, and long life.

Daoist immortality practice goes beyond even this. Its goal is the complete transformation of the material souls, the transfiguration of all instinctual patterns, into etheric, spiritual forms of being. Thus, they first
control sexual energies (kidneys, will) and food intake (spleen, intention),
then move on to work with breathing practices (lungs, material souls)
and engage in visions of the divine (liver, spirit souls) to eventually
reach oneness with Dao (heart, spirit).

Worms and Gods

A further expansion of this dichotomy within the individual is the Daoist understanding of resident body divinities that too come in yin and yang forms. Yin here manifests in the so-called Three Worms or Deathbringers, while yang appears as a set of gods known as the Three Ones.

The earliest mention of the Three Worms (*sanchong* 三蟲) occurs in Wang Chong's 王充 *Lunheng* 論衡 (Balanced Discussions) of the second century C.E. He says: "In the human body there are three worms. They correspond to creatures that live in the marshes beneath the soil. Those we call leeches. The leeches gnaw their way through the feet of people, just as the three worms gnaw through their intestines" (16.3; Forke 1962, 2:363; Kubo 1956, 192; Kohn 1995, 35).

The Three Worms here are real worms, placed solidly in the natural world; they are leeches, not divine or demons. The same idea is found in the biography of the physician Hua Tuo 華沱 in the *Sanguo zhi* 三國志 (Record of the Three Kingdoms) of the third century: "To expel the Three Worms, use a green pasty powder made from the leaves of the lacquer tree. Take it for a long time, and the three worms will be expelled, the five inner organs will be greatly strengthened. The body as a whole will feel light, and there will be no white hair" (*Weizhi* 29; DeWoskin 1983, 149). Again, the three inner parasites are plainly physical beings that cause harm to the person, who can be cured by herbal formulas.

This early medical view, supported by the growing belief in body gods, developed into a more religious vision in the third century. The Three Worms become the Three Corpses (*sanshi* 三尸)—a term that uses the word "corpse" in a causative way and thus means agents that bring about death and can thus be called Deathbringers. Their nature takes on a supernatural character. Instead of mere leeches gnawing on human intestines, they are officials of the celestial hierarchy, placed in the body to monitor human behavior and punish sins and transgressions. As the *Baopuzi* has:

> There are Three Deathbringers in our bodies. Although not fully corporeal, they are like our inner energies, like numinous powers, ghosts and spirits. They want us to die early. After our death, they become ghosts and move about at will to where sacrifices and offerings are laid out.

> On every *gengshen* 庚申 [57th] day [of the sixty-day cycle],
> they ascend to heaven and file a report on our misdeeds with
> the Ruler of Fates (Siming 司命). Similarly during the last night
> of the month, the Stove God makes a journey to heaven and
> reports on our behavior. For the more important misdeeds,
> three hundred days are deducted from our lives. For lesser sins,
> they take off three days. (6.4b; see Ware 1966, 115-16)

While the Three Worms thus graduate from a mere physical if dangerous
nuisance, to demonic deathbringers, their wormy nature is retained in a
separate group of parasites, known as the Nine Worms (*jiuchong* 九蟲).
More organic and less demonic creatures, they are like germs and bacteria yet work with the Deathbringers who summon them to cause sickness and disease. As the *Baopuzi* says:

> If you only have a faithful heart and do nothing for your spiri-
> tual wellbeing, your life expectancy will be defective and you
> will come to harm. The Three Deathbringers will take advan-
> tage of your weak months and perilous days, of all those hours
> when your longevity could easily be interrupted or sickness
> incurred, to summon vicious energies and bring in any para-
> sites they can find. The danger is great for anyone. (15.7a; Ware
> 1966, 252-53)

The Three Deathbringers have, therefore, advanced to managerial positions. They no longer bring harm themselves but order other noxious
creatures to do so. Illnesses still come from physical parasites that enter
the body in a moment of weakness, however, the agency that instigates
this invasion is now separate and has a religious character. While the
religious tradition thus supersedes the medical, it never ignores or abol-
ishes it altogether.

Due to their heightened powers, the expulsion of the Three Deathbringers also takes on a more spiritual significance. Expelling the leech-worms
can improve one's health and raise life expectancy, but getting rid of the
Deathbringers is a prerequisite for higher spiritual states. Mere concoctions of leaves, though certainly useful, no longer suffice. Ritual measures, such as night-long vigils, and ethical purity must be advanced, especially on the *gengshen* day and at other times of transition. [2] In addition,

---

[2] Holding a vigil on the *gengshen* night became a major way of eliminating
the Three Deathbringers under the Tang. Staying awake prevents them from

stronger medicines are needed, preferably the drugs of life itself, the elixirs of immortality. For example, "Take pure unadulterated lacquer and you will enter into communication with the gods. Mix it with ten pieces of crab, then take it with mica water or dissolved in jade water. The Nine Worms will drop from you, and all your bad blood will flow out in nosebleeds" (*Baopuzi* 11.10b-11a; Ware 1966, 190). Sun Simiao similarly notes in his *Qianjin fang* 千金方 (Recipes Worth a Thousand Pieces of Gold; ed. Zhonghua shuju) that the very first step in eliminating grains is the removal of the Three Worms and provides several recipes that rely heavily on digitalis extract (*dihuang chi* 地黃池) combined with clear lacquer (*qingqi* 清漆) (58.511).[3]

Present in many medieval Daoist texts, the most elaborate description of the Three Deathbringers appears again in the *Baosheng jing*. It says:

> The Upper Deathbringer is called Peng Ju, also known as Ake (Shouter). He sits in the head and attacks the cinnabar field in the Niwan Palace [center of the head]. He causes people's heads to be heavy, their eyesight blurred, their tears cold. He makes mucus assemble in their noses and their ears go deaf. Because of him, people's teeth fall out, their mouths rot, and their faces shrink in wrinkles. He further deludes people so they desire carriages and horses, crave for fancy sounds and sights, and gloat over evil and filth. . . .
>
> The Middle Deathbringer is called Peng Zhi, also known as Zuozi (Maker). He enjoys deluding people with the five tastes and makes them greedy for the five colors. He lives in the human heart and stomach and attacks the Scarlet Palace [in the heart, the middle cinnabar field] together with its central heater. He causes people's minds to be confused and for-

---

leaving the body, so they cannot file their report. If they fail to do so over seven *gengshen* nights, they will be fired from their jobs and die. The vigil soon turned into a major social event, complete with multiple forms of entertainment and extensive vegetarian feasts. In addition, the practice was linked with a Tantric protector deity known as Qingmian jingang 青面金剛 (Jap. Shōmen kongō), the Bluefaced Vajrapani. The entire complex was duly transmitted to Japan, where so-called *kōshin* vigils combined with the worship of the god are still held to the present day. See Kubo 1956; Kohn 1995.

[3] On the medical use of these substances, see Stuart 1976, 150 and 377.

getful, so that they are full of troubles, dry in saliva and low in energy. Dissipated and melancholy, they follow the false and see things in wrong perspective. . . .

The Lower Deathbringer is called Peng Qiao, also known as Jixi (Junior). He lives in people's stomachs and legs and attacks the lower parts of the body. He makes energy leak [through the genitals] from the Ocean of Qi and thereby invites a multiplicity of ills. Attracting the robbers of human intention, he makes people hanker after women and sex. Courageous and zealous only in the pursuit of passion, people suffering from him are blindly attached to things and waste away. They have no way to control themselves and hold on to life. (7a-8b)

The nine worms, in contrast, are purely organic in nature. Their names are: Twist, Coiling, White, Flesh, Lung, Stomach, Cauldron, Red, and Scavenger Worm. The *Baosheng jing* description includes their size (between one and four inches), the harm they do to which part of the body, and the most obvious countermeasures. The *Baosheng jing* also includes their pictures: they look like ordinary worms or insects, some long and slithering, others round with leg-like extensions, yet others spongy or crab-like. Their main effect is depletion of the person's qi, but they also cause pain and disease.

While adepts must, therefore, undertake physical, ethical, and spiritual efforts to rid themselves of the Deathbringers and their minions, they should also rely on help from the pure gods of Dao, visualizing them in their three elixir fields and maintaining a strong connection to Heaven through them. Most important here are the Three Ones (*sanyi* 三一), the immediate manifestation of pure primordial qi, the original material of Dao, from which all creation springs. Upon proper meditation, they come to reside in the person and aid his or her spiritual transformation.

The *Jinque dijun sanyuan zhenyi jing* 金闕帝君三元真一經 (Lord Gold-tower's Scripture of the Three Primes and Perfect Ones, DZ 253) describes them:

> The Upper One is the Celestial Emperor;
> He resides in the body's center [in the head].
> The Middle One is the Cinnabar Sovereign;
> he resides in the Crimson Palace [in the heart].
> The Lower One is the Primordial King;
> he resides in the Yellow Court [in the abdomen].
>
> `Together they supervise the twenty-four energies of the body and bring them in accord with the twenty-four deities of Great Tenuity. Through them, these energies combine in the vapor of emptiness and develop into pure spirit.
>
> The Three Ones each have a thousand chariots and ten thousand horsemen; they ride in cloud chariots with feathery canopies. . . .
>
> Concentrate firmly on them, and the Three Ones will become visible for you. Once visible, a thousand chariots and ten thousand horsemen will arrive [to escort you on your heavenly journey]. (1a; Andersen 1980)

These three deities reside originally in heaven and represent the primordial state before creation. Once called down and activated in the adept's body, they come to control it, raising the entire person to a celestial level. Powerful good forces of Dao, divine agents of longevity, good fortune, and immortality, they serve to activate the adept's heavenly nature. They help in all that is good and holy, and assist in the ascent to the divine. Like the pure gods of Dao worshiped in rituals, they dislike meat and the five strong vegetables and thrive on pure foods and the ingestion of *qi*. In their power to connect to the gods, dietary practices thus dovetail smoothly with other advanced spiritual activities, such as meditations and rituals.

Dietary Change

Changing the diet toward immortality takes place in a setting separate from ordinary society that is specially geared toward the divine effort. Predominantly an individual endeavor, the practice—even if undertaken under the guidance of a master—usually takes place in isolation, be it in the distant mountains, on the fringes of a monastic institution, or in the anonymity of the cities. As already the *Fu zhaijie weiyi jing* 敷齋威儀經 (Dignified Observances for Arranging Retreats, DZ 532) has:[4]

> A Daoist adept distances and cuts himself off from human traces and lives quietly in the mountains. He practices a perpetual retreat and lives alone in a desolate valley. He no longer selects a master of the teaching [as his preceptor] but simply makes his mind converse with his mouth. (Eskildsen 1998, 115)

Texts variously emphasize the need for physical detachment and outline the ideal setting of the practice. This means ideally staying in a small, stand-alone hut with proper ventilation and light, not unlike the oratory or quiet chamber (*jingshi* 靜室) of the Celestial Masters or the tea house in Japan. Surroundings should have greenery, freshness, and quietude, and basic foods and/or herbal supplements should be readily available. The texts also stress the need to comply with cosmic phases by observing calendar rules and daily prohibitions, thus making sure that the internal transformation of yin and yang is not hindered by external patterns.

For example, the *Shesheng zuanlu* 攝生纂錄 (Comprehensive Record on Conserving Life, DZ 578)[5] outlines the influence of earth and climate in different locations and recommends that practitioners make regular offerings to the gods of Water, Earth, and Stove. They should also bury a deer antler under their doorstep and near the toilet to ensure the prosperity needed for the practice and an ox's hoof near the four corners of the house for general good fortune (19a).

In addition, the text has various travel prescriptions, much like those found in popular almanacs. Each month divides into six different types of days, such as "robber days," during which one should not travel at all,

---

[4] On this fifth-century text of the Numinous Treasure school, see Bokenkamp 1983, 484; Yamada 2000, 235.

[5] The text probably dates from the Tang. See Despeux in Schipper and Verellen 2004, 356. For a translation, see Huang and Wurmbrand 1987, 2:75-90.

and "official days," when one can move about without harm and conduct one's affairs (23a). In addition, certain days are better than others for travel in specific directions. Also, practitioners should use various forms of magical protection to ensure their safety, such as discarding a cup of water at a certain point (24a).

Once the setting is right and the basic instructions are known, adepts pursue several different methods: reducing ordinary food, taking herbal concoctions, guiding the *qi* through breathing exercises, and absorbing cosmic energies in visualizations. Thus the *Xuanmen dalun* 玄門大論 (Great Treatise on the Gate of All Wonders),[6] outlines nine "dietary" modes that move from eating food into breathing and meditation:

1. Coarse eating: grains, "to terminate cravings and desires;"
2. Rough eating: vegetables, "to abandon fats;"
3. Limited eating: no food after noon, "to eliminate confusion and defilement;"
4. Absorbing essences: talisman water and cinnabar efflorescences, "to embody flower stems;"
5. Absorbing sprouts: directional *qi*, "to change into sprouts;"
6. Absorbing light: sun, moon, stars, "to transform into light;"
7. Absorbing *qi*: universal energy, "to become *qi* and wander into the six directions;"
8. Absorbing primordial *qi*: cosmic energy, "to merge with Heaven and Earth;"
9. Embryo respiration: pure *qi* of creation, "to become one with Dao." (8a-9a; Eskildsen 1998, 116)

To begin Daoists gradually modify their food intake in accordance with the major food groups. As the *Taiqing fuqi koujue* 太清服氣口訣 (Great Clarity Oral Instructions on the Absorption of Qi, DZ 822)[7] notes, they first take simple, grain-based food to harmonize spleen-*qi* and activate the saliva, such as rice porridge, boiled wheat dumplings, or cooked barley, often supplemented with dried meat and peppercorns. After a few weeks of breathing practice and this simple diet, they can skip one or two meals. They then replace the grains with steamed vegetables, seasoned with soy sauce or vinegar and enhanced with medicinal herbs.

---

[6] This is closely related to or identical with the *Xuanmen dayi* 大義 (DZ 1124), a seventh-century encyclopedia (Schmidt in Schipper and Verellen 2004, 439-40). The edition used is in YJQQ 37.

[7] Probably of Tang origin. See Lévi in Schipper and Verellen 2004, 369-70.

This cleanses the colon and weans the body from its need for grains. After about a week, adepts can do away with the vegetables and only take their juice. Three days later, food intake is given up completely, but liquids—such as boiled water, wine, ginger soup, or vegetable juice—are taken until such time when reliance on primordial *qi* is complete (Huang and Wurmbrand 1987, 60).

Another outline of the process appears in the *Taiqing tiaoqi jing* 太清調氣 經 (Great Clarity Scripture on Balancing *Qi*, DZ 820), also of the Tang. It says:

> Every day at breakfast, eat a little unflavored watery porridge to balance the spleen-*qi* and provide sufficient fluids to last you through the day. At noon, eat one or two unflavored slices of bread and maybe some broth that contains onions or scallions. Do not eat them hot, though.
>
> If you are hungry in the evening, take a few unflavored dumplings that you have boiled for twenty or thirty minutes. Again, make sure not to eat to fullness but three to five mouthfuls less. It is best always to leave the table with a feeling a slightly empty stomach. (11ab)

The amount of food eaten should be reduced each day while the flow of saliva is supported by sucking on plum or date pits and body fluids are maintained by drinking little sips of water. Onions, scallions, and meat—otherwise prohibited—serve to enhance yang energy. Similarly, peppercorns are used:

> Each time you eat rice, first swallow twenty or thirty raw peppercorns with some water. Only then eat the rice. Should you feel pain or fullness after a meal, you can take ten additional peppercorns. The pepper will move the Triple Heater activity downward and chase out all sorts of bad *qi*. It will also dissolve any food remnants left behind in the intestines. (12b)

The initial response of the body to this change in diet is weakening and detoxification. The *Daoji tuna jing* 道基吐納經 (Scripture of the Foundation of the Dao on Expelling [the Old] and Taking in [the New]), in a passage that is also taken up in Sima Chengzhen's 司馬承禎 *Fuqi jingyi lun* 服氣精義論 (How to Absorb *Qi* and Penetrate [Ultimate] Meaning, DZ 277, YJQQ 57), says:[8]

> When a Daoist adept has cultivated his body and fasted by means of [breathing by] expelling the old and taking in the new for ten days, his essence and *qi* will feel slightly feverish, and his complexion will become haggard and yellowish.
>
> After twenty days, he will feel dizzy, will be clumsy in his movements, and his joints will ache. His large bowel movements will become somewhat difficult and his urine will take on a reddish-yellowish color. Sometimes, he will have bowel movements that are muddy at first and firm afterwards. After thirty days, his body will be emaciated and thin; [he will feel] heavy and weary when he walks. (3.23a; Eskildsen 1998, 51-52)

Over a period of several months, however, supplemented by herbal formulas and while undertaking intense breathing and *qi*-guiding practices, adepts can cease eating altogether and will start to become stronger and more cheerful. Matching contemporary experiences, such as the regimen undergone by Hu Fuchen 胡孚琛 (b. 1945) in the 1990s (Arthur 2006b, 113-14), the text continues:

> After forty days, one's facial complexion will become cheerful [ruddy, healthy] and the mind will be at ease. After fifty days, the five organs will be harmoniously regulated and the *qi* will be nurtured within.
>
> After sixty days, the body will have recovered its former strength and its functions will be well regulated. After seventy days, his heart will dislike boisterousness and his only aspiration will be to fly up on high.
>
> After eighty days, he will be peacefully content and remain in serene solitude. He will believe and understand the techniques and methods. After ninety days, his skin will have a smooth luster of glory and elegance, and he will clearly hear all sounds. After one hundred days, his *qi* will be complete and its efficacy will increase daily. (3.23ab; Eskildsen 1998, 52)

---

[8] The text does not survive independently. The passage appears in the seventh-century encyclopedia *Sandong zhunang* 3.23ab. Sima's work dates from the 730s. For details, see Engelhardt 1987, 105-06. Cf. also Mollier 2000, 75.

Adapts may maintain this state and live vigorously without food for however long they desire. Should they, however at some point wish to return to ordinary food, the process is reversed and grains are introduced gradually. As the *Taiqing jing duangu fa* 太清經斷穀法 (Ways to Give Up Grain Based on the Scriptures of Great Clarity, DZ 846). says:

> If you wish to give up the diet and return to eating grains, first take a decoct from mallow seeds [with pork fat] and lesser formulas, then you can start eating again. Begin by taking one serving of thin rice porridge three times a day.
>
> After two more days, take two servings, increasing the amount to five servings after three more days, then seven servings after yet another three days, and finally to one pint after three more days. Continue like this for one month and you will be ready to eat ordinary food. (11b-12a)

Medicinal Formulas

Texts differ with regard to the importance of supplementary formulas or medicines (*yao* 藥). The *Taiqing tiaoqi jing* is against them. It favors relying entirely on breathing and *qi*-guiding to replace ordinary food, noting that herbs only stave off hunger for so long while creating mental agitation in a continuous search for better recipes. It says:

> Worldly people tend to be greedy for pleasure and love profit. They cannot stop their thoughts and widely search through recipe books for formulas to take for grain abstention. When such concoctions first enter the stomach, they do in fact create a feeling of fullness for a period of time. However, once their effect is exhausted, hunger will come back with a vengeance. This creates a vicious circle without end.
>
> In addition, it constantly keeps the mind involved with thoughts of formulas and the quest for apparent harmony in daily affairs. Moving to and fro, forever restless, such people do not have even a moment's rest. Their strength feeble, their thoughts drained, they continuously increase troubles and vexations and don't even need to invite misfortunes to arrive. (22a)

The opposite position is taken in most medieval texts. For example, the *Baopuzi* cites the *Shennong bencao jing* 神農本草經 (The Divine Farmer's Materia Medica), saying:

High-quality formulas put the body at ease and extend life, so that people can ascend to heaven and become immortals. Able to soar up and down in the air, they have all sorts of spirit minions at their beck and call. Their bodies grow feathers and wings, and they receive their food [spiritually] by cosmic catering [the traveling kitchen-feast]. (ch. 11; see Ware 1966, 177)

It then proceeds to list a variety of substances that will make efficacious formulas, many of them minerals, such as cinnabar, gold, silver, jade, mica, pearls, realgar, hematite, quartz, rock crystal, sulfur, and malachite (Ware 1966, 178; also Poo 2005). Among vegetal and herbal means, it emphasizes fungi, knotgrass, thistle, asparagus, atractylis, sesame, pine sap and root, as well as pepper and ginger. A very similar list appears also in the monastic *Laozi shuo Fashi jinjie jing* which defines formulas as "gold and jade, mushrooms and excrescences, yellow essence, Chinese lycium, birthwort, pine, and cypress" (l.17).

The most important early document on immortality formulas is the *Lingbao wufuxu* 靈寶五符序 (Explanation of the Five Numinous Treasure Talismans, DZ 388), a complex text in three scrolls edited over several centuries, part of which go back to the Han (see Arthur 2006a; 2009). The second scroll is entirely dedicated to immortality recipes, the essence of which is further summarized in the *Taiqing jing duangu fa*. Key ingredients, many of which are also essential to the practice according to Sun Simiao's *Qianjin fang* (28.511-12), include:

—asparagus root (*tianmen dong* 天門冬), grown in Shandong and Sichuan, which is tonic, stomachic, and expectorant, inducing sweat (Stuart 1976, 55) and, according to the *Baopuzi*, strengthens people so they can walk very fast and very far (Ware 1966, 178);

—atractylis (*shu* 朮), grown mainly in Zhejiang which is warming and stomachic, a stimulant, tonic, and diuretic that staves off old age (Stuart 1976, 57);

—birthwort (*baishu* 白朮, *aristolochia recurvilabra*), which resembles ginger root and cures digestive disorders (1976, 49-50).

—China root fungus (*fuling* 茯苓; *poria cocos*), also called "excrescences," the mushroom-like growth on tree roots considered a transformed resin, which is peptic, nutrient, diuretic, and quieting (1976, 298)

—Chinese lycium (*gouji* 枸杞), a shrub native to the northern plains which has tonic, cooling, and life-prolonging properties (1976, 250);

—jade bamboo (*weirui* 萎蕤), a northern plant with cooling, sedating, and tonifying properties (1976, 340)

—knotgrass (*bianxu* 萹蓄), helpful against itching and a diuretic, which can be poisonous if not taken with care (1976, 341; Ware 1966, 179);

—mallows or malva (*kui* 葵), a strong diuretic used to clean the stomach and lubricate internal passages (1976, 256);

—pine tree (*song* 松) in various forms, such as sap, seeds, or roots, considered nutritious, life-enhancing, and strengthening (1976, 333);

—sesame (*huma* 胡麻; *jusheng* 巨勝), introduced from the West, with cooling, expectorant, and laxative properties (1976, 404; Arthur 2006b, 106);

—thistle (*daji* 大薊), especially the root, considered a native form of ginseng, which stops hemorrhages and promotes plumpness (1976, 119);

—yellow essence (*huangjing* 黃精), also know as Solomon's Seal and botanically identified as *polugonatum canaliculatum*, a mountain plant that looks like bamboo and is also called "hare bamboo" or "deer bamboo;" it has strong medicinal properties that make it useful as a tonic and prophylactic (1976, 339-40; see also Eskildsen 1998, 60-66; Huang 2007, 55-58; 2008a, 100-29).

Most of these herbs have diuretic and tonifying qualities that make them ideal for removing stale *qi* and digestive remnants while enhancing positive energies and building strength. Being potent and effective even in small quantities, the Chinese also used them in times of famine when grains, beans, and vegetables were sparse, and people had to survive on very little. In addition, they are key plants gathered and ingested by hominids in prehistoric periods (Spencer 1993, 28-29), again showing the Daoist effort at returning to a more primordial stage in human living.

At the same time, Daoists also use soybeans and grains in their recipes. Soybeans (*dadou* 大豆, *huangdou* 黃豆) can be used as sprouts or mature legume, the former being laxative and resolvent, while the latter work toward strengthening and vitality enhancement. The same effect is also achieved by wheat (*mai* 麥), glutinous panicled millet (*chishu mi* 赤黍米), and the various forms of rice: glutinous (*dao* 稻), nonglutinous (*geng* 粳),

hulled (*mi* 米), cooked (*fan* 飯), and congeed (*zhou* 粥) (Stuart 1976, 189-90, 443, 294).

Before ingesting any herbs or grains, adepts cleaned, chopped, pounded, and cooked them, then mixed them in various combinations and formed them into pills or decocts. Secondary, binding ingredients include alcohol (*jiu* 酒), fermenting agent (*qu* 麴), yeast (*xiao* 酵), white wax (白蠟 *baila*), white honey (*baimi* 白蜜), flower water (*huashui* 華水), malt-sugar (*yi* 飴), broth (*jiang* 漿), sweet fermented soy paste (*meijiang* 美醬), as well as animal fats taken from pigs, sheep, and cattle (see Arthur 2006a). For example,

> Take five pints of China root fungus branches, seven pounds of oily pine sap, five pounds of white wax, three pounds of white honey, two pints of Sichuan thyme, and steam them all together as if you were steaming a picul of grain. When it is well cooked, take it out and form it into pills the size of cypress seeds. (*Taiqing jing duangu fa* 2b)

The formulas claim to be highly effective: all feelings of hunger and thirst evaporate, the skin is firm and glossy, the complexion smooth and soft, white hair turns black, lost teeth grow again, and unheard-of longevity is attained. As Sun Simiao says: "As you continue taking these formulas without stopping, eventually your bones and marrow become strong and full, and the five grains will be needed less and less until you can give them up naturally" (*Qianjin fang* 58.511).

Breathing Exercises

Changing the diet and taking formulas make up an intrinsic part of the practice known as "ingesting *qi*" (*shiqi* 食氣) or "swallowing *qi*" (*yanqi* 嚥 氣). This also involves the dedicated, disciplined practice of breathing exercises, which in turn become the bridge to the ultimate level of living on *qi* through the technique of "absorbing *qi*" (*fuqi* 服氣). The difference between the two is that eating *qi* replaces ordinary foodstuffs with refined foods, potent formulas, and breathing without essentially changing the body's respiratory and digestive systems. Absorbing *qi*, on the other hand, does away with food and herbs, shuts down the lungs and spleen, activates the kidneys and heart to a new level of yin-yang interchange, and thereby transforms the body's system to a primordial level that functions on a purely internal energy exchange (Jackowicz 2006, 78-79; see also Huang 2007, 59; 2008a, 130-46)

In either practice, as the *Yangxing yanming lu* describes it, adepts inhale *qi* through the nose, then hold it in the mouth to form a mixture of breath and saliva—called "jade spring" or "sweet wine." They rinse the mouth with it to gain a feeling of fullness, allowing the *qi* to envelope the tongue and teeth. Then they consciously swallow it, visualizing the mixture as it moves through the torso into the inner organs. Once the *qi* is safely stored in its intended receptacle, they exhale. As the text says, "If you can do one thousand swallowings like this in one day and night, this is most excellent" (2.1a).

The *Taiqing tiaoqi jing,* closely matching descriptions in other medieval and Tang sources, [9] adds:

> Rinse your mouth with the numinous fluid [saliva], then lie down on your back, make your hands into fists, and block [the *qi* opening at] the soles of the feet. Support your head with a pillow and breathe, keeping your mind stable and following the movement of the breath without interruption as it comes in and goes out, passing through gate [nose] and doorway [mouth].
>
> Next, close the mouth firmly and become aware of the internal *qi,* pulling it up carefully into the mouth. Softly drum [the belly] and swallow it down, using your intention to guide it or using your hands to rub it from above the heart to the lower belly. Then again balance the breath six or seven times before you proceed to swallow it once more, as before using your hands to guide it by rubbing [along the front of the torso]. Stop when you have completed twenty rounds of *qi*-work in this manner. (9b-10a)

---

[9] Texts include: *Daoyin yangsheng jing* 導引養生經 (Scripture on Nourishing Life through Healing Exercises, DZ 818); *Huanzhen xiansheng fu neiqi juefa* 幻真先生服內氣訣法 (Master Huanzhen's Essential Method of Absorbing Internal *Qi*, DZ 828, YJQQ 60.14a-25b), *Taiwu xiansheng fuqi fa* 太無先生服氣法 (Master Great Nonbeing's Method of *Qi*-Absorption, DZ 824; YJQQ 59.8b-10a); *Yanling jun lianqi fa* 延陵君煉氣法 (Lord Yanling's Method of *Qi*-Refinement, YJQQ 61.25a-26b); *Yanling xiansheng ji xinjiu fuqi jing* 延陵先生集新舊服氣經 (Master Yanling's Scripture Collecting Old and New [Methods of] Absorbing *Qi*, DZ 825), and others more. See Maspero 1981, 460-61; Kohn 2008a, 118-21.

All this serves to increase the presence of *qi* in the body and replace food intake with pure breath. It is further enhanced by guiding the *qi* through the body in concentrated visualization. As Sima Chengzhen says:

> First, visualize the *qi* in the lungs for some time, then feel it run along the shoulders and into the arms, until it reaches your hands that have been curled into fists. Next, envision it gently moving down from the lungs and into the stomach and spleen area, from where it moves into the kidneys. Allow it to flow through the thighs into the legs and feet. You will know that you are doing it right when you feel a slight tingling between skin and flesh, like the crawling of tiny insects. (7b)

Similar instructions also appear in the *Daoyin yangsheng jing*, associated with various immortals of old. One of them, ascribed to Wangzi Qiao, is called the "Eight Spirit Exercises." Practitioners begin by lying on their back, their neck supported by a pillow, their feet five inches apart, and their hands three inches from the body. Relaxing the mind, they inhale through the nose and exhale through the mouth, allowing the breath to become so subtle that it is all but inaudible but remaining aware of movements in the belly as the *qi* is swallowed together with saliva (7b). Next, they engage in a systematic vision of the body, seeing its different parts in different shapes and colors. The text says:

> See the throat as a succession of white silver rings, stacked twelve levels deep. Going downward, you reach the lungs which are white and glossy. They have two leaves reaching tall in front, and two leaves hanging low in back. The heart is connected to them underneath. Large at the top and pointed below, it is shining red like an unopened lotus bud hanging down from the lungs.
>
> The liver is connected to it underneath. Its color is a clear green like a male mallard's head. It has six leaves that envelop the stomach—two in front that reach up tall and four in the back that hang down low. The gall bladder connects to it underneath, like a green silk bag. The spleen is in the very center of the belly, enwrapped from all sides. It is bright yellow like gold, lustrous and radiant.
>
> Behind all this, see the kidneys lying back to back like two sleeping rats, curled up with elbow to navel and as if they wanted to stretch out. Their color is a thick, glossy black. Fat streaks run through them, so that the white and black glow jointly. (8a; Kohn 2008a, 124)

Following this, practitioners are to become aware of the psychological agents connected to the organs, the spirit, as well as the spirit and material souls, intention, and will. They should also note whether there are any areas in the body that are empty or full, that is, suffer from insufficient or excessive *qi*. Should there be places that are empty, it is best to keep the eyes closed during practice; for full areas, it is best to keep them open (8b). Also, the practice should be complemented by easy movement, such as walking back and forth for a few hundred steps and/or some gentle stretches of the four limbs.

Another set of instructions is associated with Master Ning. It consists of eight short instructions on how to visualize the body, including a vision of the five inner organs with their respective colors that will "allow the *qi* to flow evenly through the body" (17a). In addition, the text suggests that one should "visualize the gods of the five organs with their appropriate colors, each in his specific place" or see them "transform into dragons or fish" (17a). Practitioners should envision "the heart radiant as a fire, shining brightly like the Dipper to block out bad *qi*" (17b) and "the kidney-*qi* below the navel in bright red and white, allowing it to move along the spine, up to the head, and back down again to pervade the entire body" (17ab). The latter practice is called "reverting essence." While the expression is commonly used to refer to the refinement of sexual energy, the practice described here is more reminiscent of the microcosmic orbit where *qi* moves along the central channels up and down the torso.

Over a period of time, adepts become proficient at this *qi*-circulation and overcome the need to balance the breath and hold the *qi* in the lungs, instead directing it immediately in the digestive system. "The ideal level is reached when the *qi* moves about with rumbling noises and eventually flows to the area beneath the navel. You will have a feeling of fullness and satiation in your intestines" (*Fuqi jingyi lun* 7b). This is when one can "stop eating grain and start living on *qi*."

Absorbing Qi

Going beyond this, the absorption of *qi* connects the person more actively with the greater universe. Already the *Wufuxu* contains a variety of methods that involve the expulsion of the Three Deathbringers and absorption of stellar essences, such as the sun and the moon, and the visualization of cosmic and body gods (Yamada 1989, 107, 119; Eskildsen 1998, 56-28). It says:

> By nourishing on the essence of the sun one can attain long life. Every month on the morning of the first, third, fifth, sixth, ninth, and fifteenth day, face the sunrise with open hair and closed eyes.
>
> Concentrate on the sun and visualize a small child dressed in red in your heart. His garments are embroidered in the five colors and he emits a bright red radiance. Then rub both hands from your face down to the heart twelve times. You will see the red radiance of the sun, and a yellow *qi* will appear before your eyes. Make this enter your mouth and swallow it twice nine times. Then rub your heart and recite the following:
>
> "Ruler of the Sun! Let your primal yang energy merge its power with me! Let us together raise the immortal child in the scarlet palace of the heart!"
>
> Concentrate a little longer and the child will descend from the heart to the lower elixir field. He will stay there and make you live long. (1.18b; Yamada 1989, 119)

A variant of this, essential to *qi*-work in the Tang, is the ingestion of the five sprouts (*wuya* 五芽), a subtler and more refined version of the absorption of celestial energies.[10] It begins with swallowing the saliva while chanting invocations to the original *qi* of the four cardinal directions. Adepts face the direction in question, usually beginning with the east, and in their minds visualize the *qi* of that direction in its appropriate color. A general mist in the beginning, it gradually forms into a ball, sort of like the rising sun, then through further concentration shrinks in size and comes closer to the adept. Eventually the size of a pill, the sprout can be swallowed and guided mentally to the organ of its correspondence. A suitable incantation places it firmly in its new receptacle, and gradually

---

[10] On this practice, see Yamada 1989, 109; Robinet 1989, 165-66; 1993, 176-78; Eskildsen 1989 53-55; Jackowicz 2006, 84-87; Kohn 2008a, 155-58.

the adept's body becomes infused with cosmic energy and partakes more actively in the cosmos as a whole.

The incantations are short and to the point. As the *Fuqi jingyi lun* says:

> Green Sprout of the East:
> Be absorbed to feed my [internal] green sprout [liver].
> I drink you through the Morning Flower [root of upper teeth].
>
> Vermilion Cinnabar of the South:
> Be absorbed to feed my [internal] vermilion cinnabar [heart].
> I drink you through the Cinnabar Lake [root of lower teeth].
>
> Lofty Great Mountain of the Center:
> Be absorbed to feed my [internal] essence and *qi*.
> I drink you through the Sweet Spring [root of the molars].
>
> Radiant Stone of the West:
> Be absorbed to feed my [internal] radiant stone [lungs].
> I drink you through the Numinous Liquid [saliva inside lips].
>
> Mysterious Sap of the North:
> Be absorbed to feed my [internal] mysterious sap [kidneys].
> I drink you through the Jade Sweetness [saliva on tongue].(3ab)

The sprouts, as Isabelle Robinet points out, are "emanations of the highest poles" and as such full of the power of far-off regions (yin), the fringes of civilization where the Dao resides in a rawer state. At the same time, they are "tender like freshly sprouted plants" (yang) and as such contain the entire potential of being in its nascent state (1989, 165). In this growth potential of both yin and yang, the small and imperceptible *qi* in a state of pure becoming, lies their main attraction for the Daoist practitioner. "Sprouting" means inherent creation, purity, newness, return to youth. It also implies the prevalence of the soft over the hard and the power of yin over yang that Laozi describes in the *Daode jing*. The practice is undertaken at dawn, the time when everything awakens to life, yet another symbol of yang and of creative, unstructured potential. By ingesting the sprouts, the Daoist partakes of the inherent power of celestial bodies and feeds on the pure creative energy of the universe its most subtle form. Becoming increasingly one with the germinal energy of the universe, adepts become lighter and freer, learn to appear and disappear at will, overcome the limitations of this world, and attain immortality in the heavenly realms.

Their very bodies change under the impact of the advanced techniques. As Stephen Jackowicz puts it:

> The individual returns to the primordial state of being and is like the embryo, but instead of being supported by a mother's body, he or she is now nourished in the womb of the universe, the body corrected to be *qi*. . . . The practitioner in his or her body has returned to the stage of the primordial egg, from which the comic giant Pangu transformed and created the world. Primordial union has been reestablished, and the practitioner partakes of the unlimited supply of original, primordial, ever-circulating *qi*. (2006, 82-83)

This, in turn, means the attainment of immortality, complete with unlimited life expectancy, perfection in body and mind, supernatural powers, and control over nature and divinities. As the *Daoji tuna jing* says:

> If one practices the method without interruption, life expectancy will naturally be extended. After three years, all burns and scars will disappear, and the facial complexion will have a clear radiance. After six years, bone marrow will be abundant and the brain be filled. One will have clairvoyant knowledge regarding matters of life and death.
>
> After nine years, one can employ and command demons and spirits, taking the title of perfected. Serving as assistant to the Highest Lord, one's life matches that of Heaven while one's radiance merges with the sun. (3.23b; Eskildsen 1998, 52)

The ultimate level of Daoist dietetics is, therefore, to abandon food and drink completely. This requires, besides a firm belief and strong determination, an optimal setting in a quiet and undisturbed environment, the careful observance of moral rules and temporal taboos, as well as the systematic elimination of the Three Deathbringers in favor of the Three Ones. Once the foundation is established, practitioners move on to use herbal formulas and various techniques of breathing, exercise, meditation, and visualization to refine their personal constellation to ever greater subtlety and eventually transform the basic configuration of their system to becoming an embryo to the cosmos at large. They are, at last, fully pervaded by Dao, at one with the root of the universe, as eternal as Heaven and Earth.

Part Three

Texts on Practices

Text One

Herbal Formulas[1]

Pine Root (*songgen* 松根)

[1a] Take eastward growing pine root, peel it to remove the white skin, chop fine, fry, then pound it into a paste. Eat your fill and you can eliminate all grains. Should you be thirsty, just drink water.

China Root Fungus (*fuling* 茯苓)

[1b] Take China root fungus, scrape it to take off the black skin, then pound the branches and place them into an earthenware jar to soak in good-quality wine. Tightly seal the lid with dirt and keep the mixture buried for fifteen days. When you open it, the mixture should be firm like a cake. Cut it into lumps the size of chess pieces and take a day. You can also crumble it and take it in an inch-sized spoon. You will no longer feel hunger and thirst, be free from all diseases, and extend your years.

[2b] Take five pints of fungus branches, seven pounds of oily pine sap, five pounds of white wax, three pounds of white honey, two pints of Sichuan thyme, and steam them all together as if you were steaming a picul of grain.[2] When it is well cooked, take it out and form it into pills the

---

[1] Selections from the *Taiqing jing duangu fa* 太清經斷穀法 (Ways to Give Up Grain Based on the Scriptures of Great Clarity, DZ 846). The text contains materials that go back to the Han dynasty and refers to various recipes in the *Baopuzi* and *Wufuxu*. It was probably compiled in the late Six Dynasties. See Lévi in Schipper and Verellen 2004, 99. For a study of herbal recipes, including some translated here, see Eskildsen 1998, 62-63; for details on the *Wufuxu* and its recommendations, see Arthur 2006a; 2006b; 2009.

[2] Measurements include: pints (*sheng* 升 = ab. 0.7 liters), pecks (*dou* 斗 = ab. 7 liters), pounds (*jin* 斤 = 597 grams), and piculs (*dan* 石 = 72 kilos).

size of cypress seeds. Take ten of them, gradually decreasing their number until you feel no more hunger. After ten days, you can limit yourself to one pill. Do not overeat! But you can drink a little wine.

Atractylis (*shu* 术)

[3b] Take one picul properly cured atractylis, rinse and wash it, then pound it. Soak it overnight in two piculs of water, then boil it until the liquid is reduced by half. Add five pints of clear wine and boil again. When the mass is down to one picul, wring it out and remove the dregs. Next, simmer it over a low flame, adding two pints of soy branches and one pint of asparagus root. Mix it all into pills the size of crossbow pellets. Take three in the morning, once a day. Living in the mountains or on a long journey, you can take them with you replace food. You will be able to withstand wind and cold, extend your years, and be free from all diseases. This method was used by Cui Yezi 崔野子.[3] Oh, and make sure to take the skin off the asparagus root before adding it.

Yellow Essence (*huangjing* 黃精)

[5a] Take one picul of minced yellow essence and steam it in two-and-a-half—or, alternatively, six—pints of water, simmering it all day. [5b] When dusk arrives, it will be done. Once well-cooked, take it out and cool it. With your hands, press it and make it into small pieces. Put them into a wineskin to ferment, then extract the juice. Take the sediment and let it dry, then put it into a pot and form it into pills the size of chicken eggs. Take one pill three times a day. This will help you to eliminate grains, expel the hundred diseases, become light in body, stay vigorous, and avoid aging. Your dosage should be regular, do not take more or stop in the middle of the course. Should you be thirsty, just drink water. This method is of highest excellence. It comes from the *Wufuxu* [2.21ab].

Jade Bamboo (*weirui* 萎蕤)

[6b] Always pick the leaves in the 2nd or 9th months. Chop them, then let them dry before curing and taking them. Use an inch-sized spoon three

---

[3] An immortal of the Six Dynasties, Cui has a biography in *Lishi zhenxian tidao tongjian* 歷世真仙體道通鑒(Comprehensive Mirror through the Ages of Perfected Immortals and Those Who Embody the Dao, DZ 296), by Zhao Daoyi 趙道 — of around the year 1300 (7.13b; see Lévi in Schipper and Verellen 2004, 99).

times a day. You can also prepare the herb into cakes like you would Yellow Essence. When you take it, guide its *qi* through the channels. It strengthens muscles and bones, cures interior wind, heals tendons, knits flesh, and will also smooth out wrinkles and create a good complexion.

Asparagus Root (*tianmen dong* 天門冬)

[6b] Take three piculs of asparagus root, peel it and discard the skin, then thoroughly soak it, pound and wring it until you extract one picul of juice. On a small fire, simmer it down to about five pints of boiled extract. Add one pint of white honey and two pints of steamed sesame [*Wufuxu:* that has been boiled so it is fragrant and has a golden hue]. Stir the mixture without resting, then make it into pills the size of soybeans or into round crumb-cakes about three inches in diameter and a half inch thick.

[7a] Take one piece a day. After one hundred days, you will no longer feel hungry, your skin and flesh will be moist and glossy, [*Wufuxu:* your white hair will return to black, lost teeth will re-grow, and you can extend your years. You can also add three pints of Yellow Essence juice and cook it all together. This recipe is most excellent. It comes from the *Wufuxu* [2.30b-31a].

Sesame (Mulgedium) (*jusheng* 巨勝)

[7b] Take any amount of fat black sesame, sift, clean, and steam it. Let the steam rise so it envelopes you completely. After a while take it out and dry it. Repeat this process nine times. It is best to do it three times per day and continue the procedure for three days to make a total of nine rounds. Dry the mixture, then place it in a mortar bowl, moistening it with a little hot water, and pound it until it becomes white. Again dry it and sift it to remove excess skins. Steam it once more until it becomes fragrant, then mash it under your hands to sift out coarse parts. Take two or three pints daily, as you see fit. You can also mix it with honey and form it into egg-sized pills. Take five of these daily. You can also mix it with sugar or dissolve the mixture in wine.

Gradually reduce the dose. After one hundred days, you will be free from disease. After one year, you will have a glossy complexion. After five years, you will be invulnerable to fire and water, and when you walk you will be as swift as a horse. The Master of Embracing Simplicity says: "This is not contained in the Jiangdong edition. The recipe was used by refuges at the disorder in the first year of the Yong'an reign period [in 264, at the end of the Three Kingdoms period]. I obtained and recorded it on 8/1 in Yongxing 2 [305].[4]

Assorted Grains (*za mimai* 雜米麥)

[9a] Mix one pound each of the following ingredients: nonglutinous rice, panicled millet, buckwheat, sesame, and steamed soybeans; [9b] add one pound of white honey, fry it and soak it in cold water. Then make the mixture into pills the size of plum pits that you can swallow in one gulp. You will not be hungry to the end of your days. This comes from the *Wufuxu* [2.36a].

[9b] Take one pint common millet and three pounds red stone fat [cinnabar], mix and soak them in water, then leave the compound in a warm place for two or three days until a coat forms on top. Next, pound it into pills the size of plum pits and take three per day. You will no longer feel hungry. Should you be thirsty, just drink water. You will also be able to walk as far as a thousand *li* without getting tired. This comes from the *Wufuxu* [2.35a].

Direct Internal Preservation (*shouzhong jingyi* 守中俓易)

[10b] Take three pints of very fresh bean sprouts, place them in your hands, then visualize a radiance spreading through your body, warm and beautiful. Eat the sprouts, swallowing them quickly so they can be absorbed. After fifty to a hundred days, you will not feel hungry any longer. Should you be thirsty, just drink water. Make sure not to overeat; rather, keep reducing the amounts.

[10b] To take two pints of steamed bean porridge, use the following method: eat time first face the sun and bow repeatedly, then swallow one pint at a time. Revolve each mouthful around the mouth, then swallow it. Repeat this process three times on the first day. On the next day, split one pint into three portions. Children should use half the amount.

To Return to Eating Grains and Stop Taking Herbal Formulas (*yuhuan shigu jieyao* 欲還食穀解藥)

[11b] While taking herbal formulas for internal preservation or after eliminating grains, do not take any extraneous items. Should you be thirsty, just drink little sips of cold water. If you wish to give up the diet

---

[4] This citation is not contained in the *Baopuzi* as transmitted today. See also Lévi in Schipper and Verellen 2004, 99.

and return to eating grains, first take a decoct from mallow seeds and lesser formulas, then you can start eating again. Begin by taking one serving of thin rice porridge three times a day. After two more days, take two servings, increasing the amount to five servings after three more days, then seven servings after yet another three days, [12a] and finally to one pint after three more days. Continue like this for one month and you will be ready to eat ordinary food.

Mallow Seed Decoct (*kuizi tang* 葵子湯)[5]

[12a] Take one pint mallow seeds and one pound pork fat. Boil in five pecks of water until the liquid is reduced to two pints. Remove the sediments and take it very, very slowly. Feel it sink down to fill [the belly], then stop. You can also mix it with rice to make thin porridge. It is also excellent if drunk with Sichuan thyme.

---

[5] For a review and discussion of this recipe as well as an analysis of the chemical properties of the various herbs, see Huang 2007, 63-69.

Text Two

Giving Up Ordinary Food[1]

[9b] To live on *qi*, it is best to work after you wake up from sleep, right from around midnight to the fifth watch [3-5 a.m.]. Balance the breath, inhaling and exhaling in proper measure and with due attention to the breathing rhythm.

Rinse your mouth with the numinous fluid [saliva], then lie down on your back, make your hands into fists, and block [the *qi* opening at] the soles of the feet. [10a] Support your head with a pillow and breathe, keeping your mind stable and following the movement of the breath without interruption as it comes in and goes out, passing through gate [nose] and doorway [mouth]. Then close the mouth firmly and become aware of the internal *qi*, pulling it up carefully into the mouth. Softly drum [the belly] and swallow it down, using your intention to guide it or using your hands to rub it from above the heart to the lower belly. Then again balance the breath six or seven times before you proceed to swallow it once more, as before using your hands to guide it by rubbing [along the front of the torso]. Stop when you have completed twenty rounds of *qi*-work in this manner.

During daylight hours, again find suitable times to sit or lie down and rest in perfect calm and serenity. Practice the swallowing for at least ten rounds. Make sure to balance the breath in between each swallowing, breathing steadily forty to fifty times, then swallowing slowly and carefully. Even if you are not busy at all, do not do all the swallowings at the same time. Also, make sure each time to use your hands to rub the front

---

[1] *Taiqing tiaoqi jing* 太清調氣經 (Great Clarity Scripture on Balancing *Qi*, DZ 820), probably of Tang origin (see Lévi in Schipper and Verellen 2004, 369). Excerpts on *bigu*: 9b-14b and 22b-22b. Earlier translation in Huang and Wurmbrand 1987, 80-86 and 96-98. Subheadings added by the translator.

of the torso, guiding the *qi* downward while also using your intention to send it on its way. Then examine yourself. If the Upper Heater is open, the *qi* will move easily below the navel. If not, the *qi* will stay in the chest and heart area.

Pay particular attention to meal times and see whether the upper torso feels empty and if there is a feeling of flow below. If this is the case, the *qi* is flowing freely. [10b] Then you can go ahead and eat. However, do not eat if you are not in fact hungry, and when you do eat, do not fill up completely, since fullness hinders the absorption of *qi*. After the meal, wait until the area between heart and belly feel slightly empty, then again absorb *qi* by practicing a set of twenty swallowings. Do the same at the evening meal. Every day repeat this process around the same time, regardless of whether your are walking, standing, sitting, or lying down. Complete a hundred days like this. Always remember: Every time you swallow *qi*, use your hands to disperse it and practice at least ten balanced breaths in between. This will maximize the effect.

Levels and Precautions

In the beginning it is common that the Triple Heater is not quite clear and the various passes are not open. As long as that is the case, obstructions are common and you won't be able to absorb much *qi*. Increase your practice by three times five swallowings every ten days until the first hundred days have passed. After 150 days, again increase by four times five swallowings, until you reach 200 swallowings in a day. Once you have done the practice for a whole year, the *qi* will easily flow, passes and joints will be open, your skin and flesh will be moist and glossy, and your hair pores will be free and clear.

Having reached this level, you just need to wait until your stomach feels empty, then do three times five swallowings as appropriate. You may do them successively, without balancing the breath in between, and there is no more need for adhering to a rigorous daily schedule. [11a] Just do not overdo it: no more than 300 swallowings a day.

After three years of practice, the *qi* will flow freely all around, completely pervading the entire body. Your five organs will be well nurtured, your bones solid, your marrow full, and your skin glossy and rich. At this point, there is no more limit to the number of swallowings, and you should be able to eliminate grains with ease.

Should you go into fasting before the three years are up, you will suffer from the five exertions and seven injuries,[2] reducing the potency of your inner organs and causing the hundred joints to dry up and wither. The process will not work unless you cultivate the *qi* very gradually and never give in to the temptation of cutting out grains abruptly to quickly attain long life. It also won't work unless you eliminate all thoughts of involvement in worldly schemes, of satisfying the six senses, and of going after wealth and sensual pleasures.

Also, if you give in to a hungry stomach, letting go of grains only reluctantly and without sufficient supplementary formulas, you will cause new ailments to arise and the myriad diseases to assemble. If your thoughts and desires do not die, how can you ever reach attainment?

Another point is that, after practicing the absorption of *qi*, you need to make sure you know how to eat properly. Every day at breakfast, eat a little unflavored watery porridge to balance the spleen-*qi* and provide sufficient fluids to last you through the day. At noon, eat one or two unflavored slices of bread and maybe some broth that contains onions or scallions. [11b] Do not eat them hot, though. If you are hungry in the evening, take a few unflavored dumplings that you have boiled for twenty or thirty minutes. Again, make sure not to eat to fullness but three to five mouthfuls less. It is best always to leave the table with a feeling of slight emptiness in the stomach.

If you fill up in one batch, the passage of *qi* is blocked and it cannot flow, wasting a whole day's work. To prevent this, also avoid all greasy, fatty, and sticky foods as well as raw vegetables, root plants, and anything old, stale, smelly, or suchlike. Also, never take anything that has turbid *qi* [slaughtered and killed].

In the first thirty to fifty days, it is unavoidable to have occasional twinges of hunger. If you catch yourself thinking of food, immediately balance the breath and practice the *qi* method, then gradually your belly

---

2 The *Yangxing yanming lu* says: "The five exertions are [creating exertion through] (1) the will, (2) thinking, (3) the mind, (4) worry, and (5) fatigue. They create six forms of extreme pressure [stress] in the body, to wit, in (1) *qi*, (2) blood, (3) tendons, (4) bones, (5) essence, and (6) marrow. These six forms of extreme pressure in turn cause the seven injuries which transform into the seven pains. The seven pains create disease" (2.3a).

will feel rich and moist and you won't be tempted to think of the hundred flavors.

When we speak of taking porridge, bread, or dumplings, in all cases eat them in accordance with your schedule and convenience. There is no need to rely on a specific daily regimen of eating, but for the most part your order of food intake should follow the above outline. Establish your own schedule and rhythm and take mostly unflavored watery porridge with little bits of boiled rice here and there. This will be most excellent.

[12a] Once you have begun to successfully absorb *qi*, your Triple Heater will be clear, the stomach apertures will be open, and the five organs will be in perfect harmony. Then sweet saliva arises and the Jade Pond will be luscious. At this point any food you take will taste delicious, just like to a person just recovering from illness. The tendency at this point is to get greedy and no longer know when it is enough: it all just tastes so *good*! Curb this urge. If you give in to it, great harm will come. So, initially you must pay great attention to the times and amounts you eat.

Now, every time you eat, you are bound to ingest some toxins as well as excess heat from the five flavors. For this reason, after every meal open your mouth wide and exhale with the *he* breath. This will lessen the hot *qi* in the mouth and prevent future afflictions. Also make sure to limit your intake of salty, spicy, sour, and other strong flavors. In fact, it is best to avoid them altogether. This may be hard in the beginning, but not for long. Within even ten to twenty days, you will notice a numinous spring of sweet fluid gushing forth, which would not happen if you ate salty or spicy foods. Practicing the absorption of *qi*, you will further find that your five organs are juicy and full and that your proper *qi* sinks down to chase out any bad energies, which duly leave through the lower orifices.

To avoid harm to the already purified stomach area, you should also not eat anything sticky or greasy nor anything raw or hard. [12b] Should you inadvertently take a mouthful of such a substance, you will feel a slight pain wherever the morsel comes to rest in your system. With continued effort and a deeper awareness of your inner workings, you will realize this naturally.

To sum up: Eat only soft and well-cooked food. That is most excellent. And after every meal always exhale with *he*.

Supplements

Each time you eat rice, first swallow twenty or thirty raw peppercorns with some water. Only then eat the rice. Should you feel pain or fullness after a meal, you can take ten additional peppercorns. The pepper will move the Triple Heater activity downward and chase out all sorts of bad *qi*. It will also dissolve any food remnants left behind in the intestines.

Similarly, you should take two or three peppercorns if you feel a sense of dense and cloying [depressed] *qi* in the heart and chest area during your guiding of proper *qi*. They will in due course dissolve this feeling. The benefits of simple peppercorns are truly beyond words.

Another way to deal with bouts of fullness, a cloying feeling, or a sense of *qi* stagnation is to practice quiet-sitting and balancing the breath. The feeling will disperse quickly and the *qi* will leave through the lower orifices.

Some old texts say that one should stabilize the *qi* and not allow it to leave. In the old days when people first practiced, they accordingly stabilized the *qi*, holding on to it as much as possible. [13a] However, after a short period of time, they would feel a tension in their bellies, be beset by worries, and imagine themselves dying. The two lower orifices directly connect to the nose and mouth above. Accordingly, when there is stale or bad *qi* in the five organs, it must sink down to leave. Why should one stabilize and hold on to it?

Stabilizing the *qi* prevents it from flowing freely and leaving the body. If it does not flow freely and is prevented from leaving, pain results. This is so because, when the stale *qi* has not yet left and fresh *qi* suddenly enters, the two *qi* clash with each other and create discomfort. If is thus not necessary [or advisable] to stabilize the *qi*. Much better to have it flow freely and leave properly.

Also, every day try to drink one or two cups of liquor on an empty stomach, as your disposition allows. This is really good. But make sure that you do not get to the point of getting intoxicated or maudlin. It is even better if you can slowly sip three to five cups of liquor every day, greatly aiding your *qi*-work. In all cases, the liquor should be clear and of good quality. When you first start taking it, don't drink more than one mouthful. Be prepared for the *qi* to be unsettled for a few days.[3]

On another note, if something delightful happens to you and you wish to celebrate by drinking, you can also do so, using the method described below. The reason why ordinary people get intoxicated or maudlin when they drink liquor is that it is usually made toxic by fermenting yeast and when that toxic *qi* enters the four limbs, there is intoxication. [13b]

To drink properly, do the following. When you sit with five or ten people and the cup gets passed around, reaching you every so often, drink when your turn comes and every time afterward open your mouth and exhale with *he* seven or eight times. This way the liquor's toxin will be expelled and dispersed. Should more than one cup arrive at your place at the same time, open your mouth very wide and exhale with *he*, but if there is only one cup at a time, be subtle about it.

Generally, whenever you exhale, accompany the leaving breath with a subtle *he*. Like this you can make it through a whole banquet without stopping your practice of balancing the breath. Even better: If you can usually drink three pints, that day you can stomach ten, yet without getting inebriated and without losing the good taste of the liquor throughout the evening. Even if you drank for a whole day, the taste would not diminish. Eventually you will go to sleep, and after you wake up you swallow the *qi* and balance the breath again as described above.

Social Situations

On another note, there may be a sudden burst of *qi* leaving the body through the lower orifices at an unexpected time, such as during a meal, when with an invited guest, while riding on horseback, or when with honored relatives. So, if the *qi* comes then, what to do? You must find a suitable way to let it escape. If you keep it tight and fail to let it leave, [14a] it will reverse its course and move back into the intestines where it will cause stomach pain and irritate the heart and chest area. If not dispersed over a long period, even one mouthful of contained *qi* can cause confusion, depression, and pain.

---

[3] Huang and Wurmbrand interpret this to mean nausea, followed by a purging of the system through vomiting (1987, 84).

Should you, due to public or private affairs, have no time to undertake longevity practice, make sure to at least avoid meat and the five strong vegetables. Then, even if *qi* leaves through the lower orifices, it will not be very smelly. Once you have started the practice of avoiding grain, on the other hand, whether there is one instance of flatulence or more, the escaping *qi* will be entirely without odor.

Also, make sure to avoid any contact with birth, dirt, pollution, and various forms of serious illness. They all massively reduce proper *qi*. Should you walk along a public street and unexpectedly encounter any form of such bad *qi*, immediately enclose the *qi* [by holding your breath] and pass by quickly. Should this be impossible, drink a bit of clear liquor or have a small bite of meat or a strong vegetable. This will create a block. Should you have actually absorbed the bad *qi* and you begin to feel restless and ill at ease, practice balancing the breath to expel it.

Another precaution: Do not shout out loud, sing, cry, or wail. If in your social life you cannot avoid a situation of mourning, make some small appropriate noises but do not cry excessively. [14b] Should you feel the *qi* move upward and create a lump in your throat, do not repress it but let it rise up to a certain point, then swallow it back down. Once it has reached the belly, again take in fresh *qi* and swallow it. Repeat this three or five times. This will help you settle down. You can also help it disperse by rubbing the front of your torso down with your hands.

Taking a bit of pepper and some liquor will completely relieve the situation. However, if you are it by a sudden sob that you cannot move down, then do not force yourself to swallow. This would only cause an obstruction in the Upper Heater. Rather, breathe slowly and with conscious intention, then examine yourself. If the *qi* has not yet dispersed, do not eat, since any eating or sense of fullness will prevent you from doing a proper swallowing. Eat only after you have swallowed a few times. Otherwise, you are inviting disease.

Also, at each swallowing hold the breath and block the nose. When inhalation and exhalation are regular, use the intention to send the *qi* outward. Then watch it on the inside. It moves down the left side of the torso, along twenty-four notches. As it descends one notch at a time, you can hear it like water dripping, clear and rhythmical. If there is no sound it is because you ate something oily or heavy or did not follow the proper procedure. If it does not dissolve soon and you absorb more *qi*, it will create internal pressure and lead to disease. [15a] Be very careful!

Cutting Out Ordinary Food

[21b] If you want to fast for a period, just use the [breathing and swallowing] method spelled out earlier. After three years, your five organs will be well nurtured, your bones will be solid and your flesh full. The hundred spirits return and maintain residence, your blood arteries are open to free flow, your *qi* passageways are loose and wide, and your various body energies circulate smoothly without obstruction. You will feel light and completely renewed every day.

Once you reach this point, you naturally find yourself having less and less desire to smell the aroma of the five flavors and hardly ever think about food. It will be not difficult at all to stop eating altogether.

[22a] Worldly people tend to be greedy for pleasure and love profit. They cannot stop their thoughts and widely search through recipe books for formulas to take for grain abstention. When such herbal concoctions first enter the stomach, they do in fact create a feeling of fullness for a period of time. However, once their effect is exhausted, hunger will come back with a vengeance. This creates a vicious circle without end [yoyo dieting].

In addition, this tendency constantly keeps the mind involved with thoughts of formulas and the quest for apparent harmony in daily affairs. Moving to and fro, forever restless, such people do not have even a moment's rest. Their strength feeble, their thoughts drained, they continuously increase troubles and vexations and don't even need to invite misfortune to arrive. Also, even though they take various concoctions and things, how can they suddenly eliminate eating? So, some will suck on fruit pits to increase vigor while others ingest more complex concoctions to simulate fullness.

All this, when in fact all you need to do is increase your breath-balancing practice, keep yourself well, and nurture peaceful thoughts. The exhausting toil of chasing after the right formulas, the demeaning effort of refining various concoctions—they all strain people for months and years and uselessly labor essence and spirit. How can they ever attain the reversal of aging and a return to youth? If you just don't eat rice, how can you call it "eliminate eating"?

Indeed, there are lower-level practitioners who can't even live without grains and still work in the world by taking herbal formulas to supplement their system. Yes, they will gain some minor benefits. But higher-level practitioners do not do anything like this. [22b] They just absorb *qi* over long periods and as they perfect their practice, they come to fast naturally. Sensing that their stomachs are empty, they just swallow *qi*. Never worried whether early or late, they have no obstructions or hindrances. Swallowing whenever they feel the need, they have no limits or boundaries. They become naturally aware of their proper rhythm and timing and won't even need lots of practice sessions anymore. As they absorb *qi* like this for a very long time, they naturally reach the stage of eliminating eating. They thereby attain complete self-liberation and freedom from vexations in all they do.

To sum up: In the beginning stages of practice, if you want to take some herbal formulas to supplement the absorption of *qi*, by all means do so. However, the tendency is that those who get into taking the supplements often do not do the practice of absorption and make the quest for and ingestion of herbs their main objective.

Text Three

Guiding Qi[1]

The Scripture says:

[5b] To study Dao and practice the immortals' methods of living on *qi* you need to guide the *qi* in the 2nd and 3rd months of spring, always on the 9th, 18th, and 27th days, as well as on all days of the cyclical signs *jia-chen, yisi, bingchen,* and *dingsi*.

[6a] To guide the *qi*, set up a quiet room in the mountain forest, in a tranquil and secluded spot that is near a sweet spring, has an eastward flowing stream, and faces south. Take a bath in fragrant hot water and—as prescribed in the elixir books—focus your attention on the Jade Chamber, about one inch below the elixir field. [Note: The Jade Chamber is usually about three inches below the elixir field in the abdomen.] In the Jade Chamber you will then proceed to visualize the inner *qi* of the middle elixir field moving toward the lower field.

Before you do all this, remove the fine hairs from your nostrils, lie down flat with your feet five inches apart, and lengthen the shoulders away from the body by five inches. Close your eyes and make your hands into loose fists. [Note: Fists are the shape the hands of infants tend to be in.] Use a pillow made of rushes about three inches high. If you have an ailment in your chest, make sure the pillow is seven inches. Should you have a condition below the navel, remove the pillow altogether.

Once you begin the practice of guiding the *qi*, you must no longer eat raw food and avoid the five strong vegetables. This shows the proper respect. If your goal is to give up grains altogether and reach a state where you actually live on *qi*, every day eat one mouthful less of food. After ten days, you can stop eating. If after two or three days of this your stomach feels irritated and you have a strong sensation of hunger, take

---

[1] *Shenxian quegu shiqi* 神仙卻穀食氣 (How Immortals Give up Grain and Eat *Qi*, YJQQ 59).

nine ripe dates or nine square atractylis cakes [6b] and eat them one at a time, morning and evening. Do not take any more food than that. Really, if you don't think about food, you will find no need to eat.

As for drinking water, you take three or five pints everyday, spaced out evenly. Do not stop drinking! Also, it is a good idea to keep a date pit in your mouth. It enhances the *qi* in your body and provides a steady flow of saliva.

The Scripture says:

Dao is *qi*. Love *qi* and attain Dao. Attain Dao and live forever!

Essence is spirit. Treasure essence and spirit shines forth. Have spirit shine forth and endure in eternity!

One way of guiding the *qi* is to refine it. To do so, lie down flat on your back, then slowly rinse with Sweet Spring and swallow it. [Note: Sweet Spring means saliva.] From here, very subtly inhale *qi* through the nose and bring it slowly into the body, never pushing to extremes in any form. When you have fully inhaled five times, exhale once completely. This is one round. Count it by bending a finger each time.

When you get to ninety breaths, you may feel troubled and exhausted. In that case, finish the round and stretch briefly. After the stretch is complete, practice again later. Eventually you will be able to complete four times ninety or 360 breaths. We call this one set. Doing this over a prolonged period, you will find all sorts of diseases are naturally eliminated.

[7a] Another part of this is making the exhaled *qi* return. To do so, when you first inhale give a very short exhalation, then let the breath move in and out very, very slowly. Continue to practice like this, then pull the breath in again through the nose. Unless you follow this, you will move in the wrong direction. This would go against the usual way which is that when you inhale, the *qi* rises up; when you exhale, it flows down.

Over a long period of practice, you will become aware of the *qi* circulating through your whole body. If your practice is not quite secure and you feel some fatigue in your mind, then stop after one long round of ninety breaths. Gradually work up to three times ninety, or 270 breaths. This, too, we call one set.

In guiding the *qi*, make sure it moves evenly and fills the organs, but never expel it vigorously. On the other hand, if you hold the breath in, swallow it only after a ninety-count. If you cannot quite get to the swallowing level, just work on doing the breathing to the count of ninety. Completing three times ninety breaths should be quite sufficient. There is then no more need to count in detail.

At this point think of the *qi* as pervading the tips of your hair at the top of the head and from there flowing down all the way into your four limbs, reaching naturally down to the three luminants. [Note: The jade stalk and two gonads.]

The Scripture says:

To guide the *qi*, visualize it entering from the ten fingers between the 1st and 15th days of the month; see it coming in from the ten toes between the 16th and 30th days of the month. [7b] Over a longer period of practice you will naturally feel it in the hands and feet. If you practice without interruption, your body will start to feel lighter and more vigorous every day, *qi* and channels will be soft and supple, and the protective and defensive *qi* will pervade your limbs and joints.

The Dao of long life centers on guiding *qi*. It imitates the way of wondrous, long-lived turtles who too extend their existence by absorbing *qi*.

After some time of living purely on guided *qi* you may desire to go back to eating worldly food. Should this be the case, begin by taking small sips of rice gruel, increasing the amount gradually by one mouthful every day. After ten days, you should be ready to eat congee again—but never to satiation.

The Scripture says:

When you first start the practice of guiding *qi*, there tends to be a great deal of disharmony. It may cause coughs, [stomach] upsets, or stiffness in the four limbs. However, if you persist in your practice, things are certain to improve over time.

By the time you make it to four times ninety breaths, or one set of 360, your body will feel like a soft robe with light bones and open joints. After a very long time, you will even become aware of the *qi* moving freely throughout the physical structure, pervading and enriching the whole body. It continues to moisturize all your parts, making your skin glossy and soft, filling and enhancing the five organs and six viscera, and driving out the hundred diseases once and for all.

Always, before you set about guiding *qi*, make sure to calm the body and harmonize the physical structure. [8a] Should the *qi* appear at odds and there is a sense of unrest in yourself, stop and wait for a while. Then establish internal harmony and begin your practice.

> The *qi* in harmony—the body is fully at peace.
> The body at peace—the breath flows smoothly through the nostrils.
> The breath smooth—pure *qi* is activated.
> Pure *qi* active—the body gets naturally warm.
> The body warm—there is a rush of perspiration.

At this point, there is no more need to move around or push the *qi* intentionally. Just rest peacefully and nurture it, your main job being to make sure the prolonged continuation of breathing and internal flow.

Throughout your practice make sure you feel not even a trace of irritation, anger, anxiety, or worry in your mind. Should there by any, even a little bit, of these emotions, the *qi* will be disturbed. And if the *qi* suffers disturbance, you are running in the opposite direction from immortality.

To counteract emotional tension, think of the One. Thinking of the One, proper *qi* arrives. Proper *qi* present, there is sweetness and fragrance in your mouth. Your mouth sweet, saliva arises in plenty while the breath becomes soft and long. Saliva plentiful and the breath long, the *qi* flows about in an orderly manner. This means long life and extended years.

In the practice of guiding *qi*, you inhale very, very subtly through the nose and exhale long and soft through the mouth. This is what we call a "long breath." Also, the inhalation is just one type of breath, but the exhalation comes in six forms: *hu, chui, xi, he, xu,* and *si.* Ordinary people breathe one in and one out, without being aware of these Daoist forms of breathing. Daoists, on the contrary, balance their *qi* in this manner. When it is cold, use chui; when it is hot, use hu. Thus know:

> *Chui* dispels heat. *Hu* dispels wind. *He* dispels tension.
> *Xi* lowers *qi*. *Xu* dissolves obstructions. *Si* releases extremes.

Someone in a tight emotional state typically will breathe heavily with sobs and sighs, i.e., *xu* and *xi*. Thus these two are completely taboo when it comes to practicing the long breath. They are bad for anyone trying to study Dao and practice guiding of *qi*.

Text Four

Embryo Respiration[1]

[1a] Followers of [the] Highest Clarity [scriptures] and the *Daode jing* (Book of the Way and Its Virtue), as well as practitioners in the lineage of the *Huangting jing* (Yellow Court Scripture) and the *Yangsheng yaoji* (Essential Collection on Nourishing Life) all can use the following method to eliminate the myriad diseases and attain spirit immortality.

In general, absorbing *qi* involves visualizing the heart as if it contained a baby in the mother's womb. After ten months it is complete, tendons and bones are harmonized and supple. Breathe with concentrated mind and maintain awareness, and the harmonious *qi* will arrive of itself. If you breathe in and out as described in this method, you can swallow *qi* and not get hungry, since the hundred pores will allow the breath to enter without blockage.

Always follow the six yang hours to absorb fresh *qi*. Then the strength of your *qi* will increase daily. The method of the six yang hours is as follows:

Practice at midnight, at the *zi* hour, nine times nine or 81 times.
Practice at dawn, at the *yin* hour, eight times eight or 64 times.
Practice at breakfast, at the *chen* hour, seven times seven or 49 times. [1b]
Practice at noon, at the *wu* hour, six times six or 36 times.
Practice at mid-afternoon, at the *shen* hour, five times five or 25 times.
Practice at dusk, at the *si* hour, four times four or 16 times.

While absorbing *qi*, the tongue should be soft and mysterious [almost intangible], and the breath should follow the proper gate to enter and

---

[1] *Taishang yangsheng taixi qi jing* 太上養生胎氣經 (Highest *Qi* Scripture on Nourishing Life and Embryo Respiration , DZ 819), a short treatise compiled from a number of well-known texts, focusing on Highest Clarity visualizations and probably dating to the Tang. See Lévi in Schipper and Verellen 2004, 368-69.

163

leave. The nose is the Gate of Heaven; as you absorb *qi* the spirit and material souls return to this gate. The mouth is the Doorway of Earth; as you absorb *qi*, the spirit and material souls return here.

The *Huangting jing* says:

> The solidity of the hundred grains
> is the essence of earth and soil;
> The five flavors are attractive on the outside,
> but their evil and demonic aspects stink.
> The jade pond [mouth] is full of clear water,
> moistening the numinous root [tongue].
> If you can cultivate this,
> you will enhance your Gate of Destiny!

If you want to enhance longevity, breathe in through the nose and out through the mouth. This is cultivation in accordance with *qi*. Using this method with a perfect mind and never stopping, you can subdue and eliminate the Three Worms, expel all glory and get rid of attachments. Day by day you gradually fulfill the work and begin to get closer to Dao.

[2a] Now, the original nature of the perfected is hidden and enclosed. Only very carefully and with clear refinement does he speak. He thinks and acts in harmony with Dao and is without blemish. He rinses and swallows his numinous saliva, and in his belly the hundred flavors are naturally complete. He penetrates the three burners and regulates his upright *qi*. Thus his *qi* naturally encompasses all parts [of his body] and penetrates his five organs. His bones and marrow are accordingly strong and rich.

The Dao is the master of the myriad forms of *qi*. Actually, Dao is *qi*. *Qi* is the gate of essence. If one guards one's essence like a person in an closed room, one may last for a hundred generations. However, if one is without essence or treats it like a room with no one in it, one will fail even in this lifetime. *Qi* is protected by essence. Essence is *qi*. When they are both complete, we speak of a perfected.

People have three cinnabar or elixir fields. The upper elixir field is the Niwan Palace in the head, ruled by the Red Emperor and his son and minister. He is called Primordial Priority. The middle elixir field is the heart. It is ruled by the Perfected of Radiant Stability. He is called the Cinnabar Child. The lower elixir field is ruled by the Infant of Valley

Mystery. He is called Master of Primordial Yang. He rules the gate of both *qi* and essence.

The three fields each have three agents of spirit. As spirits expands, *qi* begins to leak out. As *qi* leaks out, essence disperses. When essence is dispersed, spirit declines. [2b] Essence is a wondrous substance. It is the root of long life in the perfected. The root of long life is the position of *qi*. If essence is complete, *qi* is complete; if essence is dispersed, *qi* is dispersed. Just focus on your *qi* and you can protect your complete perfection. The wise ones of old who realized that loved their *qi* and guarded their essence. Thus they could live long.

Now, sensuality is aroused through the emotions, whose control does not come naturally. How, then, can we stabilize them? The situation we are in [with regards to emotions] is as dangerous as a mountain tumbling or an ocean draining. The mountain is your *qi*. The treasure [it centers on] is your kidneys. The kidneys are the root of destiny. If the root has no essence, the leaves wither. Once the leaves wither, the branches dry up. And when the branches dry up, the body rots. Then you may yearn for and pine to come back to life—but how can you ever be saved?

Now, taking in *qi* is yin; expelling *qi* is yang. These two are one process. They are used equally in absorbing the essence and florescence of the sun and the moon. *Qi* is emptiness and nonbeing. Emptiness and nonbeing are spontaneity and nonaction. Nonaction means that the heart/mind is not moving, that there is no quest on the outside and only spontaneity on the inside. Everything is peaceful and calm.

> When everything is peaceful and calm, spirit is stable.
> When spirit is stable, *qi* is in harmony. [3a]
> When *qi* is in harmony, primordial *qi* arrives by itself.
> When primordial *qi* arrives by itself, the five organs are rich and glossy.
> When the five organs are rich and glossy, the hundred channels are open and *qi* flows freely.
> When the hundred channels are open and *qi* flows freely, the body fluids rise upward in proper accord.
> When the body fluids rise upward in proper accord, one does no longer think of the five flavors and will never be hungry or thirsty.
> One will expand one's years and ward off old age

.

Qi transforms into blood; blood transforms into marrow. One year of practice effects a change in the *qi*. Two years of practice effect a change in the blood. Three years of practice effect a change in the channels. Four years of practice effect a change in the flesh. Five years of practice effect a change in the marrow. Six years of practice effect a change in the tendons. Seven years of practice effect a change in the bones. Eight years of practice effect a change in the hair. Nine years of practice effect a change in the entire body and one becomes a perfected. Refining oneself through nine cycles, one penetrates to spirit immortality. It is mysterious and wondrous—unfathomable indeed!

The Secret Zi Method of Highest Clarity

Green Sprout of the east. [Note: Green Sprout matches the liver.] Absorb and eat the Green Sprout and drink the Morning Florescence [Note: Morning Florescence is the upper gum.] Use the tongue to lick the lips, then rinse and swallow. [3b]

Vermilion Cinnabar of the south. [Note: Vermilion Cinnabar matches the heart.] Absorb and ingest the Vermilion Cinnabar and drink from the Cinnabar Pond. [Note: The Cinnabar Pond is the lower gum.] Use the tongue to rub the teeth and gums, then rinse and swallow.

Bright Stone of the west. [Note: Bright Stone matches the lungs.] Absorb and eat the Bright Stone and drink the Numinous Fluid [Note: Numinous Fluid is the saliva at the lips.] Use the tongue to rub the teeth seven times, then rinse and swallow.

Mysterious Offshoot of the north. [Note: Mysterious Offshoot matches the kidneys.] Absorb and eat the Mysterious Offshoot and drink from the Jade Womb [Note: Jade Womb is the tongue.] Use the nose to pull and guide the primordial *qi* into the mouth, then inhale, exhale, and swallow.

Lofty Mount Tai of the center. [Note: Lofty Mount Tai matches the guarded essence.] Absorb and eat the *qi* and essence and drink from the Sweet Spring. [Note: Sweet Spring is the mysterious grease at the root of the teeth and just inside the lips. The Flowery Pond is beneath the root of the tongue. It is also called Jade Radiance or Golden Bridge.]As described above, rinse and swallow. Repeat each exercise three times.

Always practice *qi* at midnight, at the *zi* or *yin* hours. Stand upright, dressed in proper cap and gown. Then open your golden bridge and waken the jade radiance to balance the flowery pond. Rinse with Sweet

Spring and Numinous Fluid. Contract your nose and make the *qi* return, going up to the head and sinking down inside the mouth. There it can transform into jade spring. From here, pull the *qi* to the root of the tongue, swallow, and send it off.

[4a] As you do all this, there should be a rumbling sound in both your throat and your abdomen. As you guide the *qi* into the elixir field, it is like a child just born and already able to cry. This is called the root of long life. When hungry, eat the *qi* of spontaneity; when thirsty, drink the juice of the flowery pond. Then you can be forever full and satiated.

Part Four

Recipes

Notes

The recipes below follow the guidelines for Daoist monastics or priests during purification in that they avoid all animal products (except the occasional egg) as well as the five strong vegetables. Many are taken from the Chinese medicated diet as outlined by Drs. Engelhardt and Nögel (2009); from Michael Saso's *Daoist Cookbook* (1994); and from the five volumes on Daoist monastic cooking, available in temples on Mt. Wudang, by Peng Mingquan (2006).

They do not claim to represent classic Daoist cookery but hope to make a Daoist-inspired way of eating accessible to Westerners. To this end, the recipes also include items that are definitely not Chinese, such as, for example, chocolate-chip cookies. They also use numerous ingredients not (yet) common in China, such as whole-grain bread, peanut butter, miso, tempeh, coconut milk, and various baked dishes. And they make use of prepration methods, such as baking, that are more easily accessible in Western kitchens.

Each section describes the nature of the food discussed, then lists ingredients, outlines procedures, illuminates variations, and provides specific examples. The idea is that once readers have grasped the basic idea on how to prepare a certain kind of dish, they mix and match materials based on availability in their specific location and during different seasons as well as in accordance with their own personal taste and bodily needs.

Abbreviations
    c   cup
    lb   pound
    lg   large
    t   teaspoon
    T   tablespoon

Measurements
    1 c = 16 T = 8 oz = 250 g (3 ¼ oz = 100g)

1. Cooked Cereals

Description

Cooked cereals are the main staple of the Chinese and Daoist diet. This section deals with them in their softest form, as porridge, congee, or gruel. All grains tend to have a sweet or neutral flavor and strongly support the center of the body, the spleen and stomach systems. Their preparation as warm porridge opens them for maximal absorption into the system. Cooked cereals are warming and strengthening and provide a nice, steady boost of energy. Often mixed with little bits of fruit or vegetables, they are best used for breakfast and during convalescence, but are also excellent at other times. Alternatives include cooked grains in breads and pancakes.

Ingredients

Grains: Barley, black rice, buckwheat, corn, couscous, millet, oats, polenta, quinoa, rice.

Fruits: Apples, bananas, cherries, chestnuts, coconut, dates, figs, grapes, kiwis, mangoes, oranges, papaya, peaches, pears, pineapple, plums, strawberries.

Vegetables: Avocado, bamboo, bean sprouts, bok choy, broccoli, cabbage, carrots, cauliflower, celery, cucumber, eggplant, kohlrabi, lettuce, lotus root, mountain vegetables, spinach, sweet potato, tomato, yams.

Pickles: Artichokes, burdock, mushrooms, plums, *daikon*, turnips.

Herbs and Spices: Cinnamon, cardamom, *fuling*, ginger, ginseng, sesame.

Also: Nuts, raisins, dried fruit of various kinds, edible flowers, such as chrysanthemums and nasturtiums.

Preparation

Grains: Cook in water with a pinch of salt, in most cases 1 part grain to 2 parts water. Soak whole grains (like rolled oats) overnight; use left-over grains from previous meals with only little water. Cooking times range widely depending on the grain—aim for soft, almost liquid consistency. Add one or two items from the list above; maybe sweeten with honey.

Fruits: Use fresh and cut into bite-sized chunks or slightly cooked into a compote, with a pinch of cinnamon, cardamom, or honey, to make the fruit more warming and gentler on the stomach.

Vegetables: Use fresh, slightly steamed, or briefly fried in a miniscule amount of oil; also take pickled or left-over from main dishes (see below). Root vegetables like yams need to be cooked first, then can be slightly roasted or browned.

Herbs: Cut fine and roast slightly before sprinkling on the porridge.

Also: Breakfast cereals benefit greatly from nuts and dried fruit of all kinds—raisins, craisins, prunes, apricots, etc.

Variations

Bread: Should cooking grain not be an option, whole-grain bread with some butter and jam, peanut butter, vegetable spread, or fruit may serve as a healthy breakfast alternative.

Pancakes: Left-over porridge mixed with flour and baking powder makes excellent pancakes; so do grated potatoes. Fry in a little oil until brown on both sides, then take with fruit, syrup, apple sauce, or yogurt.

Soy: Soymilk makes a good addition to all cooked cereals and can be used in pancakes. Soy pulp (*okara*), the left-over mush after the milk is extracted from the beans, as well as soy flour are great staples to use in breads and pancakes.

Examples

Pancakes

1 ½ c flour, 1 t salt, 2 T sugar, 1 ¾ t baking powder
    – sift and mix
1 egg, 3 T melted butter, 1 c soy milk
    – add, beat into a batter, fry in pan or on griddle

Cornbread

1 ¼ c flour, ¾ c corn meal, 2 T sugar, 1 T baking powder
    – mix
1 c soy milk, ½ c yogurt, ¼ c oil, 1 egg
    – add to liquids, mix well, put in pan, bake 25 mins. @ 400° F

Scones

1 ¼ c flour, 1 T baking powder, ½ t salt, 1/3 c butter, 2 eggs, ¼ c soy milk
    – mix, add raisins to taste, bake 15 min @ 450°

Apple/Pear Compote

3 apples/pears (peeled, cubed), ½ c raisins, 1 cinnamon stick
    – place in 2c water, boil, then simmer for 10 mins.

2. Appetizers

Description

Appetizers are small items of finger food to be nibbled before a meal or as a snack. Alternatively, if one likes them very much, they may be combined into an entire meal on their own. The Chinese term for appetizers is *dianxin* 點心, which is the Mandarin pronunciation of the famous Dim Sum, which does just that: make a whole meal of appetizers. Most are filled rolls (*baozi*), dumplings, or wontons, i.e., vegetables and tofu wrapped in dough skin that are steamed, boiled, or fried. But there are also pancake-type dishes and various raw food alternatives. Typically grain-based items are warming and support the middle, while raw and cold dishes (such as tofu and avocados) have cooling and moisturizing properties that aid liver and lungs in addition to spleen.

Ingredients

Vegetables: Avocado, cabbage, carrots, leafy greens, potatoes, snow peas, spinach, sweet potatoes.

Tofu: Fresh and firm.

Noodles: Thin, glassy rice or otherwise soft and fine.

Spices: Coriander, mint, peanuts.

Skins: Buy frozen in an Asian supermarket—round thin skins for *jiaozi* or *gyoza*; square thick wrappers for wantons; square white and thin "rice paper" wrappers for spring rolls; thick white *mantou* pads for *baozi*.

Preparation

All ingredients need to be chopped fine or grated before wrapping in skin. Noodles need to be cooked; some vegetables need to be blanched or pre-cooked. Finished dumplings can be frozen for extended periods.

Variations

Fresh vegetables and/or tofu can make an excellent and refreshing snack.

Examples

Steamed Buns (*mantou*)
1 ½ c warm water, 1 T yeast, 1 T sugar
    – place in small bowl, sprinkle yeast & sugar, let sit 15 mins.
4 c flour
    – place in big bowl, add water mix gradually, stir into dough, knead well, put covered in warm place, let sit 1 hr. or until doubled; knead some more, cover again, let sit 20 mins.
    – A. shape into rolls, bring water to boil in steamer, place rolls on steam tray, leaving 1 inch gap; steam for 10 mins.
    – B. shape into flat sheets, cut into squares, roll up into buns around a filling of red or white bean paste, ground sesame, almond paste, or various vegetables (chopped fine), then steam for 10 mins.

Jiaozi
1 lb tofu, 1 lb cabbage – chop fine
3 T sesame oil, 2 T soy sauce, 1 T grated ginger, salt & pepper
    – add, mash, and mix, then wrap in skins, boil or fry

Vegetable Fritters
2 potatoes, 1 carrot, 2 zucchini, 1 sweet potato
    – grate, remove moisture
2 eggs, 2 T flour, 1 T oil
    – add, mix well, fry on both sides in a bit of oil

Fresh Spring Rolls
1 c grated carrot, 3 oz snow peas
    —mix in lg bowl
1 c rice vermicelli,
    —boil ½ min, drain
2 T coriander, 2 T mint , ¼ c peanuts
    – fresh, chop and add
12 rice paper wrappers
    – dip in water, soften; put 2 T of mix per 1 wrapper, wrap and roll
<u>Sauce</u>
1 T sugar, ¼ c warm water – mix and dissolve
2 T fish sauce, ¼ c lime juice, 1 small chili, 1 T coriander – add and stir

Avocado Sashimi
1 medium-sized avocado
    – peel and cut into thin strips
1 t soy sauce with a pinch of *wasabi* (horseradish paste)
    – dip and eat

Chilled Tofu
1 cake fresh tofu, firm or soft
    – drain, cut gently into cubes, and place in serving dish
1 T ginger, *daikon*, *shiso* leaves, *nori* seaweed, sesame seeds, *mejiso* sprouts, mint leaves, *kinome* leaves
    – select one or several, grate or chop fine, place on top
1 T soy sauce, ½ t sesame oil
    – sprinkle on top, serve cold

Tofu-Avocado Paste
6 oz tofu, 1 avocado, 1 T lemon juice, salt & pepper
    – mash tofu and avocado, add spice, serve with crackers

Zucchini Roll-ups
3 small zucchini
    – slice lengthwise into thin strips, lightly fry in 1 T oil until soft
1 c tofu (or soft cheese), chopped parsley, salt & pepper
    – mash into paste
2 c spinach, ½ c basil
    – place with paste on zucchini, roll up, and serve

Eggplant and Miso
2 eggplants, 2 T oil
    – peel, cut into long strips, lightly brown in oil
1 T miso (any type), 1 t sesame oil, 1 t soy sauce, ½ t sugar
    – mix and spread over eggplant slices, grill for 3 mins.

Miso-Sesame Paste
5 T sesame paste, 2 T miso, 1 pickled dill (chopped fine), fresh herbs
    – mix together, serve with crackers

3. Salads

Description

Salads are cold vegetables, either raw or steamed or pickled, served with fresh seasonings or dressings and in some cases with some form of grain, such as rice noodles. Chinese traditional salads would be made up mostly of blanched, cooked, and otherwise warming foods, but Westerners also use many raw materials, often on a base of leafy greens. Like appetizers and soups, salads can be both sides or main courses. They have cooling and moisturizing properties and are particularly good in the summer and to support yin *qi*. However, care should be taken not to overdo cooling or raw ingredients.

Ingredients

Vegetables: Leafy, fresh greens, supplemented with other raw vegetables plus various lightly cooked and/or pickled ones.

Also: Soft, light grains, such as couscous, rice noodles, pasta; cheeses in small amounts; tofu, especially deep fried or grilled; nuts in all forms; some fruit (grapes, pineapple).

Preparation

Vegetables: Cut fine and put together in bowl.

Dressing: Olive oil plus vinegar (rice, balsamic, apple cider) or lemon juice plus salt and pepper form a basic dressing; variations include additions of fruits or cheeses (raspberries, blue cheese) as well as condiments (mustard, sesame, tahini).

Examples

Cucumber and Tomato Salad
2 cucumbers, 1 tomato
    – slice and place in bowl
3 T rice vinegar, 2 T water, 1 T sugar
    – mix to dissolve sugar, then pour over vegetables

Noodle Salad
2 c thin noodles (rice or glass)
- boil, rinse, cool, and place in bowl
1 cucumber, 1 fried egg, ½ c seaweed
- cut fine and add
1 t sesame oil, 1 t sugar, 3 T soy sauce, 1 T vinegar, pinch hot mustard
- mix, add to noodles and vegetables, stir well

Grain Salad
2 c vegetable stock, 1 c grain (couscous, bulgur)
- bring to boil, simmer for 3 mins., turn off and let sit—do not stir
3 tomatoes, 1 cucumber, 1 red pepper
- cut and dice, add to grain
1 bunch parsley, some mint, 1 T lemon juice, 1 T olive oil, salt & pepper
- cut, mix, and add, garnish with black olives

Zucchini and Mushroom Salad
1 lb. zucchini, 1 red pepper
- cut into thin slices or strips, lightly fry in 3 T oil
¾ lb mixed mushrooms
- soak if dried, then cut into thin strips, fry separately
2 T apple cider vinegar, 3 T balsamic vinegar, salt & pepper
- mix and pour over cooled vegetables, garnish with parsley

Seaweed Salad
½ c seaweed (*wakame* or *hijiki*), 1 T oil, ½ c vegetable broth
- soak to softness (15 mins), drain, fry in oil, add broth to simmer
1 carrot
- grate, add to seaweed for 10 mins.
1 T sugar, 2 T soy sauce
- mix and add to vegetables, garnish with sesame

Cabbage Salad
3 c napa cabbage, 1 c red cabbage, 1 carrot, 4 oz water chestnuts
- shred or grate into thin strips
2 tangerines (or 1 orange) – peel and cut, add to cabbage mix
¼ c rice vinegar, 3 T soy sauce, 1 t oil, 1 T brown sugar, 1 t chili sauce, 1 t sesame oil, 1 t minced ginger
- mix and pour over salad, garnish with toasted almonds

4. Soups

Description

Soups are vegetables, mushrooms, and tofu steamed to softness and immersed in flavored stock. Like appetizers and salads, soups can be both a side dish or make up a meal. Eaten mostly warm and often including root vegetables and spices, they tend to have warming qualities, support the yang aspect of the organs, and are good in winter. Some, like miso, are predominantly salty and support the kidneys, also helping to eliminate toxins from the body. Then, again, there are certain types, such as gazpacho, which are eaten cold and serve to cool the system and support yin. They tend to be favorites in the warmer months.

Ingredients

Stock: Stock can be made from boiling vegetables with various kinds of seasonings (see below) or simply be adding soybean paste to the soup after boiling. The latter is most commonly available as miso, which originated in China but was uniquely developed in Japan. It is made by fermenting soybeans for several years in cedar kegs with a grain, such as rice, barley, or buckwheat (Mitchell 1998, xxxix). Miso comes in various different colors and intensities, from very gentle white miso through the most widespread brown variety, to the rather intense red or dark paste.

Vegetables: Root vegetables, such as carrots, parsnips, potatoes, radishes, rutabaga, sweet potatoes, turnips, and yams; leafy plants, including cabbage, celery, *qingcai*, spinach.

Beans: Red (*adzuki*), white, and black beans; kidney beans; lentils in various forms and colors—all soaked overnight before use).

Tofu: Of all types—fresh, dried, skin, marinated, deep fried (*age*), burgers, etc..

Also: Various kinds of mushrooms such as the standard white mushroom, the stringy *hinoki*, the round dark *shiitake*, the chewy *mu'er* – some found fresh, others better in dried form.

Multiple forms of seaweed, including the thick and salty *kombu*, which is great for stocks and should be cut fine; the slippery, light-green *wakame* which is also good in salads; and the small smoky-flavored *hijiki* – all available in dried form and growing to unexpected proportions when soaked in water.

Preparation

Vegetables: Peel, cut, and soak root vegetables—allow around 15 mins. for steaming; leafy greens and softer vegetables as well as mushrooms and soft seaweed (not *kombu*)—add later and cook only briefly.

Also: Beans and dried goods (mushrooms, seaweed) —soak for several hours and cook slowly and patiently, until very well done.

Examples

Vegetable Stock

4 lg carrots, 2 lg parsnips (unpeeled)
    —chop and bake in oil (400°) for 30 mins
add 5 celery sticks, 2 bay leaves, 1 t peppercorns, ¾ gal water
    – put all together in large pot, boil, and simmer for 1 hr, then strain

Vegetable Soup

2 lg potatoes, 2 carrots, 1 small celery, 2 ripe tomatoes, 3 T mushrooms
    – peel, cut into cubes, boil in 2 c water, then simmer with 1 t cumin,
2 t soy sauce, juice of ½ lemon, ½ t lemon zest, 1 t sugar, 1 c grape wine
    – simmer until vegetables are soft, thicken with corn starch

Tofu-Cucumber Soup

1 T ginger (minced)
    – fry in 1 T oil for 1 min.
4 medium dried *shiitake* (soaked and softened – keep soaking liquid), 2 ½ oz bamboo shoots (cubed), ½ cucumber (sliced),
    – add and stir fry for 2 mins.
4 c vegetable stock, *shiitake* soaking liquid,
    – add, bring to boil, skim off froth
12 oz tofu, salt & pepper,
    – add and thicken with 1 t cornstarch (dissolved in water)
2 t rice vinegar, ½ t sesame oil
    – add and stir

Miso Soup

½ c mushrooms (any kind), ½ c tofu (fresh), 1 T seaweed (*kombu* or *wakame*, soaked and cut)

    – boil in 1 pint water until soft

1 T miso paste (any kind)

    – add after water has stopped boiling by putting through a strainer

Squash Soup

1 2-pound butternut squash (peeled, seeded, and cut into 1-inch cubes)

    – fry in 1 T oil until softened (5 mins.)

6 c vegetable broth, 2 T curry powder

    – add and boil, then simmer until tender

2 T honey

    – add and put in blender, puree, taste with salt, garnish with yogurt

Tofu-Seaweed Soup

6 oz soft tofu, 1 ¾ oz dried *wakame*, 3 ¼ c vegetable stock, 2 t soy sauce

    – heat in saucepan, bring to boil, simmer for 1 min.

Carrot and Orange Soup

1 lb carrots

    – peel and slice, then fry in 1 T butter until soft

½ c orange juice, 4 c veg. stock, 3 t thyme, salt & pepper

    – simmer for 20 mins, garnish with sour cream and bit of nutmeg

Gazpacho

3 tomatoes, ½ cucumber, ½ green pepper, ½ red pepper

    – chop fine

3.5 c tomato juice, ½ t sugar, salt & pepper, ¼ c olive oil, 1 t vinegar

    – mix, stir well, and serve

5. Stews and Noodle Soups

Description

Stews or noodle soups are different from soups since they contain a large amount of grains; they are different from main dishes, commonly steamed or stir-fried, in that they are served in soup or stock. Stews and noodle soups are easy to make and ready to serve, commonly found in homes, restaurants, and street stalls all over Asia. Warming in quality and supporting the middle with their heavy emphasis on grain, they make excellent lunches and are also a favorite for breakfast.

Ingredients

Grains/noodles: The main grains used in stews or are rice, barley, and millet—mainstays in ancient China. Noodles come in many different forms. Classics include: *udon, soba,* and *ramen* in Japan; *pho* and *bun* in Vietnam; *mian* in China. Besides in soup, noodles may also be served with a dipping sauce, such as for example Japanese cold buckwheat noodles (*zaru-soba*), or Vietnamese rice noodles (*buncha*).

Vegetables: Stews tend to favor root vegetables, such as carrots, turnips, and potatoes; noodle soups usually have leafy greens, such as *qingcai,* bok choy, and spinach as well as lighter vegetables such as bean sprouts, water chestnuts, and bamboo; plus various kinds of mushrooms, seaweed, and tofu.

Preparation

Grains/noodles: They come in many kinds with different cooking times ranging from 2 to 20 mins., in each case specified on the package.

Broth/sauce: Commonly consists of vegetable stock, soy sauce, and cooking wine (*mirin* or sherry), plus maybe sugar and vinegar.

Topping: Vegetables, mushrooms, and tofu are steamed or fried separately, then added and, in the case of stews, simmered together for a period. Combinations are endless and all very tasty.

Examples

Home-made Noodles
1 egg, 5 T water, 2 c flour
    – beat egg with water, add mixture to flour, stir and knead for 5
    mins., then cover with damp cloth and let sit for ½ hr in a dry place
1 c corn starch, placed in clean cloth, tied at the top
    – roll dough out and flour with cornstarch on both sides, then cut
into thin strips, boil in water

Bamboo Noodles
½ lb egg noodles
    – cook as specified or (if home made) for 3-5 mins.
½ c crumbled tofu burger, 1 t sherry, 1 t corn starch
    – mix, fry for 1 min
½ c bamboo shoots, ½ c dried black mushroom (soaked), 2 C napa
    – cut fine, add to stir-fry and cook until soft
6 c vegetable stock, salt & pepper
    – add and bring to boil, then add noodles, boil once more briefly

Bean Stew
1 c each: red, white, and black beans
    – soak overnight, then boil and cook 2-3 hours
1 c each: green, yellow, and brown lentils; ½ c each: cornmeal, millet, lemon peel; 2 T brown sugar, 3 T soy sauce
    – add and boil together for 1 hour

Seaweed Udon
1 package udon
    – prepare as prescribed on package (if precooked, just put in water
and heat gently)
1 T seaweed (soaked), 2 shiitake mushrooms (soaked), 1c fresh or deep-fried tofu (cubed); 2 T soy sauce
    – add to noodles, including soak water, boil briefly

6. Main Dishes

Description

Main dishes in the Daoist world tend to be stir-fried or steamed vegetables, tofu, or mushrooms (each of which have a separate volume in the Wudang Daoists' collection), seasoned variably and served with rice, noodles, bread, or steamed bread (*mantou*). In addition, Western vegetarians also favor tempeh, an Indonesian form of fermented soybeans. The grain base of the main dishes again is sweet in flavor and warming in energy, supporting the middle. Beyond that, the quality of specific dishes depends largely on individual vegetables used, although cooking in either form tends to alter them in favor of warming. More salty dishes enhance the kidneys; more spicy dishes support the lungs; more sour flavors work for the liver; while bitter flavors aid the heart.

Ingredients

Rice: The Chinese today, including also Daoists in temples, still use dominantly white rice. The Japanese have graduated to a mixed form, either cooking parts of white and brown rice (and also beans) together or having their rice partially polished in specialized rice shops. Westerners tend to be in favor of brown rice, which contains all the nutrients and is more tasty in itself. In addition, there are black rice and various forms of wild rice in creative combinations, easily found in health food stores. Plus the sticky rice favored for desserts and the rice cakes (*mochi*) eaten at special occasions.

Noodles: Noodles come in many forms: *udon*, *soba*, and *ramen* in Japan; *pho* and *bun* in Vietnam; *mian* in China, as well as the numerous kinds of pasta. Some take longer to cook than others, some are longer and thicker than others, some are better for certain dishes than others. There is endless choice and limitless delight.

Vegetables: Avocado, bamboo, bean sprouts, bok choy, broccoli, cabbage, carrots, cauliflower, celery, cucumber, eggplant, endives, kohlrabi, lettuce, lotus root, mountain vegetables, *qingcai*, spinach, sweet potato, tomato, yams.

Also: Tofu of all types—fresh, dried, skin, marinated, deep fried (*age*), burgers, and so on; mushrooms in their great variety; seaweeds and nuts.

Preparation

Grains/Noodles: Cook as specified on the package.

Vegetables: Cut and stir-fry or steam.

Variations

Bread: Daoists in certain parts of China serve a flat bread not unlike pita with their meals. Fresh from the oven and very tasty, it offers welcome respite for Western guests who are craving something non-Chinese for a change. Breads can be purchased easily or made from scratch, either in a baking pan or with the help of a bread maker. If making them, make sure to use seeds, such as sesame, flaxseeds, wheat germ, and the like for added taste and nutritional value.

Steamed Buns (*mantou*): Steamed buns, besides being used as a staple with main dishes, also make a great appetizer. They are found frozen in Asian food stores or can be made from scratch. See the recipe under "Appetizers" above.

Tempeh: Tempeh is one of the most nutritious soy foods. Developed in Indonesia and now available world-wide, it is made from whole soybeans that are cooked and fermented, then mixed with rice, millet, or barley and formed into a cake, each with a slightly different flavor, but generally somewhat smoky or nutty (Mitchell 1998, xxxiii). It is highly versatile. Cut into strips or cubes, it can be sautéed, baked, grilled, or braised as well as marinated and used in salads.

Examples

Bean Sprouts and Tofu
1 package firm tofu – brown in 2 T oil
1 lb bean sprouts
     – add to stir fry for 2 mins.
1 t sugar, 2 T soy sauce, 1 c water
     – mix and add to vegetables, simmer for 6-8 mins
1 t sesame oil – add to garnish

Sweet and Sour Noodles

200 g (6 ½ oz) thin noodles
– boil and drain
4 fresh baby corn, 1 green pepper, 1 red pepper, 2 celery sticks, 1 carrot,
250 g (8 oz) mushrooms
– cut and fry in ¼ c oil, add noodles, simmer for 2 mins
2 t corn flour, 2 T vinegar
– blend until smooth
1 T tomato paste, 1 c vegetable stock, 1 t sesame oil, 2 c cubed pineapple
– add and stir, then pour over stir fry

Tofu, Celery, and Carrots

1 large carrot, 1 stalk celery, 2 T oil, ½ t ginger
– cut and cube, fry in oil with ginger for 3 mins.
1 package firm tofu, 1 c mushrooms (of any kind)
– cube and add to vegetables, simmer for 3 mins.
mushroom soaking water, 2 T soy sauce, 1 t corn starch
—mix together, add to dish, mix, simmer to thicken

Celery and Walnuts

2 c chopped celery
– fry in 2 T oil
½ c walnuts (lightly roasted), 1 T soy sauce, salt & pepper
– add, stir, and serve

Spinach and Sesame

2 c spinach, cleaned, cut
– steam for 2 mins.
1 t sesame, 1 t soy sauce
– place over spinach, serve

Winter Squash

1 lb winter squash, 2 T oil
– peel, remove seeds, cut into thick slices, fry in oil for 2 mins.
½ can bamboo shoots (sliced), ½ t sugar, 1 c bamboo water
– add, boil, simmer for 3 mins.
2 T soy sauce, 1 t cornstarch, ½ c water
– mix, add, simmer until thickens, garnish with *gouji* berries

Five Phases Vegetables

2 c each: spinach, carrots, *daikon*, mushrooms, bean sprouts
    – cut and cook lightly with bits of soy sauce, sesame, or salt
    – place into four corners & center of plate, separate with cucumber

Coconut Curry Sauce

3 T peanut butter, 1 T hoisin sauce, 1/3 c coconut milk, 2 T lime juice, 1 T sweet chili sauce
    – blend until smooth, serve over stir-fried vegetables

Family-Style Tofu

2 c deep-fried or firm tofu, 1 carrot (julienned), 1 T ginger (grated)
    – cook in oil separately, each taking turns, then mix together
1 green pepper, 1 c water chestnuts, 1 c bamboo shoots, 1 c mushrooms (soaked)
    – cut into bite-size bits, heat, simmer for 2 mins.
½ c mushroom water, 2 T soy sauce, 1 t cornstarch
    – mix and add, boil to thicken, garnish with cilantro

Pineapple Fried Rice

3 c cooked rice, 2 T oil
    – fry rice in pan
½ c diced pineapple, 1 c diced red pepper, various left-over cooked vegetables (cut fine)
    – add to rice and fry for 3-4 mins.
1 T soy sauce, salt & pepper
    – add to taste, serve in pineapple half if available

Beijing-sauce Noodles

1 lb thin spaghetti or egg noodles
    – cooked as the package prescribes
1 c crumbled tofu burger, 1 t cooking wine, 1 c brown or red miso, ½ c water, 1 T hoisin sauce, 2 T soy sauce
    – fry in 1 T oil, beginning with tofu, then simmer in water 2 mins.
½ *daikon*, ½ cucumber (peeled), 1 c bean sprouts, 1 C boiled spinach
    – shred or cut fine, place on top of noodles and sauce

7. Desserts

Description

Desserts are light and often sweet dishes served at the conclusion of the meal. In China, they are most often simply fruit, notably the ubiquitous water melon which signals the—often direly yearned-for—end of the banquet. Daoists tend to serve compotes, not unlike the steamed pears and apples mentioned above under "Cooked Cereals," which have both a warming and moisturizing effect and are thus ideal at the end of the meal. Westerners in addition like to eat cakes and puddings, which are becoming more widely available all over Asia.

Ingredients

Fruits: Apples, bananas, cherries, chestnuts, coconut, dates, figs, grapes, kiwis, mangoes, oranges, papaya, peaches, pears, pineapple, plums, strawberries

Also: Honey, sugar; puddings, whipped cream; pastry dough.

Preparation

Fruits: Peel and cut, either for stuffing or into bite-size pieces; grate for baking; add sweeteners, spices, crèmes, and puddings.

Examples

Stuffed Pears or Apples
4 pears/apples
    – peel, cut off top to make lid, remove seeds
1 T honey, 1 T crystal sugar, 1 T sticky rice (soaked overnight) + 2 T ginseng powder OR 1 T chopped almonds
    – mix and place inside pears, cover with lid, steam 45 mins

Chocolate Chip Cookies

1 c peanut butter, 1 c brown sugar, 1 egg, 1 tsp. baking soda, chocolate chips
  – mix, spread on cookie sheet, bake 8-10 minutes at 350°.

Fruit Salad with Almond Paste

1 each: banana, apple, pear, orange, plus some grapes
  – peel and chop, place in bowl
2 T almond butter, ½ t vanilla powder, 1 t cinnamon, little honey, water
  – mix together into smooth crème, spread over fruit

Apple Crisp

¼ c oat flakes, ¼ c sugar, ¼ c flour, ½ t cinnamon
  – combine, add ¼ c soft butter and crumble
6 c apples, 1 c cranberries, 1 c blueberries, 1 T flour
  – cut into cubes mix in baking pan, cover with crumble
  – bake for 55 mins. @ 350°F

Carrot Cake

2 c flour, 1 c sugar, 1 T baking powder
  – stir in bowl
4 eggs, 3 c grated carrots, ¾ c oil, ¾ dried fruit, 1 T grated ginger
  – mix in other bowl, then add to dry ingredients
  –bake for 35 mins @ 350°F, add frosting of cream cheese & nuts

Coconut Pudding

9 c fresh grated coconut, 3 c (coconut) water
  – mix, bring to boil, let sit for 15 mins., squeeze to gain 4 ½ c liquid
½ c cornstarch, ¼ c sugar
  – mix into liquid to make smooth paste, keep stirring until thickens, pour into 8-inch pan and cool, cut into squares

8. Herbal Drinks

Description

Herbal drinks or tisanes are concoctions of various flowers, fruits, grains, and vegetables boiled in water singly or in combinations to create a tasty, refreshing, and medicinal drink that can be taken at all times during day or night. Daoists are very fond of tea in all its forms (white, green, black) and also enjoy it flavored with various herbs and flowers. In addition, they also favor drinks made from a variety of plants like chrysanthemums, licorice, ginger, ginseng, radish, barley, and soybeans. Easy to make and quite tasty, these drinks are an efficient way of balancing the humors, help with various conditions, and can be matched successfully with all sorts of food combinations.

Ingredients

Grains/Beans: Barley, peas, soybeans, wheat.

Also: Carrots, chrysanthemum, dandelion, dates, figs, ginger, litchis, dragon fruit, radish, tomatoes, tangerine peel, water melon.

Preparation

Cooked: Soak grains and beans before cooking to reduce preparation time, then mix with various ingredients, boil in water, simmer for about 20 mins., then strain and drink.

Raw: Squeeze juice from fruit or vegetable, combine in cup, and thin with water if needed.

Examples

Ginger-Barley Mix (slightly cooling; good for kidney, bladder blockages)
1 cherry-sized piece of ginger (peeled, cut in large slices), ½ c barley
  – boil in water for 40 mins., strain, sweeten with honey

Ginger- Tangerine Mix (settles the stomach)
1 t fresh ginger (peeled and cut in thin slices), 1 t dried tangerine peel

– boil in 1 quart of water, then simmer for 30 mins., and strain, add honey to taste

Coriander-Pea Decoct (stabilizes the stomach, reduces dampness)
½ c dried, green peas (soaked for 2-3 hours), 1 bunch fresh coriander (leaf and root)
– boil in 1.5 c water, simmer for 1 hour, then puree in blender, strain juice, add some vegetable stock to taste

Wheat & Date Drink (sweet and calming, good for heart, spleen)
3 T rough ground whole wheat, 10 Chinese dates, 1T dragon fruit (chopped)
– boil in 1 quart of water, then simmer for 20 mins., strain

Coriander-Carrot Decoct (cooling, sweet, good for cough, digestion)
2 T (carrots (sliced), 2 T water chestnuts (canned, chopped)
– boil in 1 ¼ c water, simmer for 20-30 mins
2 T coriander greens
– add, let sit for 10 mins, then puree in blender, add vegetable stock/soy sauce or honey for taste

Fig Tea (invigorating & calming, supports the center)
1 T dried figs, chopped and slightly browed (no oil)
– soak in boiling water, add a bit of honey, drink

Ginger Tea (warming, good for colds & upset stomach)
1 T fresh ginger (peeled and cut in thin slices), 1 t brown sugar
– boil in 1 pint of water, strain

Tomato-Watermelon Juice (cools and reduces infections)
Several tomatoes, some slices of water melon
– run through blender and strain or use juicer, add water to taste

Radish Juice (cools and reduces phlegm)
1 small white radish (*daikon*), peeled
—run through juicer

Celery Juice (cool, sinking: reduces blood pressure, headache, agitation)
1 stalk celery, chopped
—run through juicer

Bibliography

Adams, Carol J. 2000. *The Inner Art of Vegetarianism: Spiritual Practice for Body and Soul*. New York: Lantern Books.

Andersen, Poul. 1980. *The Method of Holding the Three Ones*. London and Malmo: Curzon Press.

Anderson, Eugene N. 1988. *The Food of China*. New Haven: Yale University Press.

_____, and Marja L. Anderson. 1977. "Modern China: South." In *Food in Chinese Culture*, edited by K. C. Chang, 317-82. New Haven: Yale University Press.

Arthur, Shawn. 2006a. "Ancient Daoist Diets for Health and Longevity." Ph. D. Diss., Boston University, Boston.

_____. 2006b. "Life Without Grains: *Bigu* and the Daoist Body." In *Daoist Body Cultivation*, edited by Livia Kohn, 91-122. Magdalena, NM: Three Pines Press.

_____. 2009. "Eating Your Way to Immortality: Early Daoist Self-Cultivation Diets." *Journal of Daoist Studies* 2:32-63.

Asano, Haruji. 2002. "Offerings in Daoist Ritual." In *Daoist Identity: History, Lineage, and Ritual*, edited by Livia Kohn and Harold D. Roth, 274-94. Honolulu: University of Hawaii Press.

Bell, Rudolph. 1985. *Holy Anorexia*. Chicago: University of Chicago Press.

Benn, Charles. 2000. "Daoist Ordination and *Zhai* Rituals." In *Daoism Handbook*, edited by Livia Kohn, 309-38. Leiden: E. Brill.

Benn, James A. 2005. "Buddhism, Alcohol, and Tea in Medieval China." In *Of Tripod and Palate: Food, Politics and Religion in Traditional China*, edited by Roel Sterckx, 213-36. New York: Palgrave MacMillan.

Bensky, Dan, and Andrew Gamble. 1993. *Chinese Herbal Medicine: Materia Medica* Seattle: Eastland Press.

Blofeld, John. 1985. *The Chinese Art of Tea*. Boston: Shambhala.

Bokenkamp, Stephen R. 1997. *Early Daoist Scriptures*. With a contribution by Peter Nickerson. Berkeley: University of California Press.

_____. 2007. *Ancestors and Anxiety: Daoism and the Birth of Rebirth in China*. Berkeley: University of California Press.

Brownlie, Ali. 2002. *Why Are People Vegetarian?* New York: Raintreee Steck-Vaughn Publishers.

Brumberg, Joan Jacobs. 1988. *Fasting Girls: The Emergence of Anorexia Nervosa as a Modern Disease.* Cambridge, Mass.: Harvard University Press.

Buell, Paul, and Eugene N. Anderson. 2000. *A Soup for the Qan.* London: Kegan Paul International.

Butt, Gary, and Frena Bloomfield. 1987. *Harmony Rules: The Chinese Way of Health Through Food.* York Beach.: Samuel Weiser.

Bynum, Caroline Walker. 1987. *Holy Feast and Holy Fast: The Religious Significance of Food to Medieval Women.* Berkeley: University of California Press.

Callahan, Maggie, and Patricia Kelly. 1992. *Final Gifts: Understanding the Special Awareness, Needs, and Communications of the Dying.* New York: Bantam.

Campany, Robert F. 2002. *To Live As Long As Heaven and Earth: A Translation and Study of Ge Hong's Traditions of Divine Transcendents.* Berkeley: University of California Press.

_____. 2005. "Eating Better Than Gods and Ancestors." In *Of Tripod and Palate: Food, Politics and Religion in Traditional China,* edited by Roel Sterckx, 96-122. New York: Palgrave MacMillan.

_____. 2009. *Making Transcendence: Ascetics and Social Memory in Early Medieval China.* Honolulu: University of Hawai'i Press.

Ch'en, Kenneth. 1973. *The Chinese Transformation of Buddhism.* Princeton, Princeton University Press.

Chan, Alan K. L. 1991. *Two Visions of the Way: A Study of the Wang Pi and the Ho-shang-kung Commentaries on the Laozi.* Albany: State University of New York Press.

Chan, Cecilia Lai Wan, and Amy Yin Man Chow, eds. 2006. *Death, Dying and Bereavement: A Hong Kong Chinese Experience.* Hong Kong: Hong Kong University Press.

Chang, K. C., ed. 1977a. *Food in Chinese Culture.* New Haven: Yale University Press.

_____. 1977b. "Ancient China." In *Food in Chinese Culture,* edited by K. C. Chang, 23-52. New Haven: Yale University Press.

Chang, Stephen. 1987. *The Tao of Balanced Diet: Secrets of a Thin and Healthy Body.* San Francisco: Tao Publishing.

Chard, Robert L. 1995. "Rituals and Scriptures of the Stove Cult." In *Ritual and Scripture in Chinese Popular Religion*, edited by David Johnson, 3-54. Berkeley: Chinese Popular Culture Project.

Chavannes, Edouard. 1919. "Le jet des dragons." *Memoires concernant l'Asie Orientale* 1919, 55-214.

Chen, Junshi, and C. Campbell. 1990. *Diet, Life-style and Mortality in China*. New York: Oxford University Press.

Chia, Mantak, and Maneewan Chia. 1993. *Awaken Healing Light of the Tao*. Huntington, NY: Healing Tao Books.

Cohen, Kenneth S. 1997. *The Way of Qigong: The Art and Science of Chinese Energy Healing*. New York: Ballantine.

Cook, Constance A. 2005. "Moonshine and Millet: Feasting and Purification Rituals in Ancient China." In *Of Tripod and Palate: Food, Politics and Religion in Traditional China*, edited by Roel Sterckx, 9-33. New York: Palgrave.

Counihan, Carole M. 1999. *The Anthropology of Food and Body*. New York: Routledge.

_____, and Penny Van Esterik, eds. 1997. *Food and Culture: A Reader*. New York: Routledge.

Craze, Richard, and Roni Jay. 2001. *Cooking for Long Life: The Tao of Food*. New York: Sterling Publishing.

Darby, William J., Paul Ghalioungui, and Louis Grivetti. 1977. *Food: The Gift of Osiris*. New York: Academic Press.

Dean, Kenneth. 2000. "Daoist Ritual Today." In *Daoism Handbook*, edited by Livia Kohn, 659-82. Leiden: E. Brill.

DeGroot, J. J. M. 1969 [1893]. *Le Côde du Mahāyāna en Chine: Son influence sur la vie monacale et sur le monde laïque*. Wiesbaden: Dr. Martin Sändig.

Despeux, Catherine. 1987. *Préscriptions d'acuponcture valant mille onces d'or*. Paris: Guy Trédaniel.

_____. 2006. "The Six Healing Breaths." In *Daoist Body Cultivation*, edited by Livia Kohn, 37-67. Magdalena, NM: Three Pines Press.

_____. 2007. "Food Prohibitions in China." *The Lantern* 4.1:22-32.

DeWoskin, Kenneth J. 1983. *Doctors, Diviners, and Magicians of Ancient China*. New York: Columbia University Press.

Dombrowski, Daniel A. 1984. *The Philosophy of Vegetarianism*. Amherst: University of Massachusetts Press.

Douglas, Mary. 1973. *Natural Symbols*. New York: Vintage Books.

Dumoulin, Heinrich. 1988. *Zen Buddhism: A History*. Vol 2. New York: Macmillan.

Eberhard, Wolfram. 1940. "Die chinesische Küche." *Sinica* 15:190-228.

Elias, Jason, and Katherine Ketcham. 1998. *The Five Elements of Self-Healing: Using Chinese Medicine for Maximum Immunity, Wellness, and Health*. New York: Harmony Books.

Engelhardt, Ute. 1998. "The Development of the *Yaoshan* (Refined Medical Cuisine) and Its Restaurants." In *Diwuci Zhongguo yinshi wenhua xueshu yantaohui lunwen ji*, edited by Zhang Yuxin et al., 71-89. Taipei: Foundation of Dietary Culture.

_____. 2000. "Longevity Techniques and Chinese Medicine." In *Daoism Handbook*, edited by Livia Kohn, 74-108. Leiden: E. Brill.

_____. 2001. "Dietetics in Tang China and the First Extant Works of *Materia Medica*." In *Innovation in Chinese Medicine*, edited by Elisabeth Hsu, 173-90. Cambridge: Cambridge University Press.

_____, and Carl-Hermann Hempen. 1997. *Chinesische Diätetik*. Munich: Urban & Schwarzenberg.

_____, and Rainer Nögel. 2009. *Rezepte der chinesischen Diätetik*. Munich: Urban & Fischer.

Eskildsen, Stephen. 1998. *Asceticism in Early Taoist Religion*. Albany: State University of New York Press.

Eyssalet, J. M. et al. 1984. *Diététique energétique et médecine chinoise*. 2 vols. Sisteron: Henri Viaud.

Fang, Chunyang. 2000. "Die Anwendung von Rettich in der chinesischen Diätetik." *Chinesische Medizin* 4/2000: 142-44.

Farquhar, Judith. 1994. "Eating Chinese Medicine." *Cultural Anthropology* 9.4:471-97.

_____. 2002. *Appetites: Food and Sex in Post-socialist China*. Durham, NC: Duke University Press.

Forke, Alfred. 1972. *Lun-Heng: Wang Ch'ung's Essays*. 2 vols. New York: Paragon.

Fox, Michael Allen. 1999. *Deep Vegetarianism: America in Transition*. Philadelphia: Temple University Press.

Freeman, Michael. 1977. "Sung." In *Food in Chinese Culture*, edited by K. C. Chang, 141-76. New Haven: Yale University Press.

Fulder, Stephen. 1993. *The Book of Ginseng and Other Chinese Herbs for Vitality*. Rochester, VT: Healing Arts Press.

Furth, Charlotte. 1999. *A Flourishing Yin: Gender in China's Medical History, 960-1665*. Berkeley: University of California Press.

Gennep, Arnold van. 1960 [1909]. *The Rites of Passage*. Chicago: University of Chicago Press.

Goffman, Erving. 1961. *Asylums: Essays on the Social Situations of Mental Patients and Other Inmates*. Garden City, NY: Anchor Books.

Goossaert, Vincent. 2005. "The Beef Taboo and the Sacrificial Structure of Late Imperial Chinese Society." In *Of Tripod and Palate: Food, Politics and Religion in Traditional China*, edited by Roel Sterckx, 237-48. New York: Palgrave MacMillan.

_____. 2009. *Le tabou du boeuf en Chine: Agriculture, éthique et sacrifice*. Paris: Collège de France.

Groner, Paul. 1990. "The *Fan-wang ching* and Monastic Discipline in Japanese Tendai: A Study of Annen's *Futsu jubosatsukai koshaku*." In *Chinese Buddhist Apocrypha*, edited by Robert E. Buswell, Jr., 251-90. Honolulu: University of Hawaii Press.

Hackmann, Heinrich. 1920. "Die Mönchsregeln des Klostertaoismus." *Ostasiatische Zeitschrift* 8: 141-70.

_____. 1931. *Die dreihundert Mönchsgebote des chinesischen Taoismus*. Amsterdam: Koninklijke Akademie van Wetenshapen.

Halpern, Georges. 1996. *Gingko: A Practical Guide*. New York: Avery Publishing Group.

Harper, Donald. 1984. "Gastronomy in Ancient China." *Parabola* 14:39-47.

_____. 1998. *Early Chinese Medical Manuscripts: The Mawangdui Medical Manuscripts*. London: Wellcome Asian Medical Monographs.

Hawkes, David. 1959. *Ch'u Tz'u: The Songs of the South*. Oxford: Clarendon Press.

Hendrischke, Barbara. 2006. *The Scripture on Great Peace: The Taiping jing and the Beginnings of Daoism*. Berkeley: University of California Press.

_____, and Benjamin Penny. 1996. "*The 180 Precepts Spoken by Lord Lao*: A Translation and Textual Study." *Taoist Resources* 6.2:17-29.

Henricks, Robert. 1983. *Philosophy and Argumentation in Third Century China: The Essays of Hsi K'ang*. Princeton: Princeton University Press.

Holmes, Peter. 1989. *The Energetics of Western Herbs: Treatment Strategies Integrating Western and Oriental Herbal Medicine*. 2 vols. Boulder: Snow Lion Press.

Horner, I. B. 1967. *The Collection of the Middle Length Sayings*. 3 vols. London: Routledge and Kegan Paul.

Hsia, Emil C. H., Ilza Veith, and Robert H. Geertsma, trans. 1986. *The Essentials of Medicine in Ancient China and Japan: Yasuyori Tamba's Ishimpô*. 2 vols. Leiden: E. Brill.

Hsu, Vera Y. N., and Francis L. K. Hsu. 1977. "Modern China: North." In *Food in Chinese Culture*, edited by K. C. Chang, 295-317. New Haven: Yale University Press.

Huang, Hsing-Tsung. 2000. *Fermentation and Food Science*. In *Science and Civilisation in China*, vol. VI, part 5. Cambridge: Cambridge University Press.

Huang Yongfeng 黃永鋒. 2007. *Daojiao yinshi yangsheng zhiyao* 道教饮食养生指要. Beijing: Zongjiao wenhua chubanshe.

_____黃永鋒. 2008a. *Daojiao yinshi chishu zhexue yanjiu* 道教服食技术哲学研究. Beijing: Dongfang.

_____黃永鋒. 2008b. "Daojiao yinshi qinhe wuwei xiwei" 道教饮食谨和五味析微. *Daoxue yanjiu* 道學研究 2:99-105.

Inglis, Les. 1993. *Diet for a Gentle World: Eating With Conscience*. Garden City, NY: Avery Publications Group.

Ishida Hidemi 石田秀實. 1987. "Sanshi to shichibaku no ronriteki imi" 三尸と七蟲の倫理的意味. *Shakai bunka kenkyūjo kiyō* 社會文化研究所記要 21:73-94.

_____. 1989. "Body and Mind: The Chinese Perspective." In *Taoist Meditation and Longevity Techniques*, edited by Livia Kohn, 41-70. Ann Arbor: University of Michigan, Center for Chinese Studies Publications.

Jackowicz, Stephen. 2006. "Ingestion, Digestion, and Regestation: The Complexities of the Absorption of *Qi*." In *Daoist Body Cultivation*, edited by Livia Kohn, 68-90. Magdalena, NM: Three Pines Press.

Jarrett, Lonny. 2006. "Acupuncture and Spiritual Realization." In *Daoist Body Cultivation*, edited by Livia Kohn, 1-18. Magdalena, NM: Three Pines Press.

Kakuzo, Okakura. 1956: *The Book of Tea*. Boston: Tuttle.

Kanter, Rosabeth Moss. 1972. *Commitment and Community: Communes and Utopias in Sociological Perspective*. Cambridge, Mass.: Harvard University Press.

Kaptchuk, Ted J. 1983. *The Web that Has No Weaver: Understanding Chinese Medicine*. New York: Congdon & Weed.

Kaput, Jim, and Raymond J. Rodriguez, eds. 2006. *Nutrionoal Genomics: Discovering the Path to Personalized Nutrition*. Hoboken, NJ: John Wiley & Sons.

Keightley, David. 2004. "The Making of the Ancestors: Late Shang Religion and Its Legacy." In *Religion and Chinese Society*, edited by John Lagerwey, 1:3-63. Hong Kong: Chinese University of Hong Kong Press.

Kenton, Leslie, and Susannah Kenton. 1984. *Raw Energy*. New York: Warner Books.

Kieschnick, John. 2005. "Buddhist Vegetarianism in China." In *Of Tripod and Palate: Food, Politics and Religion in Traditional China*, edited by Roel Sterckx,186-212. New York: Palgrave MacMillan.

Kleeman, Terry. 1991. "Taoist Ethics." In *A Bibliographic Guide to the Comparative Study of Ethics*, edited by John Carman and Mark Juergensmeyer, 162-94. Cambridge: Cambridge University Press.

_____. 1998. *Great Perfection: Religion and Ethnicity in a Chinese Millenarian Kingdom*. Honolulu: University of Hawaii Press.

_____. 2005. "Feasting Without the Victuals: The Evolution of the Daoist Communal Kitchen." In *Of Tripod and Palate: Food, Politics and Religion in Traditional China*, edited by Roel Sterckx, 140-62. New York: Palgrave MacMillan.

Kleinman, Arthur. 1980. *Patients and Healers in the Context of Culture*. Berkeley: University of California Press.

Knoblock, John, and Jeffrey Riegel. 2000. *The Annals of Lü Buwei*. Stanford: Stanford University Press.

Kohn, Livia, ed. 1989. *Taoist Meditation and Longevity Techniques*. Ann Arbor: University of Michigan, Center for Chinese Studies Publications.

_____. 1991. "Taoist Visions of the Body." *Journal of Chinese Philosophy* 18: 227-52.

_____. 1994. "The Five Precepts of the Venerable Lord." *Monumenta Serica* 42: 171-215.

_____. 1995. "Kōshin: A Taoist Cult in Japan. Part II: Historical Development." *Japanese Religions* 20.1: 34-55.

_____. 1997. "Yin and Yang: The Natural Dimension of Evil." In *Philosophies of Nature: The Human Dimension*, edited by Robert S. Cohen and Alfred I. Tauber, 89-104. New York: Kluwer Academic Publishers, Boston Studies in the Philosophy of Science.

_____. 1998a. "Steal Holy Food and Come Back as a Viper: Conceptions of Karma and Rebirth in Medieval Daoism." *Early Medieval China* 4: 1-48.

_____. 1998b. "Counting Good Deeds and Days of Life: The Quantification of Fate in Medieval China." *Asiatische Studien/Etudes Asiatiques* 52: 833-70.

_____. 2000. "The Northern Celestial Masters." In *Daoism Handbook*, edited by Livia Kohn, 283-308. Leiden: E. Brill.

_____. 2001."Daoist Monastic Discipline: Hygiene, Meals, and Etiquette." *T'oung Pao* 87: 153-93.

_____. 2003a. *Monastic Life in Medieval Daoism: A Cross-Cultural Perspective.* Honolulu: University of Hawaii Press.

_____. 2003b "Monastic Rules in Quanzhen Daoism: As Collected by Heinrich Hackmann." *Monumenta Serica* 51: 367-97.

_____. 2004a. *Cosmos and Community: The Ethical Dimension of Daoism.* Cambridge, Mass.: Three Pines Press.

_____. 2004b. *Supplement to Cosmos and Community.* Cambridge, Mass.: Three Pines Press. E-Dao Series (electronic publication).

_____. 2004c. *The Daoist Monastic Manual: A Translation of the Fengdao kejie.* New York: Oxford University Press.

_____, ed. 2006. *Daoist Body Cultivation: Traditional Models and Contemporary Practices.* Magdalena, NM: Three Pines Press.

_____. 2008a. *Chinese Healing Exercises: The Tradition of Daoyin.* Honolulu: University of Hawai'i Press.

_____. 2008b. *Meditation Works: In the Daoist, Buddhist, and Hindu Traditions.* Magdalena, NM: Three Pines Press.

_____. 2008c. "Grand Offering in Hong Kong." *Journal of Daoist Studies* 1:188-91.

_____. 2009. *Readings in Daoist Mysticism.* Magdalena, NM.: Three Pines Press

_____. 2010. *Sitting in Oblivion: The Heart of Daoist Meditation.* Dunedin, Fla.: Three Pines Press.

_____, and Robin R. Wang. 2009. *Internal Alchemy: Self, Society, and the Quest for Immortality.* Magdalena, NM: Three Pines Press.

Komjathy, Louis. 2002. *Title Index to Daoist Collections.* Cambridge, Mass.: Three Pines Press.

Kroll, Paul W. 1996. "Body Gods and Inner Vision: *The Scripture of the Yellow Court.* In *Religions of China in Practice*, edited by Donald S. Lopez Jr., 149-55. Princeton: Princeton University Press.

Kubo Noritada 窪德忠. 1956. *Koshin shinkō* 庚申信仰. Tokyo: Yamagawa.

Kushi, Avaline, and Alex Jack. 1985. *Avaline Kushi's Complete Guide to Macrobiotic Cooking.* New York: Warner.

Kushi, Michio, and Edward Esko. 1993. *Holistic Health through Macrobiotics*. New York: Japan Publications.

_____, and Phillip Jannetta. 1991. *Macrobiotics and Oriental Medicine: An Introduction to Holistic Health*. Tokyo: Japan Publishing.

LaFleur, William R., ed. 1985. *Dogen Studies*. Honolulu: University of Hawaii Press.

Lagerwey, John. 1987. *Taoist Ritual in Chinese Society and History*. New York: Macmillan.

Lavoix, Valérie. 2002. "La contribution des laïcs au végetarisme: Croisades et polémiques en Chine du Sud autour de l'an 500." In *Bouddhisme et lettrés dans la Chine médiévale*, edited by Catherine Despeux, 103-44. Paris: Louvain.

Legge, James. 1968 [1885]. *The Li Ki—Book of Rites*. 2 vols. In *The Sacred Books of China*, Parts 3-4. Delhi: Motilal Barnasidass.

Leininger, Madeleine. 1970. "Some Cross-cultural Universal and Non-universal Functions, Beliefs, and Practices of Food." In *Dimensions of Nutrition*, edited by J. Dupont, 153-79. Denver: Colorado Associated Universities Press.

Lévi, Jean. 1983. "L'abstinence des céréals chez les taoïstes." *Etudes Chinoises* 1: 3-47.

_____. 1989. "The Body: The Daoists' Coat of Arms." In *Fragments for a History of the Human Body*, edited by Michael Feher, 1:105-26. New York: Zone.

Liu, Jilin, and G. Peck, eds. 1995. *Chinese Dietary Therapy*. New York: Churchill Livingstone.

Liu, Zhengcai. 1990. *The Mystery of Longevity*. Beijing: Foreign Languages Press.

Lo, Vivienne. 2005. "Pleasure, Prohibition, and Pain: Food and Medicine in Traditional China." In *Of Tripod and Palate: Food, Politics and Religion in Traditional China*, edited by Roel Sterckx, 163-85. New York: Palgrave MacMillan.

_____. 2010. *Healing Arts in Early China*. Leiden: E. Brill.

_____, and Penelope Barrett. 2005. "Cooking up Fine Remedies: On the Culinary Aesthetic in 16th-century Chinese *Materia Medica*." *Medical History* 49:395-422.

Loewe, Michael. 1988. "The Almanacs (*jih-shu*) from Shui-hu-ti: A Preliminary Survey." *Asia Major*, 3rd series, 1.2: 1-29.

Lu, Gwei-djen, and Joseph Needham. 1977. "A Contribution to the History of Chinese Dietetics." *Isis* 42:13-20

Lu, Henry C. 1986. *Chinese System of Food Cures: Prevention and Remedies*. New York: Sterling Publishing.

_____. 1996. *Chinese Foods for Longevity: The Art of Long Life*. Selanger, Malaysia: Pelanduk Publications.

_____. 2000. *Chinese System Foods for Health and Healing*. New York: Sterling Publishing Company.

Lupton, Deborah. 1996. *Food, the Body and the Self*. London: Sage Publications.

Major, John S. 1993. *Heaven and Earth in Early Han Thought: Chapters Three, Four, and Five of the Huainanzi*. Albany: State University of New York Press.

Malek, Roman. 1985. *Das Chai-chieh-lu*. Frankfurt: Peter Lang, Würzburger Sino-Japonica 14.

Maruyama, Hiroshi. 2002. "Documents Used in Rituals of Merit in Taiwanese Daoism." In *Daoist Identity: History, Lineage, and Ritual*, edited by Livia Kohn and Harold D. Roth, 256-73. Honolulu: University of Hawaii Press.

Mather, Richard B. 1979. "K'ou Ch'ien-chih and the Taoist Theocracy at the Northern Wei Court 425-451." In *Facets of Taoism*, edited by Holmes Welch and Anna Seidel, 103-22. New Haven, Conn.: Yale University Press.

_____. 1981. "The Bonze's Begging Bowl: Eating Practices in Buddhist Monasteries of Medieval India and China." *Journal of the American Oriental Society* 101: 417-23.

Mauss, Marcel. 1967. *The Gift: Forms and Functions of Exchange in Archaic Societies*. New York: Norton.

McCreery, John. 1990. "Why Don't We See Some Real Money Here? Offerings in Chinese Religion." *Journal of Chinese Religions* 18: 1-24.

Métailié, Georges. 1979. "Cuisine et santé dans la tradition chinoise." *Communications* 23:119-29.

_____. 2001. "The *Bencao gangmu* of Li Shizhen: An Innovation in Natural History?" In *Innovation in Chinese Medicine*, edited by Elisabeth Hsu, 221-61. Cambridge: Cambridge University Press

Miles, Elisabeth. 1998. *The Feng Shui Cookbook: Creating Health and Harmony in Your Kitchen*. Secaucus, NJ: Carol Publishing Company.

Mims, Cedric. 1999. *When We Die: The Science, Culture, and Rituals of Death*. New York: St. Martin's Press.

Mitchell, Craig, Feng Ye and Nigel Wiseman. 1999. *Shang Han Lun: On Cold Damage*. Brookline, Mass.: Paradigm Publications.

Mitchell, Pauline. 1998. *The Complete Soy Cookbook*. New York: Macmillan.

Mollier, Christine. 2000. "Les cuisines de Laozi et du Buddha." *Cahiers d'Extrême-Asie* 11:45-90.

Mote, Frederick W. 1977. "Yüan and Ming," In *Food in Chinese Culture*, edited by K. C. Chang, 193-257. New Haven: Yale University Press.

Moule, A. C., and Paul Pelliot. 1938. *Marco Polo: The Description of the World.* 2 vols. London.

Mugitani, Kunio. 2004. "Filial Piety and 'Authentic Parents' in Religious Daoism." In *Filial Piety in Chinese Thought and History*, edited by Alan K. L. Chan and Sor-hoon Tan, 110-21. London: RoutledgeCurzon.

Murdoch Books. 2007. *The Essential Vegetarian Cookbook.* Ultimo, NSW: Murdoch Magazines.

Ni, Maoshing, and Cathy McNease. 1987. *The Tao of Nutrition.* Los Angeles: Seven Star Communication Group.

Nison, Paul. 2001. *The Raw Life: Becoming Natural in an Unnatural World.* New York: 343 Publishing.

Peng Mingquan 彭銘泉. 2006a. *Daojia yangshengzhou.* 道家養生粥. Taiyuan: Shanxi kexue jishu chubanshe.

_____. 2006b. *Daojia yangsheng dianxin jingcui.* 道家養生點心精粹. Taiyuan: Shanxi kexue jishu chubanshe.

_____. 2006c. *Daojia shucai yangsheng caiyao.* 道家蔬菜養生菜肴. Taiyuan: Shanxi kexue jishu chubanshe.

_____. 2006d. *Daojia junlei yangshengcaiyao.* 道家菌類養生菜肴. Taiyuan: Shanxi kexue jishu chubanshe.

_____. 2006e. *Daojia doulei ji douzhi pin yangsheng caiyao.* 道家豆類及豆制品養生菜肴. Taiyuan: Shanxi kexue jishu chubanshe.

Pitchford, Paul. 1993. *Healing with Whole Foods: Oriental Traditions and Modern Nutrition.* Berkeley: North Atlantic Books.

Poo, Mu-chou. 1997. *In Search of Personal Welfare: A View of Ancient Chinese Religion.* Albany: State University of New York Press.

_____. 2005. "A Taste of Happiness: Contextualizing Elixirs in *Baopuzi*." In *Of Tripod and Palate: Food, Politics and Religion in Traditional China*, edited by Roel Sterckx, 123-39. New York: Palgrave MacMillan.

Porkert, Manfred. 1974. *The Theoretical Foundations of Chinese Medicine.* Cambridge, Mass.: MIT Press.

Porter, Bill. 1993. *The Road to Heaven: Encounters with Chinese Hermits.* San Francisco: Mercury House.

Prebish, Charles S. 1975. Buddhist Monastic Discipline: The Sanskrit Pratimoksha Sutras of the Mahasamghikas and Mulasarvastivadins. University Park, Penn.: The Pennsylvania State University Press.

Pregadio, Fabrizio. 2000. "Elixirs and Alchemy." In Daoism Handbook, edited by Livia Kohn, 165-95. Leiden: E. Brill.

Prout, Linda. 2000. Live in the Balance. New York: Marlowe.

Puett, Michael. 2002. To Become a God: Cosmology, Sacrifice, and Self-Divinization in Early China. Cambridge, Mass.: Harvard University Press.

_____. 2005. "The Offering of Food and the Creation of Order: The Practice of Sacrifice in Early China." In Of Tripod and Palate: Food, Politics and Religion in Traditional China, edited by Roel Sterckx, 75-95. New York: Palgrave MacMillan.

Read, Bernard. 1931. Chinese Materia Medica: Animal Drugs. Beijing: Peking Natural History Bulletin.

Reed, Barbara E. 1987. "Taoism." In Women in World Religions, edited by Arvind Sharma, 161-80. Albany: State University of New York Press.

Rister, Robert. 1999. Japanese Herbal Medicine: The Healing Art of Kampo. Garden City Park, NY: Avery Publishing Group.

_____. 1999. Japanese Herbal Medicine: The Healing Art of Kampo. Garden City Park, NY: Avery Publishing Group.

Roberts, J. A. G. 2002. China to Chinatown: Chinese Food in the West. London: Reaktion Books.

Robinet, Isabelle. 1984. La révélation du Shangqing dans l'histoire du taoïsme. 2 Vols. Paris: Publications de l'Ecole Francaise d'Extrême-Orient.

_____. 1989. "Visualization and Ecstatic Flight in Shangqing Taoism." In Taoist Meditation and Longevity Techniques, edited by Livia Kohn, 157-90. Ann Arbor: University of Michigan, Center for Chinese Studies Publications.

_____. 1993. Taoist Meditation. Translated by Norman Girardot and Julian Pas. Albany: State University of New York Press.

Romano, Rita. 1997. Dining in the Raw. New York: Kensington Publishers.

Roth, Ruby. 2009. That's Why We Don't Eat Animals: A Book about Vegans, Vegetarians, and All Living Things. Berkeley: North Atlantic Books.

Sabban, Françoise. 1986. "Court Cuisine in Fourteenth-century Imperial China: Some Culinary Aspects of Hu Sihui's Yinshan zhengyao." Food and Foodways 1.2:161-96.

_____. 1990. "De la main à la pate: Refléxion sur l'origine des pates alimentaires et les transformations du blé en Chine ancienne." *L'Homme* 113:102-37.

_____. 1993. "La viande en Chine: imaginaire et usages culinaires." *Anthropozoologica* 18:79-90.

_____. 1996. "Follow the Seasons of the Heavens: Household Economy and the Management of Time in Sixth-century China." *Food and Foodways* 6.3/4:329-49.

Saso, Michael. 1972. *Taoism and the Rite of Cosmic Renewal.* Seattle: Washington University Press.

_____. 1994. *A Taoist Cookbook.* Boston: Charles E. Tuttle.

Scapp, Ron, and Brian Seitz, eds. 1998. *Eating Culture.* Albany: State University of New York Press.

Schafer, Edward H. 1977. "T'ang." In *Food in Chinese Culture,* edited by K. C. Chang, 85-140. New Haven: Yale University Press.

Schipper, Kristofer. 2001. "Daoist Ecology: The Inner Transformation. A Study of the Precepts of the Early Daoist Ecclesia." In *Daoism and Ecology: Ways Within a Cosmic Landscape,* edited by Norman Girardot, James Miller, and Liu Xiaogan, 79-94. Cambridge, Mass.: Harvard University Press, Center for the Study of World Religions.

_____, and Franciscus Verellen, eds. 2004. *The Taoist Canon: A Historical Companion to the Daozang.* 3 vols. Chicago: University of Chicago Press.

Simoons, Frederick J. 1991. *Food in China: A Cultural and Historical Inquiry.* Boston: CRC Press.

Soymié, Michel. 1977. "Les dix jours du jeune taoïste." In *Yoshioka Yoshitoyo hakase kanri kinen Dōkyō kenkyū ronshū,* 1-21. Tokyo: Kokusho kankōkai.

Spence, Jonathan. 1977. "Ch'ing." In *Food in Chinese Culture,* edited by K. C. Chang, 259-94. New Haven: Yale University Press.

Spencer, Colin. 1993. *Vegetarianism: A History.*New York: Four Walls Eight Windows.

Stein, Rolf A. 1971. "Les fêtes de cuisine du taoïsme religieux." *Annuaire du Collège de France* 71: 431-40.

_____. 1972. "Speculation mystiques et thèmes relatifs aux cuisines du taoïsme." *Annuaire du Collège de France* 72: 489-99.

Stein, Stephan. 1999. *Zwischen Heil und Heilung: Zur frühen Tradition des Yangsheng in China.* Uelzen: Medizinisch-Literarische Verlagsgesellschaft.

Sterckx, Roel. 2005. "Food and Philosophy in Ancient China." In *Of Tripod and Palate: Food, Politics and Religion in Traditional China*, edited by Roel Sterckx, 34-61. New York: Palgrave MacMillan.

_____, ed. 2005. *Of Tripod and Palate: Food, Politics and Religion in Traditional China*. New York: Palgrave MacMillan.

Stuart, G. A. 1976. *Chinese Materia Medica*. Taipei: Southern Materials Center.

Stuart, Tristam. 2006. *The Bloodless Revolution: A Cultural History of Vegetarianism from 1600 to Modern Times*. London: W. W. Norton & Company.

Tao Bingfu 陶秉福, ed. 1989. *Nüdan jicui* 女丹集萃. Beijing: Beijing shifan daxue.

Teeguarden, Ron. 1995. *Chinese Tonic Herbs*. New York: Japan Publications.

Tsukamoto Zenryū 塚本善隆. 1961. *Gisho shakurōshi no kenkyū* 魏書釋志の研究. Tokyo: Bukkyō bungaku kenkyūjo.

Turner, Victor W. 1969. *The Ritual Process: Structure and Anti-Structure*. Chicago: Aldine.

_____. 1977. "Variations on a Theme of Liminality." In *Secular Ritual*, edited by Sally F. Moore and Barbara G. Myerhoff, 36-52. Amsterdam: Van Gorcum.

Unschuld, Paul U. 1986. *Medicine in China: A History of Pharmaceutics*. Berkeley: University of California Press.

Wagner, Rudolf G. 1973. "Lebensstil und Drogen im chinesischen Mittelalter." *T'oung Pao* 59: 79-178.

Wang Ming 王明. 1960. *Taiping jing hejiao* 太平經合校. Beijing: Zhonghua.

Ware, James R. 1966. *Alchemy, Medicine and Religion in the China of AD 320*. Cambridge, Mass.: MIT Press.

Welch, Holmes. 1967. *The Practice of Chinese Buddhism, 1900-1950*. Cambridge, Mass: Harvard University Press.

Wile, Douglas. 1992. *Art of the Bedchamber: The Chinese Sexual Yoga Classics Including Women's Solo Meditation Texts*. Albany: State University of New York Press.

Wu, David Y. H., and Sidney C. H. Cheung, eds. 2002. *The Globalization of Chinese Food*. London: Curzon.

Yamada Toshiaki 山田利明. 1999. *Rikuchō dōkyō girei no kenkyū* 六朝道教儀禮の研究. Tokyo: Tōhō shoten.

_____. 2000. "The Lingbao School." In *Daoism Handbook*, edited by Livia Kohn, 225-55. Leiden: E. Brill.

Yang Liansheng 楊聯陞. 1956. "Laojun yinsong jiejing jiaoshi" 老君音誦誠經校釋. *Zhongyang yanjiu suo lishi yuyen yanjiusuo jikan* 中央研究所歷史語言研究所集刊 28: 17-54.

Yoshioka Yoshitoyo 吉岡義豐. 1970. *Dōkyō to bukkyō* 道教と佛教. Vol. II. Tokyo: Kokusho kankōkai.

_____. 1979. "Taoist Monastic Life." In *Facets of Taoism*, edited by Holmes Welch and Anna Seidel, 220-52. New Haven, Conn.: Yale University Press.

Young, Richard. 1999. *Is God a Vegetarian? Christianity, Vegetarianism, and Animal Rights*. Chicago: Open Court.

Yü, Ying-shih. 1977. "Han China." In *Food in Chinese Culture*, edited by K. C. Chang, 53-83. New Haven: Yale University Press.

_____. 1987. "O Soul, Come Back: A Study of the Changing Conceptions of the Soul and Afterlife in Pre-Buddhist China." *Harvard Journal of Asiatic Studies* 47: 363-95.

Zürcher, Erik. 1980. "Buddhist Influence on Early Taoism." *T'oung Pao* 66: 84-147

Index